Le génitif, les noms composés ........ 88
Exercices ........ 90
Bilan ........ 92

## 7. LES ARTICLES ET LES QUANTIFICATEURS

L'article indéfini *a / an*, l'article défini *the* et l'absence d'article, les quantificateurs indéfinis *some* et *any* ........ 94
Exercices ........ 97
Autres quantificateurs indéfinis ........ 100
Exercices ........ 103
Bilan ........ 106

## 8. LES PRONOMS

Les pronoms personnels, les pronoms réfléchis et réciproques, les pronoms relatifs ........ 108
Exercices ........ 110
Les adjectifs et pronoms possessifs, les adjectifs et pronoms démonstratifs, *one / ones* ........ 112
Exercices ........ 114
Bilan ........ 116

## 9. LES ADJECTIFS ET LES ADVERBES

Les adjectifs, les adverbes ........ 118
Exercices ........ 121
Le comparatif et le superlatif, les adjectifs composés ........ 124
Exercices ........ 127
Bilan ........ 130

## 10. LES PRÉPOSITIONS

Les prépositions de temps, les prépositions de lieu et de mouvement ........ 132
Exercices ........ 134
Verbes et prépositions, verbes à particule, adjectifs et prépositions ........ 136
Exercices ........ 139
Bilan ........ 142

**Annexes**

Quelques petites astuces en plus ........ 144
L'accord sujet-verbe ........ 146
100 verbes irréguliers ........ 147
Les verbes à particule ........ 149
Les collocations ........ 150
Tableau des temps ........ 151
Les majuscules ........ 152
Les participes ........ 153
Base verbale, infinitif ou *-ing* ? ........ 154
La ponctuation ........ 155
Conjonctions et mots de transition ........ 156
Modifications orthographiques ........ 159
Les préfixes et les suffixes ........ 160

**Vocabulaire** ........ 161

**Pictogrammes utilisés dans ce livre**

Attention ! Exception EXCEPTION Propre à l'anglais À bien connaître

# Avant-propos

L'objectif de cette grammaire est de vous permettre d'acquérir le bagage grammatical suffisant pour participer activement à des échanges professionnels en anglais et pour vous préparer à des examens comme le TOEIC. De plus, la combinaison d'une partie grammaire et d'une partie vocabulaire, vous permet d'aquérir des bases solides à partir desquelles vous pourrez continuer à améliorer votre maîtrise de l'anglais.
À chaque séance de travail, donnez-vous un objectif et fixez-vous quelques règles d'apprentissage.

## 1. Peu mais souvent

30 à 60 minutes de travail par jour. N'essayez pas de tout apprendre en quatre heures un dimanche après-midi ! Soyez réaliste : vous ne pouvez pas apprendre une langue étrangère en une seule nuit !

## 2. Apprendre à mémoriser

Un mot doit être vu au moins 3 fois (de préférence dans son contexte) avant d'être mémorisé. Alors, révisez, révisez, révisez !

Une façon astucieuse d'apprendre du vocabulaire consiste, par ailleurs, à établir des familles de mots.

| Noun (thing) | Noun (person) | Verb | Adjective | Adverb |
|---|---|---|---|---|
| Information, misinformation, I.T. / I.T.C. (Information Technology (& Communication)) | Informer, informant | Inform (to) | Informative, | Informatively, informingly, |
| Competition, competitiveness | Competitor | Compete (to) | Competitive | Competitively |

Bien sûr, il y a aussi du « *mind mapping* », des « *lexical sets* », et toute simplement le fait de faire des mots croisés, mots mélangés, etc. en anglais. Plus vous vous exposerez à de l'anglais, plus vous progresserez !

Si pour des raisons professionnelles vous avez besoin d'un vocabulaire particulier qui revient souvent, faites-vous une « *reminder* » (pense-bête) à mettre à côté de votre téléphone ou de votre ordinateur.

## 3. Tout en anglais

Vous avez besoin d'au moins 2 000 mots. Pour consolider votre processus d'apprentissage, lisez des articles en anglais (commencez avec des articles courts, et rallongez-les dès que vous vous sentez à l'aise dans votre lecture). Regardez les films et les séries en anglais (ce qui est facile avec Internet). Essayez aussi « l'écoute passive ». Le matin, mettez votre radio / ordinateur sur une chaine anglophone. Écoutez sans essayer de comprendre, mais simplement pour la musique de la langue. Votre oreille va s'ouvrir à la musique de l'anglais, tout en douceur.

Lisez et écoutez la langue anglaise aussi souvent que possible !

# Le nouveau TOEIC®

## GRAMMAIRE VOCABULAIRE

Serena Murdoch-Stern

# Sommaire

Avant-propos . . . . 4

## 1. LE PRÉSENT

Le présent simple . . . . 6
Exercices . . . . 8
Le présent progressif . . . . 10
Exercices . . . . 12
Bilan . . . . 14

## 2. LE PASSÉ

Le prétérit, le prétérit progressif, *used to* . . . . 16
Exercices . . . . 18
Le *present perfect simple*, le *present perfect progressive* . . . . 20
Exercices . . . . 22
Le *past perfect simple*, le *past perfect progressive* . . . . 24
Exercices . . . . 26
Bilan . . . . 28

## 3. L'EXPRESSION DU FUTUR ET DE LA CONDITION

L'expression du futur avec le présent, l'expression du futur avec *be going to* . . . . 30
Exercices . . . . 32
L'expression du futur avec *will*, autres formes de futurs . . . . 34
Exercices . . . . 36
L'expression de la condition avec *if*, l'expression de la condition avec *should*, l'expression de la condition avec *would* . . . . 38
Exercices . . . . 40
Bilan . . . . 42

## 4. LA MODALISATION

La capacité, la probabilité / possibilité . . . . 44
Exercices . . . . 47
L'obligation, l'absence d'obligation, l'interdiction, l'autorisation . . . . 50
Exercices . . . . 53
Le conseil, la suggestion, la demande et la proposition . . . . 56
Exercices . . . . 58
Bilan . . . . 60

## 5. LES PHRASES

Les questions directes, les questions indirectes, les questions négatives . . . . 62
Exercices . . . . 65
Les *questions tags*, les questions-échos, les réponses courtes, *so / neither* . . . . 68
Exercices . . . . 70
De la voix active à la voix passive, du discours direct au discours indirect . . . . 72
Exercices . . . . 74
Les causatifs, le subjonctif, l'infinitif d'intention, les négatifs piègeuses . . . . 76
Exercices . . . . 79
Bilan . . . . 82

## 6. LES NOMS

Le pluriel des noms, les noms dénombrables et indénombrables . . . . 84
Exercices . . . . 86

## 4. Ne vous découragez pas

Il y aura des moments où vous aurez l'impression de bien avancer, d'autres où vous aurez en revanche, le sentiment de ne rien apprendre... En réalité, c'est au cours de cette étape paradoxale que vous consoliderez vos acquis.

## 5. N'ayez pas peur de faire des erreurs

Non, vous n'avez pas l'air bête ! Et puis, la plupart des anglophones seront ravis de parler avec quelqu'un qui essaie de communiquer dans leur langue. Parlez anglais autant que possible, quelles que soient les situations. N'hésitez pas « à faire le perroquet » (répéter permet réellement d'assimiler) et à pratiquer une double communication, orale et gestuelle, pour mieux vous faire comprendre dans les premiers temps. Enfin, simplifiez au besoin ce que vous voulez dire ; vous serez surpris de ce que vous pouvez exprimer avec les verbes « *do* », « *have* » et « *be* » !

## 6. Entraînez-vous régulièrement

Une fois que vous aurez l'impression de bien vous débrouiller, entretenez votre anglais avec des cours, des groupes de conversation, etc.

Il n'y a pas de secret : plus vous travaillez, plus vous apprenez, et plus vite vous avancez !

Notez que dans ce livre nous utilisons les termes :
– Base verbale (infinitif sans *to*)
– Infinitif (infinitif avec *to*)

L'auteur

L'auteur remercie sa famille, Joël, Thibaut et Anne Charlotte, Arnaud, Pauline et Camille, et Lily pour leur soutien et leur patience.

# Le présent



## Le présent simple ou *simple present*

### Quand utiliser le présent simple ?

**1.** Lorsque vous parlez d'un état de fait, d'une caractéristique.
*The factory is in the industrial estate by the river.*

**2.** Lorsque vous parlez d'une vérité générale ou d'une habitude.
*I like using a computer. He works for HSB Ltd. They go to work by car.*

**3.** Lorsque vous parlez de la fréquence à laquelle vous faites quelque chose.
*He takes his dog for a walk every day during his lunch break.*
Associez le présent simple avec les adverbes de fréquence : *always, usually, often, sometimes, (not) often, hardly ever, never*, etc.
*She hardly ever uses her computer.*

*She* [*always*] ***goes*** *to work by car.*
L'adverbe de fréquence se place avant le verbe...

*He* ***is*** [*always*] *late for the meetings.*
.. mais après l'auxiliaire.

### Comment construire le présent simple ?

| Work | | | |
|---|---|---|---|
| Positive | Negative | | Interrogative |
| | Long form | Short form | |
| *I / you / we / you / they work* | *_ _ do not work* | *_ _ don't work* | *Do _ _ work?* |
| *He / she / it works* | *_ _ does not work* | *_ _ doesn't work* | *Does _ _ work?* |

↳ La plupart des verbes se conjugue selon ce modèle (y compris *have*).
Notez le –*s* à la 3e personne du singulier et faites attention aux modifications orthographiques de certains verbes !
*He goes (go), She does (do). The plane flies (fly).*

#### L'auxiliaire *do/does*

- À ne pas confondre avec le verbe *do* (« faire ») !
- « *Dummy auxiliary* » (ou « faux auxiliaire »), il ne veut rien dire, mais est nécessaire à la construction des formes négatives et interrogatives (sauf avec *be* et *have got*). Dans les phrases affirmatives, il peut aussi être employé pour marquer l'insistance (forme emphatique) :
*She does like her job.* (Elle aime beaucoup son travail.)
*I do apologise.* (Je suis vraiment navrée.)
- La forme négative non contractée *do / does not* s'utilise dans les situations formelles (dans les lettres en particulier). La forme contractée *don't / doesn't* s'emploie à l'oral et dans les communications écrites informelles.
- *Do / does* devient *did* au prétérit.

| Be | | | | |
|---|---|---|---|---|
| Positive | | Negative | | Interrogative |
| Long form | Short form | Long form | Short form | |
| *I am* | *I'm* | *I am not* | *I'm not* | *Am I?* |
| *You / we / you/ they are* | *You're, we're, you're, they're* | *You are not, we are not, you are not, they are not* | *You're not / you aren't, We're not / We aren't, You're not / you aren't, They're not / they aren't* | *Are you? Are we? Are you? Are they?* |
| *He / she / it is* | *He's* | *He is not* | *He's not / he isn't* | *Is he?* |

Verbe/auxiliaire, *be* n'a pas besoin de recourir à l'auxiliaire *do/does* aux formes interrogative et négative.

Là où le français emploie le verbe « avoir », l'anglais utilise parfois *be*.
Il a vingt ans. → *He is twenty-years-old.*
« Vous avez » au sens de « il y a » se traduit en anglais par *there is*.
Vous avez une usine sur votre droite. → *There is a factory on your right.*

**!** Il ne faut pas confondre : *There is / there are = Il y a*
*It is / they are = C'est / ce sont*

| Have got | | | | |
|---|---|---|---|---|
| Positive | | Negative | | Interrogative |
| Long form | Short form | Long form | Short form | |
| *I have got* | *I've got* | *I have not got* | *I haven't got* | *Have I got?* |
| *You / we / you / they have got* | *You've got, We've got, You've got, They've got* | *You have not got, We have not got, You have not got, They have not got* | *You haven't got, We haven't got, You haven't got, They haven't got* | *Have you got? Have we got? Have you got? Have they got?* |
| *He has got* | *He's got* | *He has not got* | *He hasn't got* | *Has he got?* |

Comme celle de *be*, la conjugaison de *have got* ne nécessite pas *do / does*.
En revanche, si vous utilisez simplement *have*, n'oubliez pas l'auxiliaire !
*I have / I do not have / I don't have / Do I have?*

*Have got* s'utilise surtout au présent et indique la possession.
Son utilisation varie suivant les pays anglophones : *have got* en anglais britannique, mais *have* en anglais australien, et *have got / got* en anglais américain.
L'anglais ne dira pas ~~*The computer has got a mouse*~~ ; seuls les gens, les animaux et ce qui peut être considéré comme un groupe de personnes (une ville, une usine, une entreprise, etc.) peut effectivement posséder quelque chose.
*The company has got a good works committee.*
*The town has got a new cinema.*

## 1 Faites des phrases affirmatives (+), négatives (-), et interrogatives (?) en n'utilisant que *be* et *have got*.

Ex. ▶ I: 30 years old (-); hard working (+); spare time (-); 150 employees (+); a laptop (?); a CEO (+)
*I am not 30 years old. I am hard working.*
*I haven't got (don't have) any spare time.*
*I have got 150 employees. Have I got (do I have) a laptop? I am a C.E.O…*

**1.** You: MBA diploma (?); experience (-); reliable (+); married (?); three children (+); an accountant (+)

Have you got an MBA diploma ? You don't have any experience / You haven't got any experience. You are reliable. Are you married ? You've got 3 children / you are an accountant

**2.** He: a team of 10 (+); German (+); single (-); innovative (+); a patent pending (?); an engineer (+)

He has got a team of 10 / He is German / He isn't single. He is innovative. He is an engineer / Has he got a patent pending ?

**3.** It: 1500 m² (+); 3 assembly lines (+); air conditioning (-); up-to-date equipment (?); the plant (+)

It's an 1500 m² / It has got a 3 assembly lines / It hasn't got air conditionning ; Has it got up to date equipment ? It's the plant

**4.** We: new machinery (?); interested in rugby (+); protective clothing (-); on the morning shift (-); machine operators (+)

..........

**5.** They: new computers (-); cutting-edge software (?); a built-in spreadsheet (-); go-ahead (+); American I.T. specialists (+)

..........

## 2 Conjuguez les verbes entre parenthèses.

### • À la forme affirmative

**1.** An assistant: He (answer) .................... the telephone and (make) .................... appointments.

**2.** The R&D team: We (develop) .................... new products and (update) .................... existing products.

### • À la forme négative

**3.** The maintenance team: Our machines (not – work) very well so we have a lot of work to do.

..........

**4.** A financial controller: He (not – deal with) everyday accounting, but is responsible for taxation, investments and cash management.

..........

### • À la forme interrogative

**5.** The night shift: They (work) at night in the factory?

..........

**6.** A quality manager: How (control) quality checks and the conformity of the products?

..........

## 3 Conjuguez les verbes entre parenthèses.

Peter: Good morning Bob, welcome to the company. I (think) .................... it would be a good idea if I explained the company to you first, and then what I (do) ....................

Bob: What the company (make) ....................?

Peter: The company (manufacture) .................... electrical appliances. We (not – produce) .................... all the parts here, some of them (be) .................... out-sourced. We (sell) .................... mostly to the mass market and (not – deal with) .................... small retailers. We (have got) .................... factories in the U.K. and the headquarters (be) ................. in Paris. Then, there (be) ................. subsidiaries in most European countries.

The company (employ) ................. over a thousand people and our turnover (be) ................. € 6 million per annum.

Bob: How many people (work) .................... in the company?

Peter: There (be) ................ 175 people here. We also often (employ) .............. temporary workers – that (be) .................. when we (have) .............. a lot of orders of course!

Bob: What hours people (work) .................?

Peter: The machine operators (work) ................. in two shifts.

Bob: What you (do) ................. in your job?

Peter: Ah – good question! I (manage) ................. production – in other words, my team and I (plan) ................. the production schedule, and generally (run) .............. manufacturing. All our machines (be) ................. computerized so the I.T. specialist (help) ................. us to set up new parameters, etc.

## 4 À partir du texte, faites des phrases simples en utilisant les adverbes de fréquence (voir liste p. 4).

Jim is a sales manager for "Turnkey" selling ready-made factories. He gets up early almost every day, and goes to work on the underground every day - he doesn't ever take the car. About once a week he has lunch in a very smart restaurant with his boss. On the other days, he has lunch in a sandwich bar with his colleagues. He has to travel to the company headquarters in Geneva once or twice a year. Although he doesn't like flying he takes the airplane because he can get back home in time for dinner. In his spare time, he plays golf, but he finds it difficult to play very much because he takes a lot of work home for the weekend. However, he frequently works out at the gym to keep fit.

Ex. ▶ have lunch - restaurant
*He sometimes has lunch in a restaurant*

**1.** take – car

..............................................................................

..............................................................................

**2.** fly – Geneva

..............................................................................

..............................................................................

**3.** work out – gym

..............................................................................

..............................................................................

**4.** go to work – underground

..............................................................................

..............................................................................

**5.** play – golf

..............................................................................

..............................................................................

**6.** have lunch – sandwich bar

..............................................................................

..............................................................................

**7.** get up late

..............................................................................

..............................................................................

## CORRIGÉS

**1. 1.** Have you got an MBA diploma? You haven't got (don't have) any experience. You are reliable. Are you married? You have got three children. You are an accountant. **2.** He has got a team of 10. He is German. He isn't single. He is innovative. Has he got (does he have) a patent pending? He is an engineer. **3.** It is 1500 m². It has got 3 assembly lines. It hasn't got (doesn't have) air conditioning. Has it got (does it have) up-to-date equipment? It is the plant. **4.** Have we got new machinery? We are interested in rugby. We haven't got (don't have) protective clothing. We are not (aren't) on the morning shift. We are machine operators. **5.** They haven't got (don't have) new computers. Have they got (do they have) cutting-edge software? They haven't got (don't have) a built-in spreadsheet. They are go-ahead. They are American I.T. specialists.

**2. 1.** answers - makes **2.** develop - update **3.** Do not work **4.** does not deal with **5.** Do they work at night in the factory? **6.** How does a quality manager control quality checks and the conformity of the products?

**3.** think – do – What does the company make? – manufactures – don't produce – are – sell – don't deal with – have got – is – are – employs – is – work – are – employ – is – have – What hours do people work? – work – What do you do in your job? – manage – plan – run – are – helps

**4. 1.** He never takes his car. **2.** He sometimes flies to Geneva. **3.** He often works out at the gym. **4.** He always goes to work by underground. **5.** He doesn't often play golf. **6.** He usually has lunch in a sandwich bar. **7.** He hardly ever gets up late.

# Le présent progressif ou *present continuous*

## Quelle est la différence entre le présent simple et le présent progressif ?

*He **develops** new products.* → action habituelle

*He **is developing** a new product.* → action provisoire

## Quand utiliser le présent progressif ?

**1.** Lorsque vous parlez de quelque chose que vous êtes en train de faire.
*At the moment he'**s drawing** the new layout of the factory.*
*What **are** you **doing**? **I'm calling** the bank.*

**2.** Lorsque vous parlez de quelque chose qui se fait sur le long terme, mais qui a un début et une fin.
*We **are developing** a new device.*
*The company **is building** a new plant.*

**3.** Lorsque vous parlez de quelque chose en constante évolution (les taux de chômage, les chiffres de la population, etc.)
*The unemployment rate **is rising**.*
*The Chinese industrial growth rate **is going up**.*

## Comment construire le présent progressif ?

| Work | | |
|---|---|---|
| **Positive** | **Negative** | **Interrogative** |
| *I am / I'm working*<br>*You / we / you / they are / 're working*<br>*He is / 's working* | *I am not / 'm not working*<br>*You, we, you, they are not / 're not / aren't working*<br>*He is not / 's not / isn't working* | *Am I working?*<br>*Are you / we / you / they working?*<br>*Is he working?* |

↳ Le présent progressif se construit comme suit :

**auxiliaire *be* au présent + verbe *-ing***

• Le présent progressif est, en général, utilisé avec les adverbes de temps suivants : *today* (dans certaines circonstances), *at the moment, these days, this week, currently, now, meanwhile, right now.*
*We are **currently** working on supply chain improvements.*
*He is calculating the cost price **right now**.*

**!** Utilisé avec la forme progressive, *always* a une valeur de critique.
*You are always losing the keys to the conference room!*
→ Vous perdez toujours les clefs de la salle de conférence !
*He is always arriving late for the meetings!*
→ Il arrive toujours en retard pour les réunions !

## Verbes « non-progressifs »

Certains verbes, en anglais, ne peuvent pas être mis à la forme progressive. Il s'agit des verbes qui expriment :

### • 1. La pensée

| |
|---|
| *agree – advise – believe – believe in – forget – know – mean – imagine – recognize – suppose – remember – doubt – understand – think…* |

*She knows a lot about quality control.*
*Do you understand technical documents in English?*

**EXCEPTION** Au sens « actif » (réfléchir), *think* peut s'utiliser à la forme progressive.
*What are you thinking about? I'm thinking about the new factory layout.*
Notez l'utilisation du verbe *"agree"*. *I agree with you / I don't agree with you* (et ne pas ~~*I am not agree with you*~~).

### • 2. Les émotions et les sentiments

| |
|---|
| *dislike – can't stand – hate – like – prefer – love – want – care – feel – don't mind…* |

*They don't like working at the weekend.*
*She prefers the morning shifts.*
Lorsque ces verbes sont suivis d'un autre verbe, celui-ci est en *-ing*.

**EXCEPTION** Lorsque vous invoquez une émotion très forte et transitoire vous pouvez utiliser la forme progressive. → *I'm loving it!*

### • 3. Les cinq sens

| |
|---|
| *see – smell – taste – hear – feel* |

*The machine smells strange – is it working properly?*
*Do you see what I'm trying to explain?*

**EXCEPTION** *smell, taste, feel* peuvent être utilisés avec un sens progressif.
*What are you doing? I am smelling the new perfume we invented.* → d'une manière active
*Where is the switchboard operator? She is not feeling well.* → état provisoire
*Look at* et *listen to* ne sont pas des verbes non-progressifs.

### • 4. La possession

| |
|---|
| *have – own – belong…* |

*The group now owns five factories in France.*
*The new laptop computer belongs to Mark Slater.*

**EXCEPTION** Lorsque *have* est suivi d'un nom et indique une activité, il peut être utilisé à la forme progressive.
*Where is John? He is having lunch.*

### • 5. Autres verbes non-progressifs

| |
|---|
| *cost* (dans le sens de « coûter » et non de « calculer un prix de revient ») *– contain – depend – consist (of) – seem – need – be* |

**EXCEPTION** Lorsqu'il indique un changement de comportement, *be* peut être utilisé à la forme progressive.
*What's the matter with James, he's being very short-tempered today?!*
(Normalement il est plutôt calme.)

**1** **À partir des indices en italique, faites une phrase en anglais pour expliquer ce qui se passe. Attention aux pronoms !**

**1.** *Quelqu'un est en train de rentrer dans une agence pour l'emploi.* (he – go into – job centre)

..........

..........

**2.** *Quelqu'un est en train d'écrire un CV.* (she – write – CV)

..........

..........

**3.** *Je suis en train de téléphoner et non d'envoyer un email.* (I – not – send – an e-mail)

..........

..........

**4.** *Deux personnes sont en train de remplir un formulaire de demande d'emploi.* (they – fill in an application form)

..........

..........

**5.** *Des personnes sont en train de visiter des bureaux.* (we – visit – the offices)

..........

..........

**6.** *Deux / trois personnes sont en train de regarder les petites annonces.* (they – look at – the small ads in the newspaper)

..........

..........

**7.** *Quelqu'un est en train de faire passer un entretien d'embauche.* (she – interview – a candidate)

..........

..........

**8.** *Deux personnes sont en train de signer un contrat.* (they – sign – a contract)

..........

..........

**9.** *Graphique montrant les chiffres du chômage qui augmentent !* (unemployment figures – not – go down)

..........

..........

**10.** *Cherchez-vous un travail actuellement ?* (you – look for – job – at the moment)

..........

..........

**2** **Formulez les questions correspondant aux réponses.**

| Question | Answer |
|---|---|
| **1.** Write – e-mail | **1.** No, he's writing a letter. |
| **2.** do | **2.** They are discussing the new machine. |
| **3.** exchange rate – go down | **3.** No, it is going up. |
| **4.** Where – go | **4.** We are on the way to Bristol. |
| **5.** Work – new requirements | **5.** No, I'm still working on the old project. |
| **6.** Speak – Chinese | **6.** I don't think so. They're speaking Russian. |
| **7.** draw up – financial plan | **7.** Yes, they need the figures. |
| **8.** look into – customer complaint | **8.** Yes, he is trying to find the quality problem. |

**1.** ..........

..........

**2.** ..........

..........

**3.** ..........

..........

**4.** ..........

..........

**5.** ..........

..........

**6.** ..........

..........

**7.** ..........

..........

**8.** ..........

..........

## 3 Conjuguez les verbes à la forme affirmative, négative ou interrogative.

Simon: OK Eric, now that you know a bit about the company, let's take a look around and see where you'll be working, in the R&D department (that's Research and Development). Come over here, I'd like you to meet Bill. At the moment, he (draw) ………………… the new factory layout on the computer because we (not – produce – currently) ………………………… at full capacity. Excuse me...

(Simon's mobile phone (ring) ……………….) Hello, yes this (Simon – speak) ……………………………… Oh, Mr Tailor... Yes, of course I can put you up-to-date with the latest developments. We (get on) ……………………… very well, in fact, we are ahead of schedule. Hold on please – Joe, (work on – you) ………….. the road map for Mr Tailor?

Joe: I (not – do) ………………… it right now, but it'll be finished by this evening.

Simon: Great! That's all under control Mr Tailor. You'll receive an e-mail later in the day. Thank you, good bye... Now, where were we? (The phone rings again) Peter, good morning. I (show – just) ………………… Eric the department and then I'll be with you – give me half an hour. Sorry Eric. Now, what (happen) ………………… in the factory?

Oh no! – why (not – move – they) ………………… machines around? Joe – who (supervise) ………………… the shift this morning?

Joe: Bill, I think. It's 8.30, so he (take – probably) ………………… a break at the moment.

Simon: Sorry about that Eric.

Eric: That's ok. I just have to get used to working at such a pace! What about the long-term plans you were talking about?

Simon: Yes, you'll be involved in all of that as well. Firstly, as I mentioned, we (develop – currently) ……………………………… a new device which will revolutionise the housewife's working day. Our standard products (sell) ………………… well and we have to increase production, so we (build – also) finished by mid-2014. Added to this, the exchange rate (not – rise) ……………………………… which is in our favour for the export market. Our competitors (not – launch) …………………………… the same products as us for the meanwhile, so we are pretty optimistic at the moment!

Eric: I am pleased that I (work) ………………… in such an innovative and dynamic company!

Simon: Oh yes, working! Let me show you your desk and then you can settle in and get down to it!

### CORRIGÉS

**1.** **1.** He is going into the job centre. **2.** She is writing a CV. **3.** I am not sending an e-mail. **4.** They are filling in an application form. **5.** We are visiting the offices. **6.** They are looking at the small ads in the newspaper. **7.** She is interviewing a candidate. **8.** They are signing a contract. **9.** Unemployment figures are not going down! **10.** Are you looking for a job at the moment?

**2.** **1.** Is he writing an e-mail? **2.** What are they doing? **3.** Is the exchange rate going down? **4.** Where are we/you going? **5.** Are you working on the new requirements? **6.** Are they speaking Chinese? **7.** Are they drawing up the financial plan? **8.** Is he looking into the customer complaint?

**3.** 's / is drawing – 're not / aren't / are not currently producing - 's / is ringing – is Simon speaking – 're / are getting on – are you working on – 'm / am not doing – 'm / am just showing – is happening – aren't / are they not moving – is supervising – 's / is probably taking – are currently developing – are selling – are also building – isn't / is not rising – aren't / are not launching – am working

## 1 Entourez la bonne réponse.

Score : ..... / 6

1. So you're a procurement officer. What exactly do you do / are you doing in your job?
2. The purchaser often travels / is travelling abroad for her job.
3. We currently are having / have over 200 people on the payroll.
4. Only use one page for your CV – on average it is taking / takes 2 minutes to read one!
5. Mary is on "gardening leave", she is looking for / looks for a new job at the moment.
6. Unfortunately, Simon is not standing / can't stand his new job.

## 2 Rangez les adverbes ci-dessous dans la colonne qui convient.

Score : ..... / 24

most of the time – at present – sometimes – now – every day – these days – how often – usually – nowadays – always – every now and the – just – this week – often – currently – never – right now – once or twice a month – meanwhile – today – not often – at the moment – hardly ever – still

| Simple present | Present progressive |
|---|---|
| ........................ | ........................ |
| ........................ | ........................ |
| ........................ | ........................ |
| ........................ | ........................ |
| ........................ | ........................ |
| ........................ | ........................ |

## 3 Écrivez ces phrases au présent simple et au présent progressif.

Score : ..... / 8

| Simple present | Present progressive |
|---|---|
| Ex. ▶ He writes computer programs. | *He is writing a computer program right now.* |
| **1.** … | She is developing a new manufacturing process. |
| **2.** They don't sell mass market products. | … |
| **3.** … | She is giving a conference in Taiwan. |
| **4.** He prepares factories for ISO certification. | … |
| **5.** … | He is just calling the supplier. |
| **6.** I read a trade magazine every day. | … |
| **7.** … | What are you doing? |
| **8.** He draws up the P&L once a year. | … |

## 4 Entourez l'erreur et corrigez-la ! Score : ..... / 12

1. The foreman is having four new machines at the moment. ..........
2. The HR manager negotiates never! ..........
3. The quality assistant do not be very efficient. ..........
4. The methods department has got 5-years-old. ..........
5. The designer provide the most innovative products on the market. ..........
6. The purchaser is always living in London. ..........
7. The procurement officer is late always for work. ..........
8. Do the financial controller filling in the dashboards? ..........
9. The warehouseman don't use barcodes for stock taking. ..........
10. On the phone – a bad line : "Are you hearing me?" ..........
11. Our competitor hasn't very many customers. ..........
12. The plant manager is knowing a lot about manufacturing. ..........

## CORRIGÉS

**1.** 1. do you do 2. travels 3. have 4. takes 5. is looking for 6. can't stand

**2.**

| Simple present | Present progressive |
|---|---|
| most of the time – sometimes – every day – how often – usually – nowadays – always – every now and then – often – never – once or twice a month – not often – hardly ever | at present – now – these days – just – this week – currently – right now – meanwhile – today – at the moment – still |

**3.**

| Simple present | Present progressive |
|---|---|
| 1. She develops new manufacturing processes.<br>2. They don't sell mass market products.<br><br>3. She gives conferences in Taiwan.<br>4. He prepares factories for ISO certification.<br>5. He calls the supplier every Monday morning.<br>6. I read a trade magazine every day.<br>7. What do you do?<br>8. He draws up the P & L once a year. | 1. She is developing a new manufacturing process.<br>2. They are not selling mass market products at the moment.<br>3. She is giving a conference in Taiwan.<br>4. He is preparing the factory for ISO certification.<br>5. He is just calling the supplier.<br>6. I am reading a trade magazine.<br>7. What are you doing?<br>8. He is drawing up the P & L this week. |

**4.** 1. The foreman has four new machines at the moment. 2. The HR manager never negotiates! 3. The quality assistant is not very efficient. 4. The methods department is 5-years-old. 5. The designer provides the most innovative products on the market. 6. The purchaser lives (/is still living) in London. 7. The procurement officer is always late for work. 8. Is the financial controller filling in the dashboards? 9. The warehouseman doesn't use barcodes for stock taking. 10. On the phone – a bad line : "Can (/do) you hear me?" 11. Our competitor hasn't got (/doesn't have) very many customers. 12. The plant manager knows a lot about manufacturing.

# Le prétérit ou *simple past*

## Quand utiliser le prétérit ?

Lorsque vous évoquez quelque chose qui est complètement terminé et sans lien avec le présent.
*He **went** to a meeting last week. Henry Ford **was** born in 1863 and **died** in 1947.*

Le prétérit est donc toujours associé (soit dans la phrase même, soit dans le contexte sans que cela ne soit exprimé) à une expression qui ramène à un moment précis du passé (*yesterday, last year, when I was a child*, etc.).

## Comment construire le prétérit ?

| **Be** | | | | |
|---|---|---|---|---|
| | **Positive** | **Negative** | | **Interrogative** |
| | | **Long form** | **Short form** | |
| *I / he / she / it* | *was* | *was not* | *wasn't* | *Was I / he / she / it?* |
| *You / we / you / they* | *were* | *were not* | *weren't* | *Were _ _?* |

| **Work** (verbe régulier) / **Go** (verbe irrégulier) | | | | |
|---|---|---|---|---|
| | **Positive** | **Negative** | | **Interrogative** |
| | | **Long form** | **Short form** | |
| *I / you / he / she / it/ we / they* | *worked*<br>*went* | *did not work*<br>*did not go* | *didn't work*<br>*didn't go* | *Did ... work?*<br>*Did ... go?* |

↳ **Les verbes réguliers** ont leur prétérit composé par addition de *-ed* à la base verbale.
**Il faut apprendre les verbes irréguliers** (voir la liste p. 147).
Apprenez les trois colonnes « base verbale», « prétérit », et « participe passé » en même temps. N'essayez pas de retenir tous les verbes à la fois, mais sélectionnez ceux qui vous semblent les plus importants et apprenez-en un par jour.

# Le prétérit progressif ou *simple past progressive*

## Quelle est la différence entre le prétérit et le prétérit progressif ?

*He **presented** the new budget figures when the CEO arrived.*
→ Il a présenté le budget quand le directeur général est arrivé (autrement dit, il l'a attendu).

*He **was presenting** the new budget figures when the CEO arrived.*
→ Il était déjà en train de présenter le budget lorsque le directeur général est arrivé.

## Quand utiliser le prétérit progressif ?

**1.** Lorsque vous parlez d'une action en cours à un moment du passé.
*What **were** you **doing** at 10.30 yesterday? I **was having** a meeting.*

**2.** Lorsque vous évoquez l'arrière-plan d'une action.
*While he was making his presentation, my mobile phone rang.*

### Comment construire le prétérit progressif ?

| Work | | | | |
|---|---|---|---|---|
| | Positive | Negative | | Interrogative |
| | | Long form | Short form | |
| *I / he / she / it* | *was working* | *was not working* | *wasn't working* | *Was ... working?* |
| *You / we / they* | *were working* | *were not working* | *weren't working* | *Were ... working?* |

↳ Le prétérit progressif se construit comme suit : ***auxiliaire be au prétérit + verbe -ing***

## *Used to* (et *to be used to*)

### Quand utiliser *used to* ?

Pour exprimer une action / un état du passé qui n'est plus d'actualité.
*He used to have glasses.* → *Now he wears contact lenses.*
*He used to work in marketing.* → *Now he is a financial controller.*
*He used to come home late every evening.* → *Now he's always back home by six.*

Pour une activité répétée, ou une habitude, « *used to* » peut être remplacé par *would*.
*He would come home late.* → ~~*He would work in marketing.*~~

### Comment construire *used to* ?

| | Positive | Negative | | Interrogative |
|---|---|---|---|---|
| | | Long form | Short form | |
| *I / you / he / she / it / we / they* | *used to show* | *did not use to show* | *didn't use to show* | *Did ... use to show?* |

### Quand utiliser *be used to / get used to*

Pour exprimer le fait d'être (ou devenir) habitué à quelque chose.
*He wasn't used to speaking English at meetings.*
*Then he was promoted and his boss said, "you will have to get used to speaking English".*
*So, he got used to speaking English and now he is used to speaking to people from all over the world!*

### Comment construire *be used to / get used to + ing* ?

| | | |
|---|---|---|
| *Be* (conjugué au temps approprié) | + *used to* | + verbe -ING |
| *Get* (conjugué au temps approprié) | + *used to* | + verbe -ING |

## 1 Conjuguez les verbes au prétérit.

• À la forme affirmative

**1.** He (divide) his presentation into 3 parts.

....................................................................................

....................................................................................

**2.** He (show) us the sales figures.

....................................................................................

....................................................................................

**3.** He (ask) if we had any questions.

....................................................................................

....................................................................................

• À la forme négative

**4.** They (not – be) very good.

....................................................................................

....................................................................................

**5.** He said it (not – be) due to competition.

....................................................................................

....................................................................................

**6.** The meeting (not - last) too long.

....................................................................................

....................................................................................

• À la forme interrogative

**7.** Everybody (be) on time?

....................................................................................

....................................................................................

**8.** He (explain) why?

....................................................................................

....................................................................................

**9.** Anyone (suggest) any improvements?

....................................................................................

....................................................................................

## 2 Entourez la bonne réponse.

Bill: I gather they make / made some mistakes in the power-point presentation.

John: The line graph showed / shown the year-to-date sales figures, but the pie chart didn't give / didn't gave the market share. However, the flow chart deal with / dealt with the order process well.

Bill: Did the sales manager put / putted the new representatives on the organisation chart?

John: Yes, it were / was very clear. We also seen / saw the plans and the blueprint they chose / choose last week for the new sales outlet.

Bill: Did you understand / understood the polar graph?

John: Not much! To sum up, sales fell / falled because of a new competitor.

## 3 À partir des données du tableau suivant, construisez des phrases en utilisant *used to.*

| In 1995 | In 2005 |
|---|---|
| Ex. ▶ Had long hair. | Has short hair. |
| **1.** Was a marketing assistant. | Is a marketing manager. |
| **2.** Worked for IMP PlC. | Works for JMP Inc. |
| **3.** Didn't know how to use a computer. | Knows how to use a computer. |
| **4.** Earned a low salary. | Earns a good salary. |
| **5.** Don't know. | Has a company car. |
| **6.** Think he lived in London – not sure. | Now he lives in New York. |

Ex. ▶ *He used to have long hair.*

• À la forme affirmative

**1.** ....................................................................................

**2.** ....................................................................................

• À la forme négative

**3.** ....................................................................................

**4.** ....................................................................................

• À la forme interrogative

**5.** ....................................................................................

**6.** ....................................................................................

## 4 En utilisant les éléments entre parenthèses, répondez aux questions suivantes :

**1.** What was he doing at 3 pm yesterday?
(present – the sales forecast)

..............................................................................

**2.** Where were they at 10 am on Tuesday?
(be – meeting room)

..............................................................................

**3.** What was she doing when you called?
(talk about – the flow chart)

..............................................................................

**4.** Why are you annoyed? (while – explain – pie chart – marketing manager – interrupt)

..............................................................................

**5.** When did the assistant point out the mistakes?
(while – the sales manager – give a presentation)

..............................................................................

**6.** What happened to the turnover?
(we – hope for – improvement – but sales slumped)

..............................................................................

## 5 Complétez les phrases avec *used to / would / be used to / get used to* (conjugué correctement).

**1.** She doesn't mind working early in the morning every day. She (get up) .......................... at 5 am.

**2.** I preferred the seminars we had before. They always (hold) .......................... them in a very chic hotel but not any longer.

**3.** She (take) .......................... the best notes I've ever read but she doesn't any more.

**4.** He (give) .......................... the longest speeches I've ever heard.

**5.** They didn't like breakfast meetings at first but with the new C.E.O. they just had to (be) .......................... at work at 7 am.

## 6 Entourez et corrigez les 21 erreurs qui se trouvent dans la conversation suivante :

– Did Paul wrote up the minutes of the last meeting?
– I'm not sure – he didn't used to be responsible for that. However, while we was updating this year's targets, he says he will deal with the report. So maybe everyone think it was his job after that!
– Mary used to took the notes, and she do a very good job.
– Didn't the C.E.O. decided that she already have enough to do, and that someone else were to do it instead? Mary were getting very stressed about having too much to do, and I think she ask for someone to take over.
– Well, I preferred Mary. We never hadn't any mistakes and the minutes come out on time. Last week we had need of the figures when the customer comes to visit, and we hadn't nothing to show him!
– Yes but don't forgot that Mary would decided who was to receive the minutes, and often people would got forgotten – including me!

## 7 Entourez la bonne réponse.

**1.** Did the quality audit go / went well?

**2.** While we was / were checking the 5s procedure, we found a lot of mess.

**3.** Didn't you used / use to tidy every day?

**4.** Yes, but the workers came / come out on strike the day before.

**5.** So the factory didn't get / got the approval?

**6.** Yes actually, everything else were / was fine.

### CORRIGÉS

**1.** 1. He divided his presentation into 3 parts. 2. He showed us the sales figures. 3. He asked if we had any questions. 4. They were not very good. 5. He said it was not due to competition. 6. The meeting didn't last too long. 7. Was everybody on time? 8. Did he explain why? 9. Did anyone suggest any improvements?
**2.** made – showed – didn't give – dealt with – put – was – saw – chose – understand – fell
**3.** 1. He used to be a marketing assistant. 2. He used to work for IMP PLC. 3. He didn't use to know how to use a computer. 4. He didn't use to earn a good salary. 5. Did he use to have a company car? 6. Didn't he use to live in London?
**4.** 1. He was presenting the sales forecast. 2. They were in the meeting room (verb be – non-progressive) 3. She was talking about the flow chart. 4. While I was explaining the pie chart, the marketing manager interrupted. 5. While the sales manager was giving a presentation. 6. We were hoping for improvement but sales slumped.
**5.** 1. is used to getting up / got used to getting up – 2. used to hold – 3. used to take – 4. used to give / would give – 5. get used to being
**6.** write up – didn't use to – while we were – he said – he would – everyone though – used to take – and she did – Didn't the C.E.O. decide – she already had – someone else was – Mary was – she asked for – We never – had – the minutes came out – we needed – the customer came – we had nothing – don't forget – would decide – would get forgotten
**7.** 1. go 2. were 3. use to 4. came 5. get 6. was

# Le *present perfect simple*

## Quelle est la différence entre le prétérit et le *present perfect* ?

Le *present perfect* n'existe pas en français. Il vous faudra penser en anglais, en contexte, et ne pas traduire ! Par contraste avec le prétérit, on utilise le *present perfect* pour parler de quelque chose qui a un lien avec le présent. Souvenez-vous, le *present perfect* a toujours une connexion avec le moment présent. Le *present perfect* n'est pas toujours utilisé en anglais américain.

**Comparez !**

*How long did you live there?*
→ Combien de temps avez-vous habité là ? (le prétérit, donc la personne n'y habite plus)

*How long have you lived there?*
→ Depuis combien de temps habitez-vous là ? (la personne y est encore)

## Quand utiliser le *present perfect simple* ?

**1.** Lorsque vous évoquez une action qui a commencé dans le passé et qui continue jusque dans le présent.

*She **has worked** in the sales department since 1998.*
→ depuis 1998 et jusqu'à ce jour

MOTS-CLÉS *since, for, for a long time, how long?*, etc.

**2.** Lorsque vous évoquez une période de temps qui n'est pas encore terminée.

*We **have worked** on the budget this week.*
→ la semaine n'est pas encore terminée

MOTS-CLÉS *this week / year, recently, in the past few days, so far*, etc.

**3.** Lorsque vous évoquez une action qui a eu lieu dans le passé, mais dont le moment n'est pas précisé.

***Have** you ever **been** to New York?*
*Yes, I have. I **went** ten years ago.*

MOTS-CLÉS *ever, yet, already, it's the first time*, etc.

On emploie souvent le *present perfect* dans la question, alors que la réponse, qui donne des détails, utilise le prétérit.

**4.** Lorsque vous relatez une actualité récente.

*He **has been accepted** into Harvard Business School!*
*The taxi **has arrived**.*
→ sous-entendu *just*

MOTS-CLÉS *just* (mais c'est davantage une question de contexte)

## Comment construire le *present perfect simple* ?

| Verbes réguliers / irréguliers | | | | | |
|---|---|---|---|---|---|
| | Positive | | Negative | | Interrogative |
| | Long form | Short form | Long form | Short form | |
| *He / she / it* | *has written* | *'s written* | *has not written* | *hasn't written* | *Has ... written?* |
| *I / you / we / they* | *have worked* | *'ve worked* | *have not worked* | *haven't worked* | *Have ... worked?* |

↳ Le *present perfect simple* se construit comme suit :

**auxiliaire *have* au présent + participe passé du verbe**

*He has been to Italy.* → il est revenu    *He has gone to Italy.* → il y est encore

! *He got promoted in 1997.* ~~*He has been promoted since 1997*~~.
Ici, ce n'est pas possible d'interchanger. Le fait d'être promu est fini : maintenant il est le patron !

# Le *present perfect progressive*

## Quelle est la différence entre le *present perfect simple* et le *present perfect progressive* ?

*He **has written up** the contract with the supplier.* → Le contrat est déjà terminé. (cf. 3.)
*He **has been writing up** the contract with the supplier.* → Le contrat n'est pas encore terminé.

Certains verbes (*live, work*...) peuvent se mettre à la forme simple ou progressive sans changement de sens (sauf avec *always* : le verbe est obligatoirement au *present perfect simple*).
*He **has lived** / **been living** in Paris for ten years.*
*He **has always worked** for PLB.*

## Quand utiliser le *present perfect progressive* ?

**1.** Lorsque vous évoquez quelque chose qui a commencé dans le passé mais qui continue dans le présent (nous rejoignons donc le présent progressif !).
*We **have been working** hard all day!* (Nous n'avons pas fini.)
*How long **have** you **been working** on the new project?* (Le projet n'est pas terminé.)
*They **have been using** the same software for years.* (L'action continue.)
*He **has been going** to the Bonn office since 2000.* (L'action est répétée et continue aujourd'hui).

**2.** Lorsque le présent est le résultat d'une action récente.
*I am tired (now) because I **have been working** very hard.*
*What **have** you **been doing**? I **have been moving** the machines around.*

! Certains verbes ne peuvent pas se mettre au *present perfect progressive* : ils parlent d'une action qui ne peut pas durer dans le temps.
*He **bought** the chocolate factory in 1985.* (Le fait d'acheter est fini.)
*He **has owned** the factory since 1985.* (Les verbes de possession sont des verbes non-progressifs.)
*They **have been producing** the same chocolate ever since.* (Depuis l'achat et cela continue.)

## Comment construire le *present perfect progressive* ?

| Verbes réguliers / irréguliers | | | | | |
|---|---|---|---|---|---|
| | Positive | | Negative | | Interrogative |
| | Long form | Short form | Long form | Short form | |
| *He / she / it* | *has been working* | *'s been working* | *has not been working* | *hasn't been working* | *Has... been working?* |
| *I / you / we / they* | *have been writing* | *'ve been writing* | *have not been writing* | *haven't been writing* | *Have ... been writing?* |

↳ Le *present perfect progressive* se construit comme suit :
**auxiliaire *be* au *present perfect* + verbe *-ing***

**1** **À partir de chacune des listes de mots, construisez une phrase au *present perfect simple*.**

• **À la forme affirmative**

**1.** you – have the agenda – since last month

..................................................................................

..................................................................................

**2.** she – already – send – the report to the manager

..................................................................................

..................................................................................

**3.** the board – reject – the motion

..................................................................................

..................................................................................

• **À la forme négative**

**4.** they – not – vote on anything – so far

..................................................................................

..................................................................................

**5.** the Financial Controller – not – come – to an A.G.M. for a long time

..................................................................................

..................................................................................

..................................................................................

..................................................................................

**6.** sales – not – be – good this year

..................................................................................

..................................................................................

• **À la forme interrogative**

**7.** how long for – he – be – chairman?

..................................................................................

..................................................................................

**8.** he – write the minutes – yet?

..................................................................................

..................................................................................

**9.** you – ever – speak – in public?

..................................................................................

..................................................................................

**2** **À partir de chacune des listes de mots, construisez une phrase au *present perfect progressive*.**

**1.** They are still in the meeting.
how long – the meeting – go on – for?

..................................................................................

..................................................................................

**2.** She doesn't understand a thing now!
she – not – listen to – the presentation

..................................................................................

..................................................................................

**3.** What's up with Tom? He looks exhausted!
he – negotiate with the operators – for 5 hours

..................................................................................

..................................................................................

**4.** The discussion still hasn't finished!
what – they – talk about?

..................................................................................

..................................................................................

**5.** The appointment was at 10. It's now 10.15.
they – not – wait – long

..................................................................................

..................................................................................

**6.** You have got ink all over your hands!
I – take down – the minutes

..................................................................................

..................................................................................

**7.** He never reaches a conclusion!
he – sum up – for a long time

..................................................................................

..................................................................................

**8.** The budget update is started but not finished.
they – update – the budget

..................................................................................

..................................................................................

**3** **Entourez *been* ou *gone*.**

**1.** He has gone / been to Paris, he isn't back yet.

**2.** Look at all those bags! Your secretary has gone / been shopping!

**3.** He has never gone / been to Rome.

**4.** What a lot of samples! You have gone / been to a trade fair.

**5.** I'm afraid he isn't in his office – he's gone / been to a meeting.

**6.** "Look at your muddy shoes!" "I have gone / been for a walk."

**7.** He'll be back on Monday. He's gone / been to the mountains on holiday.

**8.** It is 10 am. The house is empty. Everyone has gone / been to work.

## 4 À partir des indices en italiques, formulez une phrase en conjuguant le verbe entre parenthèses au *present perfect simple* ou au *present perfect progressive*.

**1.** *You see Mary. She is looking pleased but messy, but the conference room is ready for the meeting. She tells you:*

(prepare) ..................................................................

..................................................................

..................................................................

**2.** *Bill started writing the presentation 3 hours ago. He is still writing it now.*

(write) ..................................................................

..................................................................

**3.** *You need to speak to the manager. He is in a meeting which started 40 minutes ago. His assistant says:*

(be) ..................................................................

..................................................................

..................................................................

**4.** *There is a meeting for a supplier to present his new product. You arrive late and miss the presentation, so a colleague says:*

(present – already) ..................................................................

..................................................................

..................................................................

**5.** *You are at a sales conference for the first time, and it shows! A colleague asks:*

(be) ..................................................................

..................................................................

..................................................................

**6.** *Everyone has now got a copy of the file. What was your recent activity?*

(hand out) ..................................................................

..................................................................

**7.** *We started discussing the new supply chain system 2 hours ago. The discussion is not yet finished.*

(discuss) ..................................................................

..................................................................

..................................................................

**8.** *You begin to make your presentation. Your tummy begins to rumble. You had no breakfast!*

(eat) ..................................................................

..................................................................

**9.** *The CEO arrives from office to give a presentation. He needs a beamer. The maintenance team forgot to mend it!*

(repair) ..................................................................

..................................................................

..................................................................

**10.** *You cannot find the notes you made for the meeting!*

(lose) ..................................................................

..................................................................

### CORRIGÉS

**1. 1.** You have had the agenda since last month. **2.** She has already sent the report to the manager. **3.** The board has/have rejected the motion. **4.** They haven't voted on anything so far. **5.** The Financial Controller hasn't come to an A.G.M. for a long time. **6.** Sales have not been good this year. **7.** How long has he been chairman for? **8.** as he written the minutes yet? **9.** Have you ever spoken in public?
**2. 1.** How long has the meeting been going on for? **2.** She hasn't been listening to the presentation. **3.** He has been negotiating with the operators for 5 hours! **4.** What have they been talking about?! **5.** They haven't been waiting long. **6.** I have been taking down the minutes. **7.** He has been summing up for a long time. **8.** They have been updating the budget.
**3. 1.** gone. **2.** been **3.** been **4.** been **5.** gone **6.** been **7.** gone **8.** gone
**4. 1.** I have been preparing the conference room. **2.** He has been writing the presentation for 3 hours. **3.** He has been in the meeting for 4 minutes. **4.** They have already presented their new product. **5.** Have you ever been to a sales conference before? **6.** I have been handing out the files. **7.** We have been discussing the new supply chain system for 2 hours. **8.** I haven't eaten anything this morning. **9.** They haven't repaired the beamer ( / projector)! **10.** I have lost my notes!

# Le *past perfect simple*

**Comparez !**

*When we arrived, they* ***discussed*** *the budget. (Prétérit)*
→ Quand nous sommes arrivés, ils ont commencé à discuter du budget.

*When we arrived, they* ***were discussing*** *the budget. (Prétérit progressif)*
→ Quand nous sommes arrivés, ils étaient en train de discuter du budget.

*When we arrived, they* ***had discussed*** *the budget. (Past perfect)*
→ Quand nous sommes arrivés, ils avaient fini de discuter du budget.

## Quand utiliser le *past perfect simple* ?

**1.** Pour parler d'un événement antérieur à un autre dans le passé.
*When Henry arrived, the customer* ***had gone****.*
→ Quand Henry est arrivé, le client était parti.

**2.** Pour exprimer ce que vous auriez souhaité, mais qui ne s'est pas réalisé (à utiliser en particulier avec *expect to, hope to, mean to*).

*We* ***had thought*** *about asking for early delivery, but it is not their company policy.*
→ Nous avions pensé à demander une livraison anticipée mais ce n'est pas leur politique d'entreprise.

*We* ***had hoped*** *to sign the contract this week, but there are still details to sort out.*
→ Nous avions espéré signer le contrat cette semaine, mais il reste encore des détails à régler.

*I* ***had wanted*** *to see the Japanese supplier at the trade fair, but he didn't stay all week.*
→ J'avais voulu voir le fournisseur japonais à la foire, mais il n'était pas resté toute la semaine.

## Comment construire le *past perfect simple* ?

| Verbes réguliers / irréguliers | | |
|---|---|---|
| **Positive** | **Negative** | **Interrogative** |
| *I / you / he / we / you / they had / 'd worked / written* | *I / you / he / we / you / they had not / hadn't worked / written* | *Had I / you / he / we / you / they worked / written?* |

↪ Le *past perfect simple* se construit comme suit :

**auxiliaire *have* au prétérit + participe passé du verbe**

**!** Notez que le *past perfect* est aussi le passé du *present perfect*.
*I don't know what to say. I have never been to a production meeting before.*
*I didn't know what to say. I had never been to a production meeting before.*

# Le *past perfect progressive*

**Comparez !**

- Le *past perfect simple* avec le *past perfect progressive* :

*I **had worked** hard and the report was finished.*
→ J'avais beaucoup travaillé et le rapport était fini.

*I **had been working** hard, and the report was nearly finished.*
→ J'avais beaucoup travaillé et le rapport était presque fini.

- Le *past progressive* avec le *past perfect progressive* :

*Michael **was sitting** at his desk, looking at the spreadsheet.*
→ Michael était assis à son bureau en train de regarder le tableur.

*He **had been trying** to understand it for a long time!*
→ Cela faisait longtemps qu'il essayait de le comprendre !

## Quand utiliser le *past perfect progressive* ?

**1.** Lorsque le passé est le résultat d'une action ayant eu lieu dans un passé antérieur.
*I was tired (yesterday) because I **had been working** very hard.*

**2.** Lorsqu'un événement s'est produit pendant une certaine période avant un moment du passé.
*They **had been smoking** in the room before we arrived – what a smell there was!*

**3.** Pour expliquer la durée d'une action dans le passé.
*When the customer arrived, I **had been waiting** for a long time!*

## Comment construire le *past perfect progressive* ?

| Verbes réguliers / irréguliers | | |
|---|---|---|
| **Positive** | **Negative** | **Interrogative** |
| *I / you / he / we / you / they had / 'd been working / writing* | *I / you / he / we / you / they had not / hadn't been working / writing* | *Had I / you / he / we / you / they been working / writing?* |

↳ Le *past perfect progressive* se construit comme suit :

***had been* + verbe *-ing***

**!** Noter que le *past perfect progressive* est aussi le passé du *present perfect progressive*.
*We are annoyed because we have been discussing the price for a long time.*
*We were annoyed because we had been discussing the price for a long time.*

**1 Après avoir indiqué le prétérit du verbe à l'infinitif, complétez les phrases avec le participe passé du verbe.**

**1.** Do → ..............................................................

We had ..................................... business with them for ten years, then went bankrupt.

**2.** Choose → ..............................................................

The C.E.O. had ..................................... our new manager, then he changed his mind.

**3.** Fight → ..............................................................

We had ..................................... hard for the contract, so we were pleased to get it.

**4.** Give → ..............................................................

The Japanese visitor had ..................................... me his business card before.

**5.** Ring → ..............................................................

I had ..................................... him in the morning, but I tried again in the afternoon.

**6.** Deal with → ..............................................................

They had ..................................... the quality problem, but the customer was still not satisfied.

**7.** Wind up → ..............................................................

The chairman had ..................................... the meeting when james asked a question.

**8.** Lose → ..............................................................

She had ..................................... her notes, but she found them just in time for the conference.

**9.** Begin → ..............................................................

The review meeting had ..................................... on time, when the beamer stopped working.

**10.** Wear → ..............................................................

The American had ..................................... shorts to the meeting – he regretted it after!

**2 Traduisez ces phrases en vous aidant du lexique p. 166.**

**1.** Lorsque nous sommes arrivés à la réunion, les autres attendaient depuis un certain temps.

..............................................................................

..............................................................................

..............................................................................

**2.** Aviez-vous déjà été à une réunion de comité directoire avant celle de la semaine dernière ?

..............................................................................

..............................................................................

..............................................................................

**3.** Nous n'avions pas su qu'il voulait regarder le contrat.

..............................................................................

..............................................................................

**4.** Il était satisfait hier, après qu'il ait vu les résultats financiers.

..............................................................................

..............................................................................

**5.** J'avais terminé mon explication depuis dix minutes lorsqu'il a dit qu'il ne comprenait toujours pas !

..............................................................................

..............................................................................

..............................................................................

**6.** L'année dernière, c'était la première fois que nous sommes allés à la réunion trimestrielle.

..............................................................................

..............................................................................

..............................................................................

**7.** Nous avions espéré qu'il accepterait nos conditions, mais il voulait une meilleure remise.

..............................................................................

..............................................................................

..............................................................................

**8.** Aviez-vous tout organisé avant que l'équipe de production soit arrivée pour la réunion Kaizen ?

..............................................................................

..............................................................................

..............................................................................

**9.** Hier, ils ne s'étaient pas encore mis d'accord sur le prix de vente. J'espère qu'ils feront aujourd'hui.

..........................................................................................

..........................................................................................

..........................................................................................

**10.** Depuis combien de temps avez-vous travaillé sur le projet avant qu'il ne soit enterré ?

..........................................................................................

..........................................................................................

..........................................................................................

## 3 Conjuguez les verbes de cette histoire au temps qui convient : *past perfect simple* ou *progressive*.

When Bill, the financial controller, arrived at the meeting at 14.30, they (discuss) ...................................... the new project for some time, and they still (not – finish) ... .................................. He looked around and everyone looked tired. They (be) ...................................... there since 10 am and the chairman (not even – offer) ....... ............................... them a coffee break! He asked a colleague if anyone (bring up) .................................. the subject of the budget cuts, and was told that, so far, they (talk about) ...................................... the design and development of the project, but not the finances. They (look at) ...................................... the road map. In fact, they (wait) ...................................... for Bill to arrive with the figures so that they could begin. Bill took his laptop out of his briefcase and realized, to his horror, that he (leave) ...................................... all the necessary supporting documents at home!

## 4 Complétez les phrases en conjuguant le verbe entre parenthèses.

**1.** Who was the person who arrived in the middle of the meeting? I don't know, (meet) .............................. before.

**2.** Why didn't you use the O.H.P. for your presentation? Because the maintenance department (repair) ............. ..........................................................................................

**3.** Why did you interrupt the marketing manager during his talk? Because (talk) ...................................... for a long time.

**4.** Why didn't the quality people come to the meeting? They (arrange another meeting) ................................. ..... already

**5.** Why didn't you bring the japanese supplier to the meeting? Because he (travel) .................................. all night.

**6.** Why was the financial controller embarrassed at the budget meeting? Because (calculate the figures wrong) ...................................... .

**CORRIGÉS**

**1.** 1. Did – done 2. Chose – chosen 3. Fought – fought 4. Gave – given 5. Rang – rung 6. Dealt with – 7. Wound up – wound up 8. Lost – lost 9. Began – begun 10. Wore – worn.

**2.** 1. When we arrived at the meeting, everyone else had been waiting for some time. 2. Had you ever been to a board meeting before the one last week? 3. We hadn't known that he wanted to look at the contract. 4. He was satisfied yesterday after he had seen the financial results. 5. I had been explaining for ten minutes when he said he still didn't understand! 6. Last year was the first time we had been to the quarterly meeting. 7. We had hoped he would accept our terms, but he wanted a better discount. 8. Had you organized everything before the production team arrived for the Kaizen meeting? 9. They still hadn't agreed on the sales price yesterday, I hope they will today. 10. How long had you been working on the project before it was shelved?

**3.** Had been discussing – hadn't finished – had been – hadn't even offered – had brought up – had talked about – had been looking at – had been waiting – had left

**4.** 1. I don't know. I had never met him / her before. 2. Because the maintenance department hadn't repaired it. 3. Because he had been talking for a long time. 4. They had already arranged another meeting 5. Because he had been travelling all night. 6. Because he had calculated the figures wrong.

## 1 Précisez le temps du verbe souligné et la raison de son emploi.

Score : ..... / 20

1. I have often thought of changing the meeting process. ..............................

2. He was tired when he arrived because he had been travelling all day. ..............................

3. What were those people talking about during the conference? ..............................

4. Did you know that the meeting has been cancelled? ..............................

5. When I was younger, I used to hate listening to other people talking. ..............................

6. "You look pleased!" "I've been talking to our new supplier." ..............................

7. When they met, they realised they had been doing business for several years. ..............................

8. Sorry I didn't answer the phone you rang white I was taking part in a meeting. ..............................

9. They have tried to make the meetings more efficient since the beginning of the year. ..............................

10. Last year we had many too many reports to read. ..............................

## 2 Quel temps convient pour parler de... ?

Score : ..... / 8

1. To talk about something you often did in the past: ..............................
2. To talk about a recent success (a good deal, for example): ..............................
3. To say what your movements were at a given time yesterday: ..............................
4. To talk about someone who is no longer in the company: ..............................
5. To say that you can't read the figures because you've lost your glasses: ..............................
6. To say that you are tired now because of too much work today: ..............................
7. To say that you were tired yesterday, because of too much work: ..............................
8. To say that you had done something, before you did something else: ..............................

## 3 Entourez l'erreur et corrigez-la !

Score : ..... / 10

1. She has not been to the production meeting yesterday. ..............................
2. What were the results like? Had they good sales this year? ..............................
3. How long have you been knowing the quality auditor? ..............................
4. I'm sorry I'm late. Had you been waiting long? ..............................

**5.** I am working for pbn since 1999. ..............................

**6.** John has wrote the minutes. ..............................

**7.** He was not wanting to go the meeting. ..............................

**8.** Did you have the agenda yet? ..............................

**9.** They have been brainstorming since three hours. ..............................

**10.** She has left the meeting at 3 o'clock. ..............................

## 4 Imaginez une fin aux phrases suivantes.

**Score: ..... / 6**

**1.** I wrote a letter ..............................

**2.** I was writing a letter ..............................

**3.** I have written a letter this morning ..............................

**4.** I have been writing a letter this morning ..............................

**5.** I had written the letter ..............................

**6.** I had been writing the letter ..............................

## 5 Entourez la bonne réponse.

**Score: ..... / 6**

When we decided / have decided / had decided to meet the supplier for the last time to try and reach an agreement, we negotiated / have already negotiated / had already been negotiating for several months. When we arrived, he talked / has been talking / was talking on the phone and indicated rudely that we should sit down. When he finished, he explained that he finds / has found / had found another buyer! Now the problem is that I have to explain to my boss why we lost / have lost / had lost our supplier, and what I was doing / have been doing / had been doing this week to find another one quickly!

**Score total: ..... / 50**

## CORRIGÉS

**1.** 1. Present perfect – a process started in the past, continuing up to now. 2. Past perfect progressive – the result then of something which happened before. 3. Simple past progressive – something happening around a moment in the past. 4. Present perfect – something which has happened but we don't know when. 5. Simple past – "used to" – you are no longer "young" and now you like listening! 6. Present perfect progressive – present result of a recent happening in the past. 7. Past perfect progressive – they had been doing business before they met. 8. Simple past progressive – the background to another action in the past. 9. Present perfect – from a certain point in time, up to now. 10. Simple past – a finished time in the past.

**2.** 1. Simple past 2. Present perfect 3. Past progressive 4. Simple past 5. Present perfect 6. Present perfect progressive 7. Past perfect progressive 8. Past perfect

**3.** 1. did not go 2. have they had 3. have you known 4. Have you been waiting 5. have worked / have been working 6. has written 7. didn't want 8. Have you had 9. for 10. left

**4.** (Examples) 1. I wrote a letter yesterday. 2. I was writing a letter when you called. 3. I have written a letter this morning, it's finished (but the morning isn't). 4. I have been writing a letter this morning but I haven't finished it yet. 5. I had written the letter before I received your update. 6. I had been writing the letter when I was told to wait for an update.

**5.** decided – had already been negotiating – was talking – had found – have lost – have been doing

# L'expression du futur avec le présent

En anglais, il n'existe pas vraiment de temps « futur » en tant que tel. Le futur, l'avenir, les projets, peuvent donc s'exprimer de différentes façons. Il est alors nécessaire de prendre en compte le contexte pour pouvoir déterminer la façon appropriée d'exprimer le futur.

## L'expression du futur avec le présent simple

On utilise le présent simple avec un sens de futur :

**1.** Pour indiquer un horaire officiel (transports en commun, cinéma, etc.).
*The customer's train **leaves** at 5.45 this evening.*
***Does** the plane **land** at 10.05 or 10.35 tomorrow?*
*The monthly meeting **is** next Monday at 10 am.*

**2.** Après les conjonctions de temps *when, if, as soon as, before, until (till), unless.*
***As soon as** he **comes**, show him into my office please.*
***If** the plant manager **doesn't come** tomorrow, everyone will relax!*
***Before** she **goes**, please give her the new schedule.*
***When** he **arrives**, show him straight into the showroom.*
*We will stay here **until** we **reach** a decision.*
*It will be difficult to meet **unless** you **come** to my office.*

Mais après *when*, pronom interrogatif, utilisez *will*.
***When will** he come?*

## L'expression du futur avec le présent progressif

**Comparez !**

*What time does the plane take off tomorrow? It takes off at 10.45 am.*
→ À quelle heure part l'avion demain ? (Horaire officiel)
*What time are you going tomorrow? I'm going at 10.45 am.*
→ À quelle heure avez-vous prévu de partir demain ? (Horaire personnel)

**1.** Accompagné d'une expression, ou dans un contexte, qui vous place dans le futur, le présent progressif est utilisé pour parler de ce que l'on a programmé de faire. Ce temps, aussi appelé « temps de l'agenda » ("*diary tense*") s'utilise pour toute chose que vous pourriez noter dans votre agenda, vos rendez-vous par exemple.
***He is seeing** the production manager **on Friday**.*
*What **are you doing tomorrow**? I'm going to the subsidiary in Maidstone.*
***She is working** in Manchester **next week**.*
***I am meeting** the supplier in **two weeks' time**.*

Vous pouvez aussi utiliser *be going to* + verbe (qui traduit une intention).
***I am going to meet** the supplier in two weeks' time.*

**!** La nuance entre les trois formes étant très sensible, même les « vrais anglophones » mélangent les trois. Tout dépend de la manière dont vous voyez les choses. Ces bases vous permettent d'utiliser les trois formes correctement !

**2.** Un itinéraire peut être relaté au présent simple ou au présent progressif.
*When is Mr Kibashi coming? He arrives / is arriving at 10 am on Friday.*

## L'expression du futur avec *be going to*

**Comparez !**

*I'm meeting the Australian sales manager next week.*
→ Le rendez-vous est pris : vous l'avez noté dans votre agenda.
*I'm going to meet the Australian sales manager next week.*
→ Vous avez l'intention de le rencontrer.

### Quand exprimer le futur avec *be going to* ?

**1.** Pour marquer une intention.

*Michael is going to retire before he is 65-years-old.*
→ Michael a l'intention de prendre sa retraite avant ses 65 ans.

*He is not going to work until full retirement age.*
→ Il n'a pas l'intention de travailler jusqu'à l'âge de la retraite.

*Is he going to take early retirement, then?*
→ A-t-il, alors, l'intention de prendre une retraite anticipée ?

**2.** Pour exprimer un futur proche.

*It is 10 am. John's plane is at 10.30. It takes an hour to get to the airport. John is going to miss his plane.*
→ Il est 10 heures. L'avion de John est à 10 h 30. On met une heure pour aller à l'aéroport. John va manquer son avion.

Pour évoquer un futur imminent, vous pouvez aussi utiliser *be about to* + verbe (« s'apprêter à faire quelque chose »).
*He is about to go and pick up visitor from the station.*
→ Il s'apprête à aller chercher le visiteur à la gare.

### Comment construire le futur avec *be going to* ?

| Make | | | | | |
|---|---|---|---|---|---|
| | Positive | | Negative | | Interrogative |
| | Long form | Short form | Long form | Short form | |
| *I* | *am going to make* | *'m going to make* | *am not going to make* | *'m not going to make* | *Am ... going to make?* |
| *He / she / it* | *is going to make* | *'s going to make* | *is not going to make* | *isn't going to make* | *Is ... going to make?* |
| *You / we / they* | *are going to make* | *'re going to make* | *are not going to make* | *aren't going to make* | *Are ... going to make?* |

↳ Le futur avec *be going to* se construit comme suit :

**auxiliaire *be* + *going to* + base verbale**

MAKING ARRANGEMENTS

**1** **Écrivez les phrases ci-dessous aux formes négative et interrogative.**

**1.** He is going to put off the sales meeting to a later date.

..........................................................................................

..........................................................................................

..........................................................................................

**2.** His assistant is playing golf with the CEO on Friday.

..........................................................................................

..........................................................................................

..........................................................................................

**3.** Look at the news! You are going to be delayed by the traffic on the m25!

..........................................................................................

..........................................................................................

..........................................................................................

**4.** I am picking up the customer from head office on Tuesday.

..........................................................................................

..........................................................................................

..........................................................................................

**5.** The purchaser is coming on Thursday to discuss the delivery conditions.

..........................................................................................

..........................................................................................

..........................................................................................

**6.** The review meeting begins at 17.30 on Mondays.

..........................................................................................

..........................................................................................

..........................................................................................

**7.** They are going to Malta for a management training session.

..........................................................................................

..........................................................................................

..........................................................................................

**8.** The sales team are going to set up a conference to demonstrate the new product.

..........................................................................................

..........................................................................................

..........................................................................................

**2** **Conjuguez le verbe entre parenthèses comme il convient: présent simple, présent progressif ou *be going to*.**

**1.** The meeting is next Monday. What time (begin) ...... ............................. ?

**2.** She (try) .................................. and see the supply chain manager on Monday.

**3.** What are you doing on Friday? I (take) .................... ............... the customer out to lunch.

**4.** His diary is full. He (be) .................................... very busy next week.

**5.** What time is Jonathan arriving? His train (arrive) ...... .............................. at 9.15.

**3** **À partir des indices en italique, formulez une phrase dans laquelle vous utiliserez le présent simple, le présent progressif ou *be going to*.**

**1.** *You have decided to organise a conference call for next week. It is not yet arranged. You inform your boss:*

I ..........................................................................................

..........................................................................................

**2.** *Itinerary Mr Scott: arrival factory 10.30 / Departure factory 11.30.*

Mr Scott ..........................................................................

..........................................................................................

**3.** *The quality manager has arranged to do a quality audit at a supplier on Friday. A Swedish counterpart wants to meet him at the same time. You say:*

I'm sorry but ..................................................................

..........................................................................................

**4.** *You intend to read through the sales agreement this evening when you get home. You say:*

..........................................................................................

..........................................................................................

**5.** *In Marina's diary it says: "Wednesday – meet with Fred Jones 10 am". Your colleague asks: "what is she doing on Wednesday?" You answer:*

..........................................................................................

..........................................................................................

*6. The company is spending much more money than they are earning at the moment. You can see now that the financial situation is not good for the future. You say:*

...........................................................................

...........................................................................

## 4 Entourez l'erreur et corrigez-la !

**1.** The meeting is beginning at 14.30 every other week.

...........................................................................

**2.** He is reading a newspaper this evening.

...........................................................................

**3.** What are she doing tomorrow?

...........................................................................

**4.** When he will come, we will begin the visit.

...........................................................................

**5.** They are going bring forward the date.

...........................................................................

**6.** The meeting at 6 pm is going not suit everyone.

...........................................................................

**7.** What do you tomorrow?

...........................................................................

**8.** They are about to going into a breakfast meeting.

...........................................................................

## 5 Si les phrases ci-dessous ne veulent pas dire la même chose, expliquez la différence de sens.

**1. A.** The meeting begins at 9 on Mondays.
**B.** He is having a meeting at 9 on Monday.

...........................................................................

...........................................................................

**2. A.** She is seeing the new sales outlet next week.
**B.** She is going to see the new sales outlet.

...........................................................................

...........................................................................

**3. A.** They are going to go to a trade fair in Spain.
**B.** They are going to a trade fair in Spain.

...........................................................................

...........................................................................

**4. A.** We are going to work on the report this evening.
**B.** We are working on the report this evening.

...........................................................................

...........................................................................

**5. A.** He is about to invite the auditor to lunch.
**B.** He is going to invite the auditor to lunch.

...........................................................................

...........................................................................

**6. A.** The financial year is ending in November.
**B.** The financial year ends in November.

...........................................................................

...........................................................................

### CORRIGÉS

**1.** 1. He isn't (is not) going to put off... Is he going to put off... ? 2. His assistant isn't (is not) playing golf... Is his assistant playing golf...? 3. You aren't (are not) going to be delayed... Are you going to be delayed...? 4. I am not picking up... Am I picking up...? 5. The purchaser isn't (is not) coming... Is the purchaser coming...? 6. The review meeting (doesn't not) begin at... Does the review meeting begin at... ? 7. They aren't (are not) begin to Malta... Are they going to Malta...? 8. The sales team aren't (are not) going to set up... Are the sales team going to set up...?
**2.** 1. The meeting is next Monday. What time does it begin? (It's totally impersonal.) 2. She is going to try and see the supply chain manager on Monday. 3. What are you doing on Friday? I am taking the customer out to lunch. 4. His diary is full. He is going to be very busy next week. 5. What time is Jonathan arriving? Oh, his train arrives at 9.15.
**3.** 1. I'm going to organize a conference call for next week. 2. Mr Scott arrives / is arriving at 10.30 and leaves at 11.30. 3. I'm sorry but he is doing a quality audit on Friday. 4. I'm going to read through the sales agreement this the sales agreement this evening. 5. She is meeting Fred Jones at 10 am. 6. They are going to go bankrupt.
**4.** 1. The meeting begins at 14.30 every other week. 2. He is going to read a newspaper this evening. 3. What is she doing tomorrow? 4. When he comes, we will begin the visit. 5. They are going to bring forward the date. 6. The meeting at 6 pm is not going to suit everyone. 7. What are you doing tomorrow? 8. They are about to go into a breakfast meeting.
**5.** 1. A. A regular meeting B. Just one meeting 2. A. It has been arranged B. She intends to see it 3. A. They intend to B. At the moment (there is no expression to put you in the future) 4. A. We intend to B. It has been arranged (but the report will probably be written in both cases!) 5. A. He will do so in one or two minutes B. An intention only 6. A. This one time B. Every year

# L'expression du futur avec *will*

## L'auxiliaire du futur *will* (ou *'ll*) s'utilise :

**1.** Pour une décision spontanée, comme, par exemple, promettre ou offrir un service, dire que l'on est d'accord, demander à quelqu'un de faire quelque chose.
*I'll ring you back. I will not forget to write. Will you let me know?*

*Won't* (= *will not*) peut être utilisé aussi pour exprimer un refus.
*The computer* ***won't work****!* → L'ordinateur ne veut pas fonctionner !
*They* ***will not listen****!* → Ils ne veulent pas écouter!

**2.** Pour une prédiction, une estimation ou un calcul concernant le futur.

*Will* est souvent associé à des verbes tels que *think, expect, be sure, wonder*.
***I wonder*** *if / I'm sure they'****ll*** *change the date.*
***I expect*** *they'****ll*** *cancel the meeting.*
***I don't think*** *I'****ll*** *set up a meeting.* (Et non: *I think they won't set up a meeting.*)

*Will* est aussi souvent associé aux adverbes de probabilité *certainly, possibly, probably, maybe, perhaps*, etc.
*She'****ll certainly*** *put back the appointment.*
*I* ***probably won't*** *make it.*

**3.** Pour exprimer un fait simple, sans nuance, ou pour être plus formel.
*Mr Jones* ***will visit*** *the factory next week.*
*He* ***will be*** *49 next year.*

Encore plus formel (et utilisé dans les journaux notamment), *be to* est équivalent à *will* (et peut également servir à l'expression de la condition).
*The president* ***is to*** *visit Hong Kong on Tuesday.*
*If we* ***are to*** *succeed, we must launch our product now.*

**!** N'oubliez pas : pas de *will* après *when, if, as soon as, before, until (till), unless*, sauf dans une question.

### Shall

Peu utilisé dans les phrases affirmatives en anglais courant (et uniquement pour *I* et *we*), *shall* est utilisé dans les phrases interrogatives pour :

- Proposer de faire quelque chose : *I have to get to the airport. Shall I take you?*
- Demander un conseil : *I have to go London this evening. How shall I go?*
- Faire une suggestion : *Shall we go? / Let's go, shall we?*
- Notez la différence entre *shall* et *will* dans une question :

| | |
|---|---|
| *Shall I give the salesman a lift home?* | *Will you give the salesman a lift home?* |
| *Do you want me to give him a lift?* | *I want you to give him a lift.* |

- *Shall not* se dit *shan't* en anglais courant.
*We shan't be here tomorrow.*
- *Shall* s'utilise aussi à la place de *will*, dans un langage formel (dans les lettres notamment).
*I shall be pleased to meet you next week.*

# Autres formes de futur

## Le futur progressif

**Comparez !**

*Come at 8 am and we'**ll show** the customer around the factory.*
→ Venez à 8 heures et nous ferons le tour de l'usine avec le client.

*Don't come between 8 and 10 am, we'**ll be showing** the customer around.*
→ Ne venez pas entre 8 et 10 heures, nous serons en train de faire le tour de l'usine.

On utilise le futur progressif :

**1.** Pour exprimer une action que l'on sera en train de faire à un certain moment dans le futur.
*Can I call you at 8.30 am? Preferably not, we'**ll be having** our weekly meeting.*

**2.** Pour parler de ce que quelqu'un a déjà organisé (à la place du présent progressif).
*We are meeting / **will be meeting** the supplier next week.*

**3.** Pour demander un service à quelqu'un (à la place du présent progressif).
*If you **will be seeing** the supplier, could you pick up the contract?*

## Le *future perfect*

On utilise le *future perfect* pour parler de quelque chose qui sera terminé/complété à un certain moment dans le futur.
*Shall I call you at 8.30 am? Yes, we'll have finished our weekly meeting by then.*

On peut aussi alors remplacer *will* par un auxiliaire modal. (Voir chapitre 4)

## Le *future perfect progressive*

On utilise le *future perfect progressive* pour exprimer la durée d'une action en train de se dérouler à un moment précis du futur ; le moment auquel se déroule action et durée de l'action (*for*...) doivent être mentionnés.
*By the time they get here, we **will have been waiting** for 2 hours!*
→ Le temps qu'ils arrivent, nous aurons attendu 2 heures !

**!** Le *future perfect* et le *future perfect progressive* sont souvent accompagnés par l'expression « *by the time / by then* ».

## Le futur dans le passé

Pour parler de quelque chose que l'on avait l'intention de faire à un certain moment dans le passé, on utilise le passé de la forme verbale que l'on utiliserait normalement pour parler du futur.
***I am going to** ring you later.* → Je vous appelle plus tard.
***I was going to** ring you later, but...* → J'avais l'intention de vous appeler plus tard, mais...

## 1 Conjuguez les verbes entre parenthèses en utilisant *will / shall.*

**1.** Do you want a lift back to the office? No thank you, I think (walk) .................................... .

**2.** Can you give me their contact address? Yes, I (call back) .................................... this afternoon.

**3.** I'm running out of time to get the sales contract finished. Don't worry I (help) .................................... there.

**4.** Are you coming to the meeting on Friday? No, I'm afraid I (not be) .................................... there.

**5.** How is the conference organisation getting on? PMB Inc (certainly – not – come) .................................... on time.

**6.** The Marshes said they were coming but I'm sure they (not be) .................................... on time.

**7.** Oh look at the time, it's 13.15! (We – go) .................................... to lunch?

**8.** I've decided to show them the company film. Do you think they (like) .................................... it?

**9.** I'm not sure about coming on Tuesday. (Let know – me) .................................... a.s.a.p.?

## 2 Lisez les données en italique et faites une phrase en utilisant *will* ou *shall.*

**1.** *You are trying to finish a spreadsheet on the computer. It doesn't work.*

..........................................................................................

..........................................................................................

**2.** *You want to offer to help someone.*

..........................................................................................

..........................................................................................

**3.** *You think that it is only possible the purchaser will sign the contract.*

..........................................................................................

..........................................................................................

**4.** *You promise not to tell anyone about a new patent.*

..........................................................................................

..........................................................................................

**5.** *You want someone to organise the meeting.*

..........................................................................................

..........................................................................................

**6.** *You don't know whether or not to buy a new machine. You ask a colleague.*

..........................................................................................

..........................................................................................

**7.** *Next year is the company's 10-year anniversary.*

..........................................................................................

..........................................................................................

**8.** *You were going to visit a supplier. Now you decide not to go.*

..........................................................................................

..........................................................................................

## 3 Reliez le début et la fin de phrase.

| | | | |
|---|---|---|---|
| By the time you get to the office | **1.** • | • **A.** | the meeting lasted until 7 pm. |
| The sales conference is to | **2.** • | • **B.** | working together for 10 years. |
| Shall we | **3.** • | • **C.** | he'll be busy. |
| I'm not sure, but I don't think he will | **4.** • | • **D.** | they will be finalizing the agreement. |
| Next year we will have been | **5.** • | • **E.** | won't have time to go through everything. |
| I was going to call you this afternoon but | **6.** • | • **F.** | they will have finished the negotiations. |
| We shall be pleased to provide you with | **7.** • | • **G.** | want to put forward the meeting. |
| Unless he comes soon, we | **8.** • | • **H.** | take place at the Signal Hotel. |
| At 8 o'clock tomorrow morning | **9.** • | • **I.** | any further information. We look forward... |
| I wouldn't disturb the auditor now, | **10.** • | • **J.** | have a break now? |

## 4 Répondez à chacune des questions suivantes.

**1.** What will you do to make the customer happy?

..............................................................................

..............................................................................

**2.** Can I see you at 12.30 tomorrow? – No,

..............................................................................

..............................................................................

**3.** Can I see you at 12.30 tomorrow? – Yes,

..............................................................................

..............................................................................

**4.** What were you planning to do, but you had to change your mind?

..............................................................................

..............................................................................

**5.** What can you do to give me the information I need quickly?

..............................................................................

..............................................................................

**6.** Will you be working next week?

..............................................................................

..............................................................................

**7.** Will you take the customer back to the airport?

..............................................................................

..............................................................................

**8.** Do you think that the trade fair will be called off because of the snow?

..............................................................................

..............................................................................

## 5 Dans chacune des listes suivantes, entourez l'intrus.

**1.** I will drive – I will be driving – I was going to drive – I am to drive.

**2.** Will you send the fax? – How shall we calculate it? – Shall I take you home? – Shall we go?

**3.** I won't be in Italy next week – He won't do the job – We won't have finished – They won't be long.

**4.** He expects ... – He wonders ... – I think ... – I hope ... – I'm sure ...

**5.** She won't be coming – They won't be eating with us – We won't be at the meeting.

## 6 Entourez la bonne réponse.

– The RDI department will have / has the new product ready by 1st September.

– Good, we will certainly / certainly will need to organize a reception to launch it.

– Yes, and quickly, otherwise our competitors will have show / shown their product on the market too.

– Let's set a date – say 1st October.

– The marketing team will be working / worked day and night to meet that deadline!

– Shall / will you make sure they are on time?

– Yes, what else do you think we will to need do / need to do?

– Someone will had to / have to send out the invitations.

– Will / shall I do that?

– I was going to suggest / will have suggested using on agency, but if you like it not will / will not cost so much that way.

### CORRIGÉS

**1.** **1.** I'll walk **2.** I'll call back **3.** I'll help **4.** Won't (will not) be **5.** Certainly won't (will not) come **6.** Won't (will not) be **7.** Shall we go **8.** They'll like **9.** Will you let me know?
**2.** (Examples) **1.** The computer just won't work! **2.** Shall I help? **3.** The purchaser will possibly / may / might sign. **4.** I promise I won't tell anyone. **5.** Will you organize the meeting? **6.** Shall I buy it? **7.** The company will be ten years old next year. **8.** I don't think I'll go to the supplier.
**3.** **1.** F ; **2.** H ; **3.** J ; **4.** G ; **5.** B ; **6.** A ; **7.** I ; **8.** E ; **9.** D ; **10.** C
**4.** (Examples) **1.** I'll probably take him out to lunch. **2.** No, I'll be having lunch with a customer. **3.** Yes, we'll have finished our meeting. **4.** I was going to put forward the meeting, but I decided to change nothing. **5.** I'll ring you back/send you a fax/send you an e-mail. **6.** Yes, I will. (Oh, could you check my e-mails for me then?). / No, I won't. **7.** Of course. / I'm afraid I can't because... **8.** It'll probably not be called off.
**5.** **1.** I was going to drive – the past **2.** Will you send the fax? – Asking someone else to do something **3.** He won't do the job – a refusal **4.** I hope – followed by the infinitive not will **5.** We won't be at the meeting – the others can be replaced by the present progressive future sense.
**6.** Will have – will certainly – shown – working – will – need to do – have to – shall – was going to suggest – will not (won't)

# L'expression de la condition avec *if*

Afin de savoir quel conditionnel utiliser, il faut bien regarder le contexte.

| Pour exprimer... | Type de conditionnel | Exemples | Remarques |
|---|---|---|---|
| une vérité générale<br>une consigne | CONDITIONNEL (0)<br>*If + present,*<br>*.... present* | *– If you **fill in** your diary, you **don't make** miss meetings.*<br>*– The computer **books** the room if you **press** that switch.* | *If* peut être traduit par « quand » ou « à chaque fois que ». |
| une situation réelle et possible dans le présent et le futur | CONDITIONNEL (1)<br>*If + present,*<br>*... will* | *We **won't have** time to do everything if you **don't arrange** an all-day meeting.* | On utilise la même structure pour *when, after, before, until, as soon as, unless, providing (that)*, etc.<br>*We **won't begin** the conference until the manager **arrives**.* |
| une situation irréelle et hypothétique dans le présent et le futur | CONDITIONNEL (2)<br>*If + simple past,*<br>*... modal (would / should / could / might / may) + infinitive* | *If we **went** to their factory, we **would see** their quality process.* | Le modal ne s'utilise pas dans la partie de *if*, sauf pour demander à quelqu'un de faire quelque chose.<br>*– I **would be** grateful if you **would confirm** the appointment.* |
| une situation dans le passé avec un sens de regret | CONDITIONNEL (3)<br>*If + past perfect ,*<br>*... modal + present perfect* | *If I **had known**, I **wouldn't have come**.*<br>*If he **had had** more time, we **could have talked** about the contract.* | |

↳ Si *if* figure dans la deuxième partie de la phrase, les deux propositions ne sont pas séparées par une virgule. *I would bring forward the meeting if I were you.*

Pour traduire « étant donné que ... », l'anglais utilise *if / given that + past, ... will.*

*If / given that he came yesterday, he won't come today.*

Dans le conditionnel (2), on utilise comme forme du verbe *be* à la 1re et 3e personne du singulier *were* (et non ~~*was*~~). Cependant, en anglais courant vous entendrez souvent l'erreur « *If I was...* ».

Les modaux à utiliser avec le conditionnel sont : *would, should, might, may.*

• Il est aussi possible d'exprimer la forme conditionnelle par l'inversion du sujet et du verbe avec les verbes *be* et *have*.

***If he were** free tomorrow, we could go and see him.*

→ ***Were he** free tomorrow we could go and see him.*

***If she had been available**, we could have discussed the problem this afternoon.*

→ ***Had she been available**, we could have discussed the problem this afternoon.*

• Nous utilisons le *be to* dans les conditionnels (1) et (2) pour exprimer une condition préalable.

*If she were to cancel her other appointment, would you guarantee to come to the office?*

## Wish

- Exprime un souhait pour une réalité potentielle dans le futur.
*I wish they would get their dates organised.*
- Exprime un regret dans le présent lorsqu'il est employé avec le conditionnel (2).
*If I knew the answer, I would tell you.* = *I wish I knew the answer.*
- Exprime un regret dans le passé lorsqu'il est employé avec le conditionnel (3).
*If I had known Peter was at the factory, I would have given him the documents.*
= *I wish I had known Peter was at the factory so I could have given him the documents.*

! Pas de *would* après *wish*
*I wish I had seen the product presentation on Monday.* (Et non : *I wish I would have seen...*)

# L'expression de la condition avec *should*

### On utilise *should* en tant qu'auxiliaire du conditionnel :

**1.** Pour remplacer *if* dans un anglais très formel.
*Should you require any further information, please do not hesitate to contact us.*

**2.** Dans les conditions de forte probabilité.
*Should you be / if you should happen to be in Paris, drop into the office.*

**3.** *Should* sert aussi à exprimer...

- Comme *ought to* (voir chapitre 4) :
– la probabilité : *Are you coming to the conference? It should be interesting.*
– l'anticipation : *The customer left his office at 9, so he should have arrived by now.*
– le regret : *We should have used our former supplier, the new one isn't reliable.*
– le reproche : *You should (might/could) have told us you couldn't make the appointment.*

- Associé à *that* :
– le conseil (*be* + adjectif – *crucial, important*...)
*We think that, if possible, the quarterly meetings should be shorter.*
*It is imperative that you (should) go through all the items on the agenda.*
– le discours indirect (utilisé avec *advise, ask, beg, command, demand, intend, instruct, order, request, require, stipulate, warn*)
*He was warned that he shouldn't be late.*
– une réaction (généralement négative) (*be* + adjectif – *amazed, disappointed, worried*...)
*He was surprised (that) they should think he would prepare the presentation.*
*It's strange (that) they should think we would fix a meeting at 9 pm!*

# L'expression de la condition avec *would*

L'auxiliaire du conditionnel *would* (ou *'d*) s'utilise :

**1.** Pour une situation ou une action hypothétique au présent (« si cela était possible »).
*Would you like to discuss this next week (if I can find the time)?*

**2.** Au passé, avec un sens de regret (*would* + *have* + participe passé).
*We would have persuaded him to come if we thought it would have done any good.*

**3.** Avec *rather* pour exprimer une préférence.
*I would rather the delivery terms were ex. works, if possible.*

## 1 Reliez le début et la fin des phrases.

| | | |
|---|---|---|
| What would happen if | 1. • | • A. they might be able to come too. |
| I wouldn't ask that question, | 2. • | • B. if we invited customers together. |
| If you wanted to visit the pilot plant, | 3. • | • C. we were to cancel the tour? |
| What would you say | 4. • | • D. they would make great savings. |
| If he asked the suppliers | 5. • | • E. if everyone were ready. |
| If they held more in house meetings | 6. • | • F. if they used computerized organizers. |
| We could put forward our appointment | 7. • | • G. you would need special authorization. |
| If the products were "hazardous" | 8. • | • H. if I asked you to take the client to lunch? |
| We wouldn't need so many audits | 9. • | • I. we would need safety measures for the visit. |
| They wouldn't forget so many dates | 10. • | • J. if I were you. |

## 2 Complétez les phrases suivantes à l'aide des verbes entre parenthèses.

**1.** If you (book) ................................ a table, you (be) ................................ well placed.

**2.** We (have) ................................ lunch at 12.30 am if it (suit) ................................ you.

**3.** If you (agree) ................................, I ..................... ........... (pick up) at your office.

**4.** If we (have) ................................ time, we (visit) .... ............................ the factory in the afternoon.

**5.** I (invite) ................................ the quality manager too if you (not – mind) ................................ .

**6.** The customer (appreciate) ................................ if you (take) ................................ him to a good restaurant.

## 3 Suivant les indices, donnez les instructions en utilisant le conditionnel (0).

**1.** If / you / input / participants names = the computer/ send / the invitations

..............................................................................................

..............................................................................................

**2.** The red light / flash = if / people / cannot come

..............................................................................................

..............................................................................................

**3.** The meeting room / not be reserved = if / you / not press/ the return key

..............................................................................................

..............................................................................................

**4.** If / you / input / all requirements = computer / organise/ the meeting

..............................................................................................

..............................................................................................

## 4 Faites une phrase en utilisant le conditionnel (3).

**1.** She didn't look so she bumped her head on the overhead conveyor.

..............................................................................................

..............................................................................................

**2.** There were no safety barriers, so they touched the chemical products.

..............................................................................................

..............................................................................................

**3.** He forgot to shut the door, so the goods got covered in dust.

..............................................................................................

..............................................................................................

**4.** The fork lift truck driver was driving so fast he knocked the goods off the pallets.

..............................................................................................

..............................................................................................

**5.** They didn't tidy the spare parts, so they were all over the floor.

..........................................................................................

..........................................................................................

**6.** She wasn't wearing protective clothing so she dirtied her dress.

..........................................................................................

..........................................................................................

## 5 En utilisant les conditionnels (2) et (3), exprimez vos regrets.

**1.** What a pity that the C.E.O. wasn't there.

I wish ..........................................................................

**2.** If we had more time, we could organise a much better presentation.

I wish ..........................................................................

..........................................................................................

**3.** We should see the sales department more often to avoid mistakes.

I wish ..........................................................................

**4.** If we had known their arrival time, we wouldn't have missed them at the airport.

I wish ..........................................................................

..........................................................................................

**5.** If you had told me about the meeting I could have made sure to be available.

I wish ..........................................................................

**6.** My diary is so full; I cannot fit in any more appointments.

I wish ..........................................................................

..........................................................................................

## 6 Entourez l'erreur et corrigez-la !

**1.** Would you like to visit Japan during the trip? Yes, I would like.

..........................................................................................

**2.** He advised us that we don't should cancel the meeting if we could avoid it.

..........................................................................................

**3.** If I went to visit the new manufacturer, would you to come with me?

..........................................................................................

**4.** They would have took him out to lunch if they knew he had the time.

..........................................................................................

**5.** Should you being near the office, let's have lunch.

..........................................................................................

**6.** If you require an appointment, please do not hesitate to contact my assistant. (Formal)

..........................................................................................

**7.** You should had invited the general manager to the last audit.

..........................................................................................

## CORRIGÉS

**1.** 1. C ; 2. J ; 3. G ; 4. H ; 5. A ; 6. D ; 7. E ; 8. I ; 9. B ; 10. F
**2.** 1. If you book a table, you will be well placed. 2. We will have lunch at 12.30 am if it suits you. 3. If you agree, I will pick you up at your office. 4. If we have time, we will visit the factory in the afternoon. 5. I will invite the quality manager too if you don't mind. 6. The customer will appreciate it if you take him to a good restaurant.
**3.** 1. If you input the participants' names, the computer sends the invitations. 2. The red light flashes if people cannot come. 3. The meeting room is not reserved if you don't press the return key. 4. If you input all your requirements, the computer organises the meeting.
**4.** 1. If she had looked, she wouldn't have bumped her head. 2. If there had been safety barriers, they wouldn't have touched the chemical products. 3. If he hadn't forgotten to shut the door, the goods wouldn't have got covered in dust. 4. If he hadn't been driving so fast, he wouldn't have knocked the goods off the pallets. 5. If they had tidied the spare parts, they wouldn't have been all over the floor. 6. If she had been wearing protective clothing, she wouldn't have dirtied her dress.
**5.** 1. I wish the C.E.O. had been there. 2. I wish we had more time. 3. I wish we saw the sales dept. more often. 4. I wish we had known their arrival time. 5. I wish you had told me about the meeting. 6. I wish my diary weren't so full.
**6.** 1. Would you like to visit Japan during the trip? Yes, I would. 2. He advised us that we shouldn't cancel the meeting if we could avoid it. 3. If I went to visit the new manufacturer, would you like to come with me/would you come with me? 4. They would have taken him out to lunch if they knew he had the time. 5. Should you be near the office, let's have lunch. 6. Should you require an appointment, please do not hesitate to contact my assistant. (Formal) 7. You should have invited the general manager to the last audit.

# 3. L'EXPRESSION DU FUTUR ET DE LA CONDITION

## MAKING ARRANGEMENTS

### 1 Conjuguez les verbes entre parenthèses au temps qui convient : présent simple, présent progressif, *will* ou *be going to* ?

**Score: ..... / 10**

– Hello, could I speak to Tom, please.

– I'm afraid he's not here. I think he (be back) ............................ at 4 o'clock. He's away on business.

– Oh dear. I have to talk to him as soon as possible. This afternoon I (go) .............................. to Blois and later we (eat) .............................. at a restaurant. When could I get hold of him?

– His flight (arrive) .............................. at 14.15.

– I (telephone) .............................. our client to make sure that he (come) .............................. to the meeting next week. At 5 o'clock I (visit) .............................. the factory.

– I (tell) ..... him you called. I (take) .............................. my lunch break now.

– I can see today (be) .............................. very busy!

### 2 Classez chacune de ces phrases dans la catégorie qui convient.

**Score : ..... / 14**

1. The conference always starts at 9.30 am.
2. The company will be 10-years-old next year.
3. He's going to call you later on.
4. She is visiting the supplier on Wednesday.
5. It is 2 pm. The meeting started at 13.30. Sally is going to be late.
6. His train leaves at 14.43.
7. She'll certainly get back to you before the end of the week.
8. I'll set up a meeting for next week.
9. John picks up the phone. "I'm going to postpone the appointment".
10. They are having a conference call on Friday.
11. The trade fair is to be in Germany.
12. I'm going to be on time at every meeting this year.
13. I expect that they'll want to see the R&D laboratory.
14. I'll let you know as soon as possible.

| Intention |
|---|
| |
| Already planned |
| |
| Spontaneous |
| |
| Simple fact |
| |
| Official / timetable |
| |
| Immediate future |
| |
| Think / forecast |
| |

### 3 Pour chacune des phrases, précisez quel conditionnel est utilisé et pourquoi.

**Score : ..... / 8**

1. If you prepare the visit, it will be easier.

.......................................................................................................................................

2. People participate better if you say "have you got any questions?".

.......................................................................................................................................

3. If I had put the key words on the visuals, I wouldn't have forgotten them.

.......................................................................................................................................

4. The operators won't get much work done if we talk to them.

.......................................................................................................................................

5. If it were possible, we would like to visit R&D.

..........................................................................................

6. If we walk slowly, we can see all the process.

..........................................................................................

7. If you had warned us, we could have tidied the workshop!

..........................................................................................

8. We couldn't go into the workshop if we weren't wearing protective clothing.

..........................................................................................

## 4 Entourez la bonne réponse.

Score: ..... / 10

1. I think I'll be / I'm being away until the end of the month.
2. The supplier is in town this week. I know I visiting / I'm visiting him tomorrow.
3. The C.E.O. has announced that all meetings will be starting / are to start on time.
4. Can you let me know? Yes, I'll get / I'm getting back to you A.S.A.P.
5. Please tell me as soon as you will have decided / you have decided.
6. I have to withdraw from our agreement with Tom. How shall I / will I tell him?
7. What are you going to do / are you doing this afternoon?
8. The purchaser is looking cross now. He will refuse / is going to refuse our tender.
9. The meeting is on Monday? I think it won't be / I don't think it will be convenient.
10. We won't go and bother the technicians now – they be tied up / they'll be tied up.

## 5 Entourez la bonne réponse.

Score: ..... / 8

1. If you cancel too often, you lost / you lose your customer.
2. Would you like to suggest / suggest another date?
3. If we had checked / if we checked, we wouldn't have missed the appointment.
4. If all goes well, we should to be able to / we should be able to come later.
5. If we work late / if we will work late, we'll finish today.
6. I wish the schedule would have been / had been computerized.
7. You wouldn't like to come earlier, would you? / will you?
8. I should be grateful if you confirm me / would confirm.

Score total: ..... / ...50

## CORRIGÉS

**1.** 'll be back – am going – are eating – arrives – 'll telephone – is coming – am visiting – 'll tell – 'm going to take – is going to be

**2.** Intention: 3, 12 / Already planned: 4, 10 / Spontaneous: 8, 14 / Simple fact: 2, 11 / Official/timetable: 1, 6 / Immediate future: 5, 9 / Think / forecast: 7, 13.

**3.** 1. 1 (Real situation) 2. 0 (Cause = effect) 3. 3 (Regret) 4. 1 (Real situation) 5. 2 (Polite, hypothetical request) 6. 0 (Cause = effect) 7. 3 (Regret) 8. 2 (Hypothetical – warning)

**4.** 1. I'll be 2. I'm visiting 3. Are to start 4. I'll get 5. You have decided 6. Shall I 7. Les deux! 8. Is going to refuse 9. I don't think it will be 10. They'll be

**5.** 1. you lose 2. to suggest 3. If we had checked 4. we should be able to 5. If we work late 6. had been computerized 7. would you 8. Would confirm

# 4 La modalisation



## Comparez !

*He **can** sign the agreement.* → Il peut signer le contrat.
*He **has to** sign the agreement.* → Il doit signer le contrat.
*He **should** sign the agreement.* → Il devrait signer le contrat.
*He **may** sign the agreement.* → Il se peut qu'il signe le contrat.

Notamment par l'intermédiaire d'auxiliaires particuliers, la modalisation permet d'exprimer le possible, le nécessaire, le probable, l'obligation, le permis, le conseil, etc.

| Auxiliaires modaux | Formes à sens modal | Quasi-modaux |
|---|---|---|
| *can, could, may, might, shall, should, will, would, must* | *be able to, have (got) to, be allowed to, be likely to, be forbidden to, be bound to, be to, be supposed to* | *had better, ought to, would rather* (*Dare* et *need* peuvent se comporter comme un modal, ou comme un verbe ordinaire.) |
| suivis d'une base verbale (jamais précédés de *to*) | suivies d'une base verbale (le *to* fait ensemble avec le verbe) | suivis d'une base verbale (jamais précédés de *to*) (*Ought to* : le *to* fait ensemble avec le verbe.) |

↳ Pas de -*s* à la 3<sup>e</sup> personne.

Différentes modalisations peuvent être utilisées au sein d'une même phrase.
*He **must be able to** make a compromise.*
La négation se trouve généralement après le modal sauf ceux qui contient un *to* :
*You **should not** take him so seriously. You **cannot** really **believe** them!*
*You **are not allowed to** give away trade secrets.*

## La capacité

*can – could – be able to*

*Can* (*could* au prétérit) exprime généralement une capacité physique ou intellectuelle; *can't* (ou *cannot*) (*couldn't* au prétérit) une incapacité.
*He **can speak** English so well – you **can't (cannot) tell** he is French!*
*I spoke to the supplier but **I couldn't hear** him very well.*

Toutefois, on utilise la forme *be able to* à la place de *can* :

**1.** Pour exprimer une capacité momentanée, la vraie capacité de faire quelque chose.
*The lawyer drew up the contract for them. They **are able to** see clearer now.*
*The machine was broken. Michael's team **were able to** mend it.*

**2.** À la place de l'infinitif d'intention.
*He learnt english **to / in order to** speak with foreign suppliers.*
*He learnt english **to be able to** speak with foreign suppliers.*

**3.** Après le -*ing* ou un autre auxiliaire modal.
*It is a pity not having **been able to** make a deal with them.*
*We might **be able to** offer you a discount.*

**4.** Pour la forme future.
*By the time we finish the negotiations, he **will have been** able to reduce the cost.*

! C'est le verbe *be* qui est conjugué.

# La probabilité / possibilité

*must – should – could – may – might – cannot – couldn't – bound to – likely to*

## Choix de l'auxiliaire

**1.** Différents modaux permettent d'exprimer un fait probable.
Le choix de l'auxiliaire modal dépend du degré de probabilité.

| Faits probables à... | Auxiliaire modal | Exemples | Remarques |
|---|---|---|---|
| 90 % | *must* | *He **must** be tired, he's been talking about the joint venture all day.* | *He **has to** be tired, ...* (plus formel)<br>*He'**s got to** be tired, ...* (informel) |
| 70 % | *should* | *He **should** be at the meeting tomorrow, he negotiated everything.* | |
| 60 % | *could* | *It **could** be a good idea to review the contract.* | *Could have* + participe passé exprime quelque chose de possible mais de non réalisé.<br>*We **could have sold** more goods.* |
| 40 – 35 % | *may – might* (*May* est un peu plus probable que *might*.) | *They **may** / **might** have been thinking of investing in a foreign country.* | • Pour exprimer un doute : *He may/might not agree to being in the advert.*<br>• Ajouté à *may* et *might*, *well* augmente la probabilité. *They **may well** talk us into it. (It is likely they talk us into it).*<br>• *Might* s'utilise aussi pour une déduction formelle, qui devient une menace. ***Might** you be suggesting that you want to withdraw from our agreement?* |
| 0 % (faits improbables) | *can't / couldn't* | *They **can't/couldn't** be going to renew the out-sourcing contract.* | |

↳ La forme négative s'utilise pour exprimer un doute.
*They **may not** finish making our new products by the end of the year.*

**2. *Would be able to*** permet d'exprimer un fait possible (souvent dans une forme conditionnelle).
→ *If you increased your quantities, we **would be able** to give you a discount.*

**3. *Be bound to*** exprime une forte probabilité.
→ *He's **bound** to choose the other supplier because they are offering a better deal.*

**4. *Be likely to*** exprime une probabilité.
→ *They **are likely to** try and negotiate a quantity discount.*

Les modaux ont la même nuance de possibilité que de probabilité.
→ *Simon **might be able to** help draw up the contract.*

**Conjugaison des auxiliaires**

| | Auxiliary | Present | Past | Future |
|---|---|---|---|---|
| *1: I / you / he / she / it / we / they* | *must / could / can't ...* | *be + adjective / noun* | *have been + adjective / noun* | |
| *2: I / you / he / she / it / we / they* | *must / could / can't ...* | *be + present participle* | *have been + present participle* | *be + going to +* base verbale |
| *3: I / you / he / she / it / we / they* | *must / could / can't ...* | *+ base verbale* | *have + past participle* | |

1: *It can't be true. / It could be a good deal. / It must have been interesting.*

2: *She must be thinking about it. / It should have been done. / He must be going to sign soon.*

3: *They can't pull out now. / We might have guessed they would.*

## 1 Révisez les règles d'utilisation des auxiliaires modaux en répondant aux questions suivantes.

**1.** What is a modal for?

..............................................................................

..............................................................................

..............................................................................

**2.** What follows a modal?

..............................................................................

..............................................................................

..............................................................................

**3.** With or without to?

..............................................................................

..............................................................................

..............................................................................

**4.** Do you put an "s" on the 3rd person single in the present?

..............................................................................

..............................................................................

..............................................................................

**5.** Is the question order the same or does it change?

..............................................................................

..............................................................................

..............................................................................

**6.** Does the negation go before or after the modal?

..............................................................................

..............................................................................

..............................................................................

**7.** Can you see several modals together or should there only be one?

..............................................................................

..............................................................................

..............................................................................

## 2 Complétez les phrases suivantes par *can* ou *could*.

**1.** The purchaser's English is very bad, I ...................... understand him at all!

**2.** He lived in Italy as a child so when he was 7 he .......... ............ speak fluent Italian.

**3.** I'll be busy on Wednesday, but I ...................... see you on Thursday.

**4.** We got the deal because we ...................... offer a quantity discount.

**5.** I am sorry, but we ...................... give you more than a 5% price reduction.

**6.** ...................... you understand the point I'm trying make?

**7.** I ...................... tell you like our offer.

**8.** Sorry we are late for the meeting, we ...................... find anywhere to park the car.

## 3 Complétez les phrases suivantes en utilisant *be able to*.

**1.** He's been learning Italian for 5 years. Last year he ...................... negotiate with PLB in Italian.

**2.** We ...................... sign the agreement for the tooling next Monday.

**3.** He went to China .................. meet up with potential suppliers.

**4.** We could ...................... deliver within 10 days, I'm not sure.

**5.** I'm not sure it's a good idea, being ...................... order from so many suppliers.

**6.** When we get through these discussions, we will ............ convince them of our terms.

**7.** We had a successful meeting: we ...................... convince them we were right.

**8.** I'm sorry, we won't ...................... to sign with this clause added to the contract.

## 4 Complétez les phrases suivantes par *can, could,* ou *be able to.*

**1.** When he was a child, he spoke Chinese. He ...................... speak Chinese as a child.

**2.** When he was a child, he spoke Dutch. Now he doesn't. He used to ...................... speak Dutch.

**3.** How many languages ...................... he speak now? He speaks 10 different languages!

**4.** He's now learning Hindi. Next year he ...................... speak 11 languages – can you imagine!

**5.** He's also good at figures. He ...................... read a spreadsheet like a book.

**6.** That's why he .................. correct the supplier on the order quantities yesterday, but he ................. give him the sales forecast because he didn't have the figures.

**7.** When he was in his last job, he ...................... travel for business because there was no budget.

**8.** By the end of this year, he ...................... re-negotiate all our supplier contracts.

## 5 En tenant compte des indices entre parenthèses, complétez les phrases suivantes par le modal qui convient.

**1.** (60 % probable)
We ...................... offer you a discount, depending on your delivery terms.

**2.** (90 % probable)
It ...................... have been difficult, persuading them to change the payment terms.

**3.** (70 % probable)
We are expecting a call from the logistics manager, that ...................... be him now.

**4.** (40 % probable)
They ...................... well win this round of discussions!

**5.** (0 % probable)
It ...................... be Fred who signed this, that's not his signature.

**6.** (90 % probable)
It ...................... be our lawyer who wrote up this agreement, I recognise the style.

**7.** (40 % / 35 % probable)
I think Simon ...................... be able to get a better price from them.

**8.** (0 % probable)
You ...................... still be hoping that they'll change their minds about the price.

**9.** (35 % probable)
It's a pity we didn't think of that before, we ...................... have got a better deal.

**10.** (threat)
...................... you be saying that you cannot deliver within ten weeks?!

**11.** (60 % probable)
They ...................... just want delivery franco and not ex-works.

**12.** (70 % probable)
If we offer a quantity discount, we ...................... get the market.

## 6 Corrigez par le modal qui convient en prenant en compte le contexte.

Last week, John went off to negotiate new terms with his supplier in Canada. He thought it was lucky as he ~~must~~ ...................... speak fluent English but he won't ~~be able to~~ ...................... speak French, and his supplier was in Quebec!
However, he ~~could~~ ...................... find an interpreter so that he ~~can't~~ ...................... negotiate.
He learnt, however, that it ~~has got to~~ ...................... be risky negotiating in a language you ~~couldn't~~ ...................... speak, because not everyone is 100% honest. They ~~were able to~~ ...................... be a friend of the person you are negotiating with, in which case, they ~~can't~~ ...................... be more on their side, and

they ~~must~~ ........................ not translate properly. Also, they ~~have to have had~~ ........................ a bad experience before with another British purchaser, and they ~~couldn't~~ ........................ just not like English people! If you have to negotiate in a foreign country, you should ~~can~~ ........................ find someone to help, but remember, you ~~will can~~ ........................ pick and choose. It's a pity, not ~~being to be able to~~ ........................ speak every language in the world, but remember, if John had learnt French, he ~~would have~~ could ........................ negotiated himself!

## 7 Choisissez la bonne réponse.

**1.** We ........................ be able to agree if you bring forward the delivery date.
**A.** must
**B.** might

**2.** He is not going to ........................ increase the order quantity.
**A.** be able to
**B.** can

**3.** ........................ I be right in understanding you are going to back out of the agreement?
**A.** Couldn't
**B.** Might

**4.** We should finalise the details to ........................ sign the final contract.
**A.** can
**B.** be able to

**5.** You ........................ possibly expect us to agree to these terms!
**A.** can't
**B.** mustn't

**6.** That ........................ be the right total. We've double- and triple-checked the figures.
**A.** can
**B.** must

**7.** We ........................ have asked them for a discount. I think they might have agreed to it.
**A.** could
**B.** must

**8.** It ........................ have been a great relief when they finally agreed to meet your conditions.
**A.** can
**B.** must

**9.** If you ........................ insist we can agree to packaging the goods in waterproof bags.
**A.** must
**B.** can

**10.** They ........................ be here on time; after all, it's them who set up the meeting.
**A.** couldn't
**B.** should

## CORRIGÉS

**1.** 1. To add a nuance to what the person says. 2. The verb. 3. Without. 4. Certainly not! 5. It's the same. 6. After. 7. You can see two together.
**2.** 1. cannot/can't 2. could 3. can / could (less likely) 4. could 5. cannot / can't 6. can 7. can 8. couldn't
**3.** 1. was able to 2. will be able to 3. to be able to 4. be able to 5. able to 6. have been able to 7. were able to 8. be able to
**4.** 1. could 2. be able to 3. can 4. will be able to 5. can 6. could / was able to – couldn't / wasn't able to 7. couldn't 8. will have been able to
**5.** 1. could 2. must 3. should 4. may 5. can't / couldn't 6. must / has to be 7. may / might 8. can't 9. might 10. might 11. could 12. should
**6.** Last week, John went off to negotiate new terms with his supplier in Canada. He thought it was lucky as he **can** speak fluent English but he **can't** speak French, and his supplier was in Quebec! However, he **was able to** find an interpreter so that he **could** negotiate. He learnt, however, that it **can** be risky negotiating in a language you **are not able to** speak, because not everyone is 100% honest. They **may / might / could** be a friend of the person you are negotiating with, in which case, they **must** be more on their side, and they **may / might / could** not translate properly. Also, they **could have had** a bad experience before with another British purchaser, and they **may** just not like English people! If you have to negotiate in a foreign country, you **should be able to** find someone to help, but remember, you **can / must** pick and choose. It's a pity, not **being able to** speak every language in the world, but remember, if John had learnt French, he **could have** negotiated himself!
**7.** 1. A. might 2. A. be able to 3. B. Might 4. B. be able to 5. A. can't 6. B. must 7. A. could 8. B. must 9. A. must 10. B. should

# L'obligation

*must – have to – have got to – need – be supposed to*

## Comparez !

*When you negotiate, you must stick to what you think.* → Avis personnel, subjectif.
*If you conclude a contract, you have to sign it.* → Obligation légale, objectif.

Utilisez *have to* et non *must* :

**1.** Si vous avez un doute sur la source de l'obligation, ou si l'obligation vient d'un tiers ou une autorité.
→ *The customs official says we **have to** pay duty on our goods.*

**2.** Pour les phrases interrogatives (n'oubliez pas l'auxiliaire *do/does* !)
→ ***Do you have** to increase the price by 5%?*

**!** Pour la négation utilisez *don't have to* (et ne pas *haven't to*)

*Must* s'utilise (surtout avec *I* et *we*) dans un langage plus formel.
→ ***Must we** deal with the same supplier all the time?*

**3.** Pour les formes passée et future (*Must* ne s'utilise qu'au présent et au *present perfect*).
→ *He **has had** to go back on his agreement.*
→ *He **had to** look through the agreement.*
→ *They **will have to be** at the meeting.*
→ *You **won't have** to go.*

*Have got to* exprime une obligation très forte, dans certains cas une urgence :
→ *I've got to get the customer to sign today or I won't get my bonus.*

*Need* exprime un besoin.
→ *We **need** them to agree to our terms and conditions.*

**!** Deux formes différentes pour la voix passive (qui veulent dire la même chose) :
*The agreement **needs to be translated** into Italian.*
*The agreement **needs translating** into Chinese.*

*Be supposed to* est une obligation culturelle ou d'usage (au présent et au prétérit seulement).
*In certain countries you **are not supposed to give** a gift as it could be seen as a bribe.*

## L'obligation, par l'impératif à la forme affirmative

***Shut** the door behind you, will you?*
***Be** careful!*
***Take** care of yourself!*

Pour renforcer votre ordre, vous pouvez :
- Ajouter un auxiliaire.

→ *Do pay attention to the small print.*
- Ajouter *always*.

→ *Always check the figures in a contract.*

# L'absence d'obligation

*don't have to – needn't*

| | Present | Past | Future |
|---|---|---|---|
| *don't have to* | *Don't worry, you **don't have to** include the transport costs.* | *You **didn't have to** change the deadline.* | *You **will not (won't) have to** sign today.* |
| *don't need to / needn't* | *You **don't need to / needn't** put in a tender until next week.* | *You **didn't need to** worry so much, they agreed in the end. You **needn't have** worried so much, they agreed in the end.* | *You **will not (won't) have to** deal with that person.* |

↳ Notez la particularité des constructions négative *need not / needn't* et passée *needn't have* + participe passé.
N'utilisez pas ~~*you haven't need to*~~…

Notez la différence entre *didn't need to (do)* et *needn't have (done)*
*He **didn't need to** do something* = ce n'était pas nécessaire et il le savait sur le moment.
*He paid by credit card so he **didn't need to** take out extra insurance, but he did it anyway.*
*He **needn't have done** something* = ce n'était pas nécessaire mais il ne le sait que maintenant.
*He **needn't have called** the purchaser; his assistant had already done so.*

# L'interdiction

*mustn't – cannot – be not allowed to – may not – be forbidden to*

**1.** *Mustn't, cannot* et *be not allowed to* sont généralement utilisés pour exprimer l'interdiction.
*You **mustn't** / **cannot** / **are not allowed to** change the price once we've signed.*
→ Vous ne devez pas / ne pouvez pas / n'êtes pas autorisé à changer les prix une fois le contrat signé.

**2.** *May not* s'utilise pour s'exprimer de façon plus formelle, ainsi que pour une interdiction officielle.
*You **may not** try to convince him. (Even if you want to!)*
→ Vous n'avez pas le droit d'essayer de le convaincre. (Même si vous le voulez !)

**3.** *Forbidden to* est souvent utilisé dans une forme passive :
*It is **forbidden to** accept gifts from suppliers / accepting gifts from suppliers is forbidden.*
→ Il est interdit d'accepter les cadeaux des fournisseurs. / Accepter des cadeaux des fournisseurs est interdit.

Sinon, la forme active : *The boss **forbode** the purchaser to accept gifts from suppliers.*
→ Le patron a interdit à l'acheteur d'accepter les cadeaux des fournisseurs.

**!** Ne confondez pas interdiction et absence d'obligation !
*You **mustn't deal** with that supplier.*
→ Vous ne devez pas traiter avec ce fournisseur. (Interdiction)
*You **don't have to** deal with that supplier.*

### L'interdiction, par l'impératif à la forme négative

***Let's not*** *bother the sales team now!*
***Don't touch*** *that!*
***Don't let*** *the customers go into the lab!*
***Don't be*** *late!*

Pour renforcer votre ordre, vous pouvez :
• Ajouter *never*
*Never sign without reading everything!*
• Commencer par le pronom
*You, don't deal with that man, he's untrustworthy!*

→ Vous n'êtes pas obligé de traiter avec ce fournisseur. (Absence d'obligation)

# L'autorisation

## Demander l'autorisation

*be (not) allowed to – can – could – may*

**1.** Dans un ordre croissant de politesse :
*We are seeing the supplier again. Can we try and lessen the price?*
*Could I /do you think I could just take another look at that proposal?*
*May I leave the meeting early this evening please?*

**2.** *Is he allowed to sign for the company?*

## Donner l'autorisation

*be allowed to – can – may*

*You are allowed to / can / may take clause 15 out of the contract.*

NEGOTIATING

## 1 Classez les modaux suivants dans la catégorie qui convient.

*be (not) allowed to – can – cannot – could – have to – don't have to – may – may not – must – mustn't – needn't – don't need to*

**1. Obligation**

**2. No obligation**

**3. Prohibition**

**4. Permission**

## 2 Complétez par *must* ou *have to* au passé, au présent ou au futur.

**1.** I think you .............................. try and persuade him to agree to our tender.

**2.** You know, we will .............................. withdraw our offer if you don't compromise.

**3.** If you want to make an order, you .............................. fill out a purchase order.

**4.** I .............................. remember to tell them about our efficient after-sales service.

**5.** She .............................. negotiate hard to bring them round to her terms last week.

**6.** .............................. you always make a counter-offer every time?!

**7.** I'm afraid that we .............................. terminate the contract because of quality defects.

**8.** Do we .............................. send you a certificate of origin with every delivery?

**9.** To my mind, we .............................. ask for a price reduction for large quantities.

**10.** In the future, you will .............................. get better terms of sale.

## 3 Complétez les phrases ci-dessous par *must, have to, don't have to* ou *needn't*.

**1.** We .............................. offer a trade discount, our prices are very competitive already.

**2.** In my opinion, you .............................. shorten your delivery time.

**3.** You .............................. cover the handling charges, it's not our problem.

**4.** We .............................. give them an answer this week, they can wait.

**5.** It's not standard practice – we .............................. pay all the additional expenses on the last delivery.

**6.** We .............................. deliver within tight deadlines – it's in the contract.

**7.** They .............................. pay duty on those goods – there's no import duty.

**8.** We .............................. to have a lawyer to draw up the contract, we can do it ourselves.

## 4 Complétez les phrases par les modaux d'interdiction ou d'autorisation qui conviennent.

**1.** You .............................. change the prices now – we agreed on them last week.

**2.** James, what do you think, .............................. we ask them to sign ex-works – is it possible?

**3.** You .............................. let the customer get the upper hand.

**4.** (In a formal situation – being polite) you ....................... rewrite that clause, if you wish.

**5.** Are you .............................. sign for your company?

**6.** We .............................. forget to add the schedule about logistics to the contract.

**7.** .............................. I just go through that point again, if you will allow me?

**8.** You .......................... go ahead with the negotiations, the CEO agrees on all the points.

**9.** (In a formal situation) you ........................... go back on your decision now.

**10.** .......................... I just use your telephone to check with the financial controller?

## 5 Classez les phrases suivantes dans la colonne appropriée et complétez la conclusion.

**1.** Be careful – there may be import taxes.

**2.** Don't accept brides.

**3.** Do be sure the goods are properly packaged.

**4.** Always ask for an order acknowledgement.

**5.** Never sign without reading everything.

**6.** Don't let the supplier see the competitor's tender.

**7.** Make sure the delivery times are clear.

| Advising | Forbidding |
|---|---|
| | |

Conclusion:

A positive imperative is for .............................. .

A negative imperative is for .............................. .

## 6 Remettez chacune des phrases suivantes dans le bon ordre.

**1.** I thought: "Wonderful, I may be able to do some shopping at the same time".

**2.** I thought I could probably leave early.

**3.** He answered: "Of course you can".

**4.** But, I was surprised, I didn't have to sign the form.

**5.** Usually I have to work from 9 am to 6 pm, but the dentist closes at 5 pm.

**6.** My boss confirmed: "You needn't sign this time".

**7.** So I went to my boss and asked: "Please may I go now?"

**8.** Then he said "You will have to make up the time tomorrow!"

**9.** I asked him: "Must I fill in the time-off form?"

**10.** I had a terrible toothache, so I thought to myself, I must see the dentist.

Order: 10 – ..... – ..... – ..... – ..... – ..... – ..... – ..... – ..... – ..... –

## 7 Complétez les phrases par le modal qui convient.

**1.** We .............................. do something, the operators are threatening to strike.

**2.** They .............................. be on strike again – it's not allowed every month!

**3.** We .............................. to have a meeting with the trade union reps soon.

**4.** I personally think we .............................. try talking to the workers first.

5. We ............................. talk to all of them – just a few.

6. ............................. I have a word with them?

7. Yes, but you ............................. make them any offers – you are not authorized to do so.

8. Last time, I ............................. – it wasn't necessary. They were complaining about their manager's attitude.

9. Yes, but we ............................. tell him to treat the operators with more respect – remember?

10. Well, I ............................. to offer anything for now, just listen to their complaints.

11. That's a good idea. I think you ............................. see them A.S.A.P.

12. On top of that, explain to the workers that they ............................. to strike every time there's a problem.

## 8 Reliez le début à la fin des phrases.

| | |
|---|---|
| **1.** Don't worry, you needn't sign • | • **A.** to buy any components you need. |
| **2.** You must see a lawyer about • | • **B.** before next week, we can wait until then. |
| **3.** You don't have to use our • | • **C.** a penalty clause in case the building work runs late. |
| **4.** I am sorry, but we have had to withdraw • | • **D.** that confidentiality clause before you sign. |
| **5.** You needn't have taken so much trouble • | • **E.** the customs officer to get the goods on time. |
| **6.** They had to bribe • | • **F.** a gentleman's agreement. |
| **7.** You have to fill out a purchase order • | • **G.** but I am very grateful to you. |
| **8.** You mustn't go back on • | • **H.** ends before we conclude the deal. |
| **9.** You really must agree on • | • **I.** from our agreement owing to financial problems. |
| **10.** We need to tie up the loose • | • **J.** freight forwarder, but we would prefer you did. |

## 9 Choisissez la bonne réponse.

**1.** *We can to / Are we allowed to* re-negotiate the terms after a year?

**2.** *Could I / am I allowed* come back to you next week on that one?

**3.** You are *allowed to / permissioned to* return the goods if there is a defect.

**4.** *I may / May I* consult my lawyer before I sign?

**5.** You *may / allowed to* check with your legal department if you like.

**6.** *Can / may* you sign on behalf of your C.E.O.?

### CORRIGÉS

**1.** 1. Have to – must 2. Don't have to – needn't – don't need to 3. Be not allowed to – cannot – may not – mustn't 4. Be allowed to – can – could – may
**2.** 1. must 2. have to 3. have to 4. must 5. had to 6. must 7. have to 8. have to 9. must 10. have to
**3.** 1. don't have to / needn't 2. must 3. have to 4. don't have too / needn't 5. had to 6. have to 7. won't have to/won't need to 8. don't have to /needn't
**4.** 1. cannot / can't 2. can 3. mustn't 4. may 5. allowed to 6. mustn't 7. could / may 8. can 9. may not 10. may / could
**5.** Advising: 1. 3. 4. 7. Forbidding: 2. 5. 6.
Conclusion: a positive imperative is for advising. A negative imperative is for forbidding.
**6.** 10. – 5. – 2. – 7. – 3. – 9. – (1.) – 4. – 6. – 1. – 8.
**7.** 1. Have got to / have to / must 2. Can't / couldn't 3. Have 4. Must 5. Needn't / don't need to / don't have to 6. May 7. Are not allowed to / may not 8. Didn't need to / didn't have to 9. Had to 10. Needn't / don't need to / don't have to 11. Must 12. Mustn't
**8.** 1. B – 2. D – 3. J – 4. I – 5. G – 6. E – 7. A – 8. F – 9. C – 10. H
**9.** 1. Are we allowed to 2. Could I 3. allowed to 4. May I 5. may 6. Can

## Le conseil

*must – should – ought to – had better*

**1.** Pour exprimer un conseil, on utilise généralement *should*.
→ *You **should** discuss that with the supply chain manager.*

**2.** Pour insister davantage et exprimer que quelque chose est vivement conseillé, utilisez *must*, ou la forme subjonctive* (voir page 77).
→ *You **must** take a look at this.*
**I suggested he (should) speak to the financial controller.*

**3.** Pour donner un conseil plus personnel, utilisez *ought to*.
→ *You **ought to** give your assistant some time off.*

Notez la distinction formelle à l'interrogatif et au négatif :

| Formal | Informal |
|---|---|
| *Do you think we should?* | *Should we?* |
| *Do you think we ought to?* | *Ought we?* |
| *I don't think you should.* | *You shouldn't.* |
| *I don't think you ought to / You ought not to* | *You oughtn't.* |

**4.** *Had better* (il vaudrait mieux)
→ *We **had better** reduce our prices. You **had better not** lose this contract.*

Nuances de *should* :
1. Probabilité : *It **should** be a profitable promotion. We'll make good money.*
2. Anticipation: *The competition **should** be launching their product soon.*
3. Regret: *We **shouldn't (ought not to)** have entrusted them with the advertising.*
4. Reproche : *You **should (might/could)** have told us you were leaving the company.*

## La suggestion

*Shall – could – might*

**1.** *Shall* et *could* sont généralement utilisés pour exprimer la suggestion.
***Shall** we call it a day?*
*We **could** take a break for lunch.*
*I think we **could** take another look at that agreement before signing.*
***Couldn't** we ask for a discount?*

**2.** *Might* s'utilise pour s'exprimer de façon plus formelle.
***Might** we talk about this later?*

### Autres formules introductives

*Why don't we... (+ V + base verbale)?*
*How / what about ... (+ V-ing)?*
*What if we... (+ V simple past)?*
*Suppose we... (+ V simple past)*

***Why don't we** increase our selling price?*
***How about** asking for a discount?*
***What if we** changed supplier?*
***Suppose we** accepted their offer.*

*Might I suggest ... (+ V-ing)?* — *Might I suggest updating the contract?*
*Let's... (+ V + base verbale)!* — *Let's get this finished!*
*Would you like... (+ V infinitive)?* — *Would you like to go through that again?*

# La demande et la proposition

can – could – may – would – will

## La demande

**1.** Demander à quelqu'un de faire quelque chose.

• Par ordre croissant de politesse :
***Can you*** *give me more details?*
***Could you*** *give me more details?*
***I wonder if*** *you could give me more details.*
***Do you think*** *you could give me more details?*

• Pour insister davantage, utilisez *will* ou *would*.
***Will you*** *get back to me before tomorrow?*
***Would you*** *please not change your mind again!*

**2.** Demander quelque chose.

• Par ordre croissant de politesse :
***Can I have*** *your confirmation tomorrow?*
***Could I have*** *your confirmation tomorrow?*
***May I have*** *your confirmation tomorrow?*

• Pour simplement dire ce que vous voulez, utilisez *would like*.
***I would like*** *to see you at 8 in the morning.*
***We would like*** *some information about your products.*

**3.** *Dare* exprime le fait d'oser quelque chose.
→ *He* ***dared (to) ask*** *me to let them pay within 6-months!*

## La proposition

**1.** (Se) proposer de faire quelque chose.
***Can*** *I call you back later?*
***I'll call*** *you back later.*

**2.** Proposer ou inviter.
***Would you like*** *a cup of coffee?*
***Would you like*** *to come to the meeting tomorrow?*

**3.** Utiliser "would rather" pour montrer une préférence dans votre réponse.
→ *I* ***would rather come*** *to the meeting next week.*

**4.** Pour dire clairement ce que l'on veut.
→ *I* ***would like you*** *to be here at 7 sharp tomorrow.*

### Quelques formulations

**Standard**
*If you need more information ...*
*Please / Could you ...?*
*I / we will ...*
*Sorry about ...*
*That suits me.*

**Formal**
*Should you require further information ...*
*I / we would / should be grateful if you could ...*
*We should be pleased to ...*
*I / We would like to apologise for ...*
*That would be convenient.*

**1** **À partir des éléments ci-dessous, formulez un conseil, en tenant compte des indications suivantes :**

| | |
|---|---|
| ++ = insisting advice | p = personal advice |
| + = advice | oe = « or else » |

**1.** We – establish a procedure for negotiations

(+) ..............................................................................

..............................................................................

**2.** You – find a new supplier

(++) ..............................................................................

..............................................................................

**3.** You – open minded about negotiations

(p) ..............................................................................

..............................................................................

**4.** We – talk this through with the manager

(oe) ..............................................................................

..............................................................................

**5.** You – not guarantee 0 defects

(+) ..............................................................................

..............................................................................

**6.** You – think it through before you decide

(++) ..............................................................................

..............................................................................

**7.** You – re-write the agreement before they see it

(oe) ..............................................................................

..............................................................................

**8.** You – not wear jeans to the meeting

(p) ..............................................................................

..............................................................................

**2** **Reformulez les phrases suivantes, en utilisant *should* ou *ought to*.**

**1.** They like our product – it is likely we get the business.

..............................................................................

..............................................................................

**2.** If we had known we wouldn't have done it – why didn't you tell us before?

..............................................................................

..............................................................................

**3.** If you want more information – just give us a ring.

..............................................................................

..............................................................................

**4.** I am disappointed – they are withdrawing from negotiations.

..............................................................................

..............................................................................

**5.** We were given advice to change – the freight forwarder is unreliable.

..............................................................................

..............................................................................

**3** **Complétez les phrases suivantes par le modal qui convient.**

**1.** ...................... you like to talk about that later?

**2.** Do you think you ...................... improve your lead time.

**3.** We thought that you ...................... approve of the terms of sale.

**4.** I don't think you ...................... get so upset during negotiations.

**5.** We are convinced that the packaging ...................... be stronger.

**6.** ...................... tie up the loose ends before ending the meeting?

**4** **À partir des indices, formulez une phrase en utilisant un modal.**

**1.** You want to offer a customer something to drink.

..............................................................................

..............................................................................

**2.** You want someone to draw up a contract for you.

..............................................................................

..............................................................................

**3.** You want to see a sample.

..................................................................................

..................................................................................

**4.** You really want the specifications by this evening.

..................................................................................

..................................................................................

**5.** You propose to your customer to send him an e-mail later in the day.

..................................................................................

..................................................................................

**6.** You want to ask, very politely, for a customer's decision tomorrow.

..................................................................................

..................................................................................

**7.** You want to insist that someone must confirm delivery next Tuesday.

..................................................................................

..................................................................................

**8.** You want to ask someone, very politely, to increase their minimum order quantity.

..................................................................................

..................................................................................

## 5 Entourez l'erreur et corrigez-la !

**1.** What will you do in my position?

..................................................................................

**2.** I think we couldn't improve on our current offer.

..................................................................................

**3.** We should to finalize today.

..................................................................................

**4.** I send you an e-mail to confirm this afternoon.

..................................................................................

**5.** He would better be sure about what he offers us this time.

..................................................................................

## 6 À partir des indices en italique, formulez une suggestion plus ou moins formelle.

**1.** We go to a restaurant for lunch?

(Shall) ..................................................................................

..................................................................................

**2.** We go through the details again.

(Might) ..................................................................................

..................................................................................

**3.** We come back to that point later.

(Could) ..................................................................................

..................................................................................

**4.** To a colleague. Go and see the supplier tomorrow.

(Let's) ..................................................................................

..................................................................................

**5.** We add penalty clause for late delivery?

(Why not?) ..................................................................................

..................................................................................

**6.** Give us a deposit?

(How) ..................................................................................

..................................................................................

### CORRIGÉS

**1. 1.** I think we should establish a procedure. **2.** You must find a new supplier. **3.** You ought to be more open minded about the negotiations. **4.** We had better talk this through with the manager. **5.** I don't think you should guarantee 0 defects. **6.** You must think it through before you decide. **7.** You had better rewrite the agreement before they see it. **8.** I don't think you ought to wear jeans to the meeting.
**2. 1.** We should get the business **2.** You should / ought to have told us before. **3.** Should you require further information, please do not hesitate to contact us. **4.** I am disappointed that they should withdraw from the negotiations. **5.** We were advised that we should / ought to change freight forwarder.
**3. 1.** Would **2.** could **3.** would(n't) **4.** should/ought to **5.** should **6.** Should we / do you think we should
**4. 1.** Would you like something to drink? **2.** Could you draw up the contract for me? **3.** We would like to see a sample. **4.** Will you send me the specifications by this evening? **5.** I'll send you an e-mail later on. **6.** May I have your decision tomorrow? **7.** Would you please confirm delivery next Tuesday? **8.** Do you think you could increase your MOQ?
**5. 1.** What would **2.** I don't think we could **3.** We should finalize **4.** I'll send **5.** Had better
**6. 1.** Shall we go to a restaurant for lunch? **2.** Might we go through the details again? **3.** We could come back to that point later. **4.** Let's go and see the supplier tomorrow! **5.** Why don't we add / Why not add a penalty clause for late delivery? **6.** How about / what about giving us a deposit?

## 1 Soulignez les 12 modaux du texte ci-dessous et expliquez ce qu'ils expriment.

**Score :..... / 12**

Before signing an agreement with a supplier, you have to settle your terms. I think you must also sign a contract, which may be drawn up by a lawyer or not. When signing the contract, you might have several different authorized signatures. If you are dealing on an international basis, you ought to have a copy in English. It can be translated by a specialist. You should check the details carefully. You are allowed to add schedules to the end for extra information. The parties are not allowed to change the contract without common agreement; you ought to have this in writing. You'd better know what you really want before starting because, once signed, you cannot change anything.

**1.** ............................................................ **2.** ............................................................

**3.** ............................................................ **4.** ............................................................

**5.** ............................................................ **6.** ............................................................

**7.** ............................................................ **8.** ............................................................

**9.** ............................................................ **10.** ............................................................

**11.** ............................................................ **12.** ............................................................

## 2 Associez la phrase anglaise à sa traduction française.

**Score :..... / 12**

| | | | |
|---|---|---|---|
| She can write it. | **1.** • | • **A.** | Il se peut qu'elle l'écrive. |
| She could write it. | **2.** • | • **B.** | Elle aura à l'écrire. |
| She was able to write it. | **3.** • | • **C.** | Il se pourrait qu'elle l'écrive. |
| She will be able to write it. | **4.** • | • **D.** | Elle devrait l'écrire. |
| She must write it. | **5.** • | • **E.** | On ne lui a pas permis de l'écrire. |
| She will have to write it. | **6.** • | • **F.** | Elle a pu l'écrire. |
| She had to write it. | **7.** • | • **G.** | Elle n'est pas obligée de l'écrire. |
| She should write it. | **8.** • | • **H.** | Elle a dû l'écrire (obligation) |
| She may write it. | **9.** • | • **I.** | Elle peut l'écrire. |
| She might write it. | **10.** • | • **J.** | Elle pourra l'écrire. |
| She wasn't allowed to write it. | **11.** • | • **K.** | Elle pourrait l'écrire. |
| She doesn't have to write it. | **12.** • | • **L.** | Elle doit l'écrire. |

## 3 Classez chacune des phrases suivantes dans la colonne qui convient.

**Score : ..... / 10**

**1.** You've got to be sure that the technical specifications and norms are right.

**2.** They may be able to offer extended credit.

**3.** They product has to be properly packaged and comply with regulations.

**4.** They could deliver the goods in part-orders to quicken delivery.

**5.** You had better be certain that the goods can be delivered from stock.

**6.** You must pay cash on delivery to have better terms.

**7.** You don't have to pay for transport.

**8.** We cannot accept to pay the customs duties.

**9.** You mustn't ship the goods any later than the 10th of each month.

**10.** They should leave a deposit as a sign of goodwill.

| Obligation or lack of obligation | Advice | Possibility or lack of possibility |
|---|---|---|
| | | |

## 4 Indiquez tous les modaux que vous pouvez utiliser pour...

**Score : ..... / 6**

**1.** To talk about a physical or intellectual ability: ..........

**2.** To talk about probability or possibility: ..........

**3.** To talk about an obligation / something forbidden: ..........

**4.** To talk about no obligation / permission: ..........

**5.** To suggest / ask / offer: ..........

**6.** To give advice: ..........

## 5 Complétez le tableau à l'aide des modaux suivants.

**Score : ..... / 10**

*be able to – can – can't be – could – don't have to – have to – may – must – ought to – should*

| Synonyms | Opposites |
|---|---|
| **1.** can – | **A.** mustn't – |
| **2.** had better – | **B.** have to – |
| **3.** may – | **C.** cannot – |
| **4.** must – | **D.** must be – |
| **5.** should – | **E.** needn't – |

**Score total : ..... / 50**

**CORRIGÉS**

**1.** 1. Have to (obligation) 2. Must (personal obligation) 3. May (possibility) 4. Might (possibility) 5. Ought to (advice) 6. Can (capacity) 7. Should (advice) 8. Allowed to (authorization) 9. Are not allowed to (lack of authorization) 10. Ought to (advice) 11. Had better (advice) 12. Cannot (not allowed)
**2.** 1. I 2. K 3. F 4. J 5. L 6. B 7. H 8. D 9. A 10. C 11. E 12. G
**3.** Obligation or lack of obligation : 1. 3. 6. 7. 9. Advice: 10. Possibility or lack of possibility: 2. 4. 8.
**4.** 1. Can / cannot / could / be able to / (manage to) 2. Must / could / may / might /can't / couldn't 3. Must/ have to / cannot / mustn't / may not / not allowed to 4. Don't have to / needn't / may (not) / could / can (not) allowed to 5. Could / shall / might / (let's) / would / can / will 6. Should / ought to / could / must / had better
**5.** 1. Be able to 2. Should 3. Could 4. Have to 5. Ought to
A. Can B. Don't have to C. May D. Can't be E. Must

# 5 Les phrases



## Les questions directes

### Deux types de questions

On distingue en anglais deux types de questions.

**1. Les « questions fermées »**

Appelées "*Yes / No questions*", ce sont toutes les questions qui pourraient commencer en français par « est-ce-que... ? ». Ces dernières suscitent généralement une réponse courte mais il peut y avoir des réponses plus indirectes.

*Do you like your job?* *No, I don't / not really / I'd rather be playing golf.*
*Are you efficient?* *Yes, I am. They say I get the job done.*

**2. Les « questions ouvertes »**

Appelées "*Wh questions*", ce sont toutes les questions introduites par les mots interrogatifs *when*, *where*, *what*, *which*, *who*, *whom*, *whose*, *why* et *how*.

Ces dernières suscitent généralement une réponse plutôt longue.

→ *Where is he going?*
→ *What time is your interview?*

Notez que *how*, *what* et *which* peuvent être composés.

→ ***What time*** *do you usually start work?*
→ ***How much*** *is your current salary?*

**!** Pour exprimer un choix en termes réduits, on emploie *which* et non *what*.
***Which language*** *do you speak better, French or German?* ***Which*** *one ...?*
***What languages*** *do you speak?*

Le mot interrogatif *who* concerne le sujet de la phrase, alors que le mot *whom* concerne l'objet. *Whom* est peu utilisé dans l'anglais courant de nos jours.

→ ***Who*** *applied for the job at the factory?*
→ ***To whom*** *are you sending your CV? / Who are you sending your CV to?*

### Ordre des éléments dans une question directe

| | Question word (facultative) | Auxiliary | Subject | Verb | Complement (facultative) |
|---|---|---|---|---|---|
| *"Yes / No questions"* | | *Do* | *you* | *work?* | |
| | | *Would* | *you* | *like?* | *some coffee?* |
| | | *Has* | *Simon* | *filled out* | *the application form?* |
| | | *Are* | *you* | - | *German?* |
| *"Wh questions"* | *Where* | *does* | *Mary* | *work?* | |
| | *How many copies* | *did* | *Peter* | *make?* | |
| | *Which job* | *have* | *you* | *applied* | *for?* |
| | *What* | *is* | *his first name?* | | |

↳ Une question directe est toujours formulée selon l'ordre suivant : **auxiliaire + sujet + verbe**
On dira donc : ***Has he got?*** ou ***Does he have?*** mais jamais uniquement *has he*....
Dans une question directe, les prépositions se placent en fin de phrase (*hanging preposition*).
*What are you thinking **about**? What is he looking **for**?*

**EXCEPTIONS**

- Verbe / auxiliaire, *be* se met toujours à la place de l'auxiliaire.
- Si *who*, *what* et *which* sont en position sujet, on n'utilise pas d'auxiliaire.

***Who did Sylvie** write to?* → auxiliaire (sujet = Sylvie)
mais ***Who wrote** to Sylvie?* → pas d'auxiliaire (sujet = who)

## Les questions indirectes

**Comparez !**

*How old are you?* (question directe)
*Could you tell me how old you are?* (question indirecte)

L'interrogation au style indirect permet une formulation moins directe de la demande et, de ce fait, plus polie. Celle-ci est souvent utilisée pour poser des questions plus délicates.

### Comment construire une question indirecte ?

**1.** Si la question directe à partir de laquelle on forme la question indirecte est une "*Yes / No question*", on utilise indistinctement *if* ou *whether*.
*Do you have any experience?*
→ *Would you mind telling me **if** / **whether** you have any experience?*

**2.** Si la question directe à partir de laquelle on forme la question indirecte est une "*Wh question*", on reprend le pronom interrogatif introductif de la question directe.
*Why do you want the job?*
→ *Would you mind if I asked **why** you want the job?*

**!** L'ordre des mots dans la seconde partie d'une question indirecte est celui de l'affirmation (et non celui de l'interrogation) : il n'y a pas d'inversion du sujet.

| Introduction* | Mot interrogatif / if / whether | Comme une affirmation |
|---|---|---|
| *He asked her* | *which position* | *she was applying for.* |
| **Will / can / could you tell me explain / I wonder* | *what* | *you think of this?* |
| **Do you know*<br>*Would you mind telling me* | *if* | *he has any experience?* |
| **Do you mind if I ask* | *whether* | *she speaks German?* |
| **Would you mind if I asked* | *why* | *you want the job?* |
| *What do you advise / propose / recommend / say / suggest / suppose / think* | *(that)* | *he should do?* |
| *Why do you say* | *(that)* | *you don't like your job?* |

*Formules introductives les plus polies, et par ordre croissant de politesse.

**!** Attention aux réponses:

*Could you tell me…*
→ *Yes of course.* ≠ *I'd rather not.*

*Would you mind telling me / if…*
→ *Not at all.* ≠ *I'd rather not.*

*Would you mind if I.....*
→ *Not at all* ≠ *I'd rather you didn't.*

## Les questions négatives

Pour poser des questions négatives, on choisit des formules introductives en fonction de ce que l'on cherche à exprimer.

| Sens recherché | Formules introductives |
|---|---|
| *open* | *Don't you want… + infinitif?*<br>→ ***Don't you want** to try for the new job?* |
| *suggestion* | *Why don't we + base verbale...? / Why not + base verbale?*<br>→ ***Why not** take a break?* |
| *persuasion* | *Wouldn't it be + comparative + infinitive...?*<br>→ ***Wouldn't it be** better to take a break?* |
| *criticism* | *Can't you (just) + base verbale…?*<br>→ ***Can't you** just take a break?* |
| *surprise* | *Didn't you + base verbale…?*<br>→ ***Didn't you** take a break?* |
| *waiting a positive answer* | *Haven't we + past participle...?*<br>→ ***Haven't we** met before?* |

## 1 Formulez les questions correspondant aux réponses données en italique.

1. ....................................................................................

....................................................................................

*– Simon*

2. ....................................................................................

....................................................................................

*– I'm from the USA.*

3. ....................................................................................

....................................................................................

*– I live in Oxford.*

4. ....................................................................................

....................................................................................

*– I'm single.*

5. ....................................................................................

....................................................................................

*– I'm 31-years-old.*

6. ....................................................................................

....................................................................................

*– I was a maintenance manager.*

7. ....................................................................................

....................................................................................

*– No, I don't (speak French).*

8. ....................................................................................

....................................................................................

*– I ride horses (during my spare time).*

9. ....................................................................................

....................................................................................

*– (I live in Oxford) for 5 years.*

10. ....................................................................................

....................................................................................

*– (I heard about the job) from a newspaper ad.*

## 2 Remettez dans le bon ordre les mots des questions suivantes.

1. is / the / salary / what?

....................................................................................

....................................................................................

2. working hours / are / what / the?

....................................................................................

3. have / experience / I / should / any?

....................................................................................

4. do / qualifications / I / what / need?

....................................................................................

5. I / apply / to / who / should?

....................................................................................

6. closing date / miss / I / did / the?

....................................................................................

## 3 Reliez début et fin de dialogue.

| | |
|---|---|
| How is she? **1.** • | • **A.** She's very well. |
| What is she like? **2.** • | • **B.** How do you do? |
| What does she look like? **3.** • | • **C.** I'm a computer scientist. |
| Who does she look like? **4.** • | • **D.** Historical novels and music. |
| What does she like? **5.** • | • **E.** She prefers a laptop. |
| What sort of computer does she like? **6.** • | • **F.** She's got dark hair and blue eyes. |
| How do you like it? **7.** • | • **G.** Black with two sugars please. |
| What do you do? **8.** • | • **H.** She's pretty, tall and very kind. |
| How are you? **9.** • | • **I.** Like her father. |
| How do you do? **10.** • | • **J.** Fine thank you, and you. |

## 4 Formulez des questions en utilisant les pronoms interrogatifs donnés.

**1.** Somebody sent in an application.

Who ..............................................................................

.............................................................................. ?

**2.** She applied for a job.

Which job ......................................................................

.............................................................................. ?

**3.** She called someone.

Who ..............................................................................

.............................................................................. ?

**4.** Someone wrote her an e-mail.

Who ..............................................................................

.............................................................................. ?

**5.** Something happened to the computer.

What ............................................................................

.............................................................................. ?

**6.** She passed the English test.

Which test ....................................................................

.............................................................................. ?

**7.** Someone selected her for the job.

Who ..............................................................................

.............................................................................. ?

**8.** Some people are on the short list.

Who ..............................................................................

.............................................................................. ?

## 5 Transformez les questions directes suivantes en questions indirectes.

**1.** Do I get paid leave?

Do you mind if I ask ......................................................

..............................................................................

..............................................................................

**2.** Do I have to work overtime?

Could you tell me whether ............................................

..............................................................................

..............................................................................

**3.** What are the chances of promotion?

Would you mind if I asked ............................................

..............................................................................

..............................................................................

**4.** What is the holiday entitlement?

Do you know what .........................................................

..............................................................................

..............................................................................

**5.** Why do you want to work here?

Tell me why ...................................................................

..............................................................................

..............................................................................

**6.** What salary do you expect to earn?

Would you mind telling me ............................................

..............................................................................

..............................................................................

**7.** What are your strengths and weaknesses?

Have you any idea ..........................................................

..............................................................................

..............................................................................

**8.** How often were you absent from your last job?

I need to know ...............................................................

..............................................................................

..............................................................................

**9.** How long does it take you to get here from home?

Can you tell me ..............................................................

..............................................................................

..............................................................................

**10.** In your opinion, what does the job entail?

Explain what you think ..................................................

..............................................................................

..............................................................................

## 6 Formulez des questions négatives en tenant compte du sens recherché.

| Nuance | Question |
|---|---|
| Ex.: Expecting positive answer | apply for a job here before |

| | |
|---|---|
| **1.** Persuasion | be easier to be honest about your experience |
| **2.** Surprise | read the job description |
| **3.** Suggestion | go through the contract |
| **4.** Surprise | speak any foreign languages |
| **5.** Criticism | give a straight answer |

Ex. ▶ Haven't you applied for a job here before?

**1.** ..........................................................................

..........................................................................

**2.** ..........................................................................

..........................................................................

**3.** ..........................................................................

..........................................................................

**4.** ..........................................................................

..........................................................................

**5.** ..........................................................................

..........................................................................

## 7 Complétez la conversation en replaçant les réponses sous les questions correspondantes.

**1.** Why are you looking so worried?

..........................................................................

**2.** Haven't you read up about the company?

..........................................................................

**3.** Would you mind if I looked over your notes?

..........................................................................

**4.** Do you know what the interviewer is like?

..........................................................................

**5.** Who asked you to come to the interview?

..........................................................................

**6.** Lucky you! What time is your appointment?

..........................................................................

**7.** Would you mind telling me what salary you are looking for?

..........................................................................

**8.** How many languages do you speak?

..........................................................................

**9.** Oh look! Who is coming towards us?

..........................................................................

**10.** Good luck! I wonder if you could give me a lift to the station after my interview.

..........................................................................

**Réponses**

**A.** It's at 10.30, but I think they're running late.

**B.** I think it's the H.R. manager's secretary.

**C.** Because I've got an interview in 5 minutes and I'm not ready for it!

**D.** The H.R. manager. She's a friend of my father's.

**E.** I'm reading about it now. I know the turnover, the number of employees, but that's about it.

**F.** Oh, so you're a competitor!! Of course I can – we can swop notes.

**G.** I'm told she's pretty tough and asks lots of difficult questions.

**H.** I'd rather not, but it's my first job so I don't expect much.

**I.** Not at all – help yourself.

**J.** Only 5 and my Russian is pretty weak.

## CORRIGÉS

**1.** 1. What is your first name? 2. Where are you from? 3. Where do you live? 4. Are you married or single? 5. How old are you? 6. What was your previous job? 7. Do you speak French? 8. What do you do in your spare time? 9. How long have you lived (/have you been living) in Oxford? 10. How did you hear about the job?
**2.** 1. What is the salary? 2. What are the working hours? 3. Should I have any experience? 4. What qualifications do I need? 5. Who should I apply to? 6. Did I miss the closing date?
**3.** 1. A 2. H 3. F 4. I 5. D 6. E 7. G 8. C 9. J 10. B
**4.** 1. Who sent in an application? 2. Which/what job did she apply for? 3. Who did she call? 4. Who wrote to her? 5. What happened to the computer? 6. Which test did she pass? 7. Who selected her? 8. Who is on the short list?
**5.** 1. Do you mind if I ask if I get paid leave? 2. Could you tell me whether I have to work overtime? 3. Would you mind if I asked what the chances of promotion are? 4. Do you know what the holiday entitlement is? 5. Tell me why you want to work here? 6. Would you mind telling me what salary you expect to earn? 7. Have you any idea what your strengths and weaknesses are? 8. I need to know how often you were absent from your last job. 9. Can you tell me how long it takes you to get here from home? 10. Explain what you think the job entails.
**6.** 1. Wouldn't it be easier to be honest about your experience? 2. Didn't you read the job description? 3. Why don't we go through the contract? 4. Don't you speak any foreign languages? 5. Can't you just give me a straight answer?
**7.** 1. C / 2. E / 3. I / 4. G / 5. D / 6. A / 7. H / 8. J / 9. B / 10. F

# Les *question tags*

## Qu'est-ce que les *question tags* et à quoi servent-ils ?

Très fréquents en anglais, les *question tags* sont des mini-questions posées en fin de phrases et qui servent à :

**1.** Poser une vraie question (intonation montante).
*You're German, aren't you?* → Tu es allemand, pas vrai?

**2.** Inviter le locuteur à être d'accord avec vous (intonation descendante).
*It isn't an interesting proposal, is it?* → Ce n'est pas une offre intéressante, n'est-ce pas ?

**3.** Demander un service ou des informations.
*You couldn't give me hand, could you?* → Tu peux me donner un coup de main?

## Comment se construisent les *question tags* ?

**1.** Si la phrase de départ est affirmative, le tag est négatif.
*Those contracts are out-of-date, aren't they?* → auxiliaire + *n't* + pronom personnel sujet

**2.** Si la phrase de départ est négative, le tag est affirmatif.
*You didn't go to the meeting, did you?* → auxiliaire + pronom personnel sujet

**!** Notez la construction particulière des tags suivants :
*That's good, isn't it?*
*I'm early, aren't I?*
*Everyone / someone wants the job, don't they?*
*Nobody wants the job, do they?*
*Let's look through the file, shall we?*
*Don't work too hard, will you?*

# Les questions-échos

Répondre sous la forme d'une question permet :

**1.** De montrer votre intérêt à ce que vous dit votre interlocuteur.
*I've invited over 400 people to the seminar in July. – Have you?*
*I don't think he'll bother to come. – Don't you?*

**2.** D'exprimer votre surprise.
*John has got the job. – Has he?! I never thought he would!*

**3.** De renforcer votre propre question.
*So, he took over from James Dean, did he?* → Reprise de l'auxiliaire et du pronom personnel.

# Les réponses courtes

On utilise des "*short answers*" pour :

**1.** Ne pas répondre par un simple *yes* ou *no* (ce qui ne se fait pas en anglais).
*Do you agree to the conditions? – Yes, I do. / No, I don't.*

*Are you looking for a job?* – *Yes, I am. / No, I'm not.*
*Have you met the manager?* – *Yes, I have. / No, I haven't.*

! Notez les réponses à une question négative :
*Don't you want to try for the job?* – *Yes, I do. (= Yes, I want to*)*
– *No, I don't. (= I don't want to*)*

**2.** Répondre aux questions introduites par un pronom interrogatif portant sur le sujet.
*Who's next?* – *I am. / Mary (is).*
*Which applicant didn't fill in the form?* – *He didn't. / Michael (didn't).*

! Notez que la reprise de l'auxiliaire est facultative quand la réponse est un nom, obligatoire quand celle-ci est un pronom personnel.

## So / neither

Pour exprimer un accord ou une identité de goût ou d'action, on utilise *so* et *neither*.

| | | Agree | Don't agree |
|---|---|---|---|
| **Positive statement** | *I like looking for a new job.* | *So do I. / Me too.* | *I don't.* |
| | *Bill's had a promotion.* | *So has Jane.* | *I haven't.* |
| **Negative statement** | *I don't like their company policy.* | *Neither do I. / Nor do I. / Me neither. / I don't either.* | *I do.* |
| | *She never wanted the job.* | *Simon didn't either.* | *Sarah did.* |

***So*** s'utilise également après des verbes comme *be afraid, expect, guess, hope, suppose, think,* etc. pour éviter la reprise de la phrase.
*Will you get there on time? – I hope so (= to get there on time)!*

! Notez la forme négative :

| | Positive | Negative |
|---|---|---|
| *don't* | *I think so. I expect so.* | *I don't think so. I don't expect so.* |
| *not* | *I hope so. I'm afraid so. I guess so.* | *I hope not. I'm afraid not. I guess not.* |
| *don't / not* | *I suppose so.* | *I don't suppose so. I suppose not.* |

Vous pouvez aussi employer l'auxiliaire seul pour éviter une répétition.
*George is going to job centre, but Harry isn't.*
*I think he should go to a head hunter, but I'm sure he won't.*

***To****: vous pouvez utiliser *to* pour éviter une répétition après *be supposed / allowed, have to, know how, like, tell, want, prefer*

*Why didn't you report the breakdown?*
→ *I didn't know I was supposed to. (Report it)*

*Will you set the printing machine?*
→ *I don't know how to. (Set it)*

*Why didn't you fill in the quality form?*
→ *I wasn't aware I had to. (Fill in the form)*

**1** **Répondez à chacune des questions. Vos réponses seront courtes et peu aimables.**

**1.** – Can I speak to the human resources manager?

– ................................................ . What is it about?

**2.** – Was it you I spoke to yesterday?

– .................................................... . I had a day off.

**3.** – Could you spare me a few minutes?

– ......................................... . If you are not too long.

**4.** – Have you read my letter?

– ............. . You know, we receive a lot of applications.

**5.** – Should I send in my curriculum vitae?

– .................................. . You can always give it a try!

**6.** – Do I have to have a medical test?

– ...................... . We deal with very sensitive products.

**7.** – Would you like me to come and see you?

– ................................ . I'm a bit busy at the moment.

**8.** – Are there any possible openings in your company?

– ................................ . For people who fit the profile.

**2** **Complétez chacune des questions posées par le tag qui convient.**

**1.** – You've put in your personal details, ......................

.................................................................................. ?

– Yes, address, phone number, etc.

**2.** – You aren't going to put in that you were fired, .....

..................................................................................

– No, I'd better just say I left the job.

**3.** – You got your driving licence, .............................. ?

– Yes, after three tries!

**4.** – You're learning french, ...................................... ?

– Yes, at evening classes.

**5.** – Nobody puts their primary school in, ....................

.................................................................................. .

– No, just secondary school.

**6.** – You haven't got any spare time activities, .............

.................................................................................. ?

– Yes, I play chess.

**7.** – You have put that you are honest and efficient .....

.................................................................................. ?

– Yes, and dynamic, and keen.

**8.** – Don't go over the page, .......................................

.................................................................................. ?

– No, just one page is enough.

**9.** – You would like me to read it through, ..................

.................................................................................. ?

– Yes please, that would be kind.

**10.** – Let's send it off then, ....................................... ?

– Yes, and keep your fingers crossed!

**3** **Formulez une question réponse pour manifester votre intérêt à ce que vous dit votre interlocuteur.**

**1.** I've got a new job!

..................................................................................

..................................................................................

**2.** He can speak 14 languages.

..................................................................................

..................................................................................

**3.** She went to the interview yesterday.

..................................................................................

..................................................................................

**4.** We are going to see the applicants tomorrow.

..................................................................................

..................................................................................

**5.** They have been looking for someone for some time.

..................................................................................

..................................................................................

**6.** I don't think he'd be very good at the job.

..................................................................................

..................................................................................

**7.** He would like to work abroad.

..............................................................................

..............................................................................

**8.** I wonder if she'll have a trial period.

..............................................................................

..............................................................................

**9.** His starting salary will be $125,000 per annum.

..............................................................................

..............................................................................

**10.** He's going to work at least 55 hours a week.

..............................................................................

..............................................................................

## 4 Complétez le tableau suivant.

| Statement | Agree | Don't agree |
|---|---|---|
| Ex. ▶ She doesn't know where to start looking. | Neither do I. | I do. |
| **1.** I'm sure he'll find a job soon. | | |
| **2.** I can't ever decide what to wear for the interview. | | |
| **3.** She enjoys working with a team. | | |
| **4.** He gets a good bonus. | | |
| **5.** They are entitled to luncheon vouchers. | | |
| **6.** I would like a company car. | | |
| **7.** We have got a good pension plan. | | |

## 5 À l'aide des éléments entre parenthèses, formulez des réponses courtes.

**1.** Do you think you've got the job?
(I – hope)

..............................................................................

..............................................................................

**2.** Who is responsible for that task?

She ............................... / Simon ...............................

**3.** Can you do the costing for that?
(I – not – know how)

..............................................................................

**4.** Will they be laying off people?
(I – not – to guess)

..............................................................................

**5.** Can he take time off for Christmas?
(He – not – allowed)

..............................................................................

**6.** Which of you wrote this letter?

I ............................... / Sandra ...............................

**7.** You should be more insistent.
(I – suppose )

..............................................................................

**8.** Who would like to come?

They ........................ / John and James ......................

### CORRIGÉS

**1.** (The right answer in the context is underlined, the others are for information). **1.** Yes, you can / no, you can't. (It would be better to say "yes, certainly" on the telephone). **2.** Yes, it was / no, it wasn't. **3.** Yes, I can / no, I can't. (Could = polite form because you asking for something). **4.** Yes, I have / no, I haven't. **5.** Yes, you should / no, you shouldn't. **6.** Yes, you do / no, you don't. **7.** Yes, I would / no, I wouldn't. **8.** Yes, there are / no, there aren't.

**2.** **1.** Haven't you? **2.** Are you? **3.** Didn't you? **4.** Aren't you? **5.** Do they? **6.** Have you? **7.** Haven't you? **8.** Will you? **9.** Wouldn't you? **10.** Shall we?

**3.** **1.** Have you? Where are you going to work? **2.** Can he? What languages can he speak? **3.** Did she? What was the answer? **4.** Are you? How many are there? **5.** Have they? Have they found anyone yet? **6.** Don't you? Why? **7.** Would he? Where? **8.** Do you? People usually do. **9.** Will it? – That's not bad! **10.** Is he? That's a lot.

**4.** **1.** So am I / I'm not **2.** Neither can I / I can **3.** So do I / I don't **4.** So do I / I don't **5.** So am I / I'm not **6.** So would I / I wouldn't **7.** So have we / we haven't.

**5.** **1.** I hope so. **2.** She is / Simon. **3.** I don't know how to. **4.** I guess not. **5.** He's not allowed to. **6.** I did / Sandra. **7.** I suppose so. **8.** They would / John and James.

# De la voix active à la voix passive

## Comparez !

*The company puts an advertisement in the job centre.* → Voix active
*An advertisement is put in the job centre (by the company).* → Voix passive

## Formation du passif

La voix passive est très employée dans l'anglais des affaires.

| | Active | Passive |
|---|---|---|
| Simple present | *Peter uses the computer.* | *The computer is used (by Peter).* |
| Past progressive | *Peter was using the computer.* | *The computer was being used (by Peter).* |
| Present perfect | *Peter has used the computer.* | *The computer has been used (by Peter).* |
| Futur ("will") | *Peter will use the computer.* | *The computer will be used (by Peter).* |
| + Modal | *Peter might use the computer.* | *The computer might be used (by Peter).* |
| + Phrasal verb | *Peter writes up the software.* | *The software is written up (by Peter).* |
| Negative | *Peter doesn't use the computer.* | *The computer isn't used (by Peter).* |
| Interrogative | *Is Peter using the computer?* | *Is the computer being used (by Peter)?* |

↳ Le passif se construit comme suit : **auxiliaire *be* + participe passé du verbe**
Attention : *She was born in 1997.* (Elle est née en 1997).

Le complément d'agent, désignant celui qui accomplit l'action, est généralement introduit par *by* (ou *with*). *The boxes were packed by Bob. They were lined with tissue paper.*

! D'autres prépositions existent :

| | |
|---|---|
| *The product was made BY MIK PIC.* | (producteur) |
| *The product was made IN Spain.* | (lieu géographique) |
| *The picture is drawn IN pastel.* | (matière) |
| *The box is lined WITH plastic film.* | (instrument) |
| *Paper is made FROM wood.* | (processus : changement de matière) |
| *Wood is made INTO paper.* | (processus : changement de matière) |
| *The door is made OF wood.* | (pas de processus) |
| *The shoes are made (OUT) OF calf's leather.* | (matière spécifique) |

## L'auxiliaire *get*

En anglais courant, *get* est souvent substitué à *be* à la forme passive :

- quand quelque chose est inattendu.
*The night watchman was employed because he can handle dogs.*
*He got bitten by his dog last night!*

- quand on parle d'un changement d'état (cf. *get married / divorced, get dressed*).
*We have to wear lab coats for hygiene. Could you please get changed?*

Dans les titres des journaux, les présentations … le passif est souvent utilisé en « forme raccourcie » :
*New smart phone presented last week. (The new smart phone was presented last week).*

# Du discours direct au discours indirect

## Discours direct

Lorsque l'on rapporte les paroles de quelqu'un au discours direct, les paroles de la personne sont citées mot pour mot et la phrase est encadrée par des guillemets.
*Bill said, "I'm applying for that position."*

## Discours indirect

Lorsque l'on rapporte les paroles de quelqu'un au discours indirect, cela entraîne une série de transformations de la phrase initiale.
*Bill said (that) he was applying for that position.*

**1.** La phrase commence par un verbe du type *say, tell, answer, ask* (souvent au passé).

**2.** On utilise *that* (« que »), souvent omis (notamment en anglais parlé).

**3.** Les pronoms personnels et réfléchis, ainsi que les possessifs changent.
*"I can't give you an answer."* → *He said he couldn't give me an answer.*

**4.** Il faut respecter la concordance des temps.

| Direct speech | Reported speech |
|---|---|
| *"I am / she is / they are (going to)..."* | *He said he / she was / they were (going to)...* |
| *"you have / she has (interviewed)..."* | *He said I / she had (interviewed)...* |
| *"I was / we were..."* | *He said he was / had been / we were / had been* |
| *"It will / can..."* | *He said it would / could...* |
| *"I do / It does / you work / we go..."* | *He said he / it did / I worked / we went...* |

**EXCEPTION** Si vous parlez de quelque chose qui est resté vrai au moment où vous parlez, il n'est pas nécessaire de changer le temps du verbe.
*John said, "the applicant's level of English isn't good enough."*
*John said (that) the applicant's level of English is / was not good enough.*

**!** L'impératif au discours indirect :
*"Make sure to be on time!"* → « Soyez à l'heure ! »
*She told them to make sure they were on time.* → Elle leur a dit d'être à l'heure.
*"Don't do that!"* → « Ne faites pas ça ! »
*She told them not to do that.* → Elle leur a dit de ne pas faire ça.

JOB SEEKING

**1** **À partir de chacune des listes de mots suivantes, formulez une phrase à la voix passive.**

**1.** Put – advert – in local paper

........................................................................................

........................................................................................

**2.** Advert – read – by potential applicants

........................................................................................

........................................................................................

**3.** HR manager – call – by people interested

........................................................................................

........................................................................................

........................................................................................

**4.** CV and cover letter – request

........................................................................................

........................................................................................

**5.** Fix – appointment – for interview

........................................................................................

........................................................................................

**6.** Interview – several applicants

........................................................................................

........................................................................................

**7.** Draw up – short list – by personnel assistant

........................................................................................

........................................................................................

........................................................................................

**8.** Interview – applicants – by C.E.O.

........................................................................................

........................................................................................

**9.** Offer the job – successful applicant

........................................................................................

........................................................................................

**10.** Applicant – accept the offer – and – contract – sign

........................................................................................

........................................................................................

........................................................................................

**2** **Transformez les phrases actives suivantes en phrases passives.**

**1.** They treat the in-house applications first.

........................................................................................

........................................................................................

**2.** The personnel assistant has filed all the applications.

........................................................................................

........................................................................................

**3.** Are they going to take on the French engineer?

........................................................................................

........................................................................................

**4.** The human resources manager promises training with the job.

........................................................................................

........................................................................................

**5.** They didn't replace the foreman when he retired last year.

........................................................................................

........................................................................................

**6.** If the results are good, the director awards operators a productivity bonus.

........................................................................................

........................................................................................

**7.** They should change the working hours if they want anyone to take the job.

........................................................................................

........................................................................................

**8.** They have not computerized the application form yet.

........................................................................................

........................................................................................

**9.** Will they standardize the recruiting system in the future?

........................................................................................

........................................................................................

**10.** They fired the sales manager last week – maybe you should try for the job.

........................................................................................

........................................................................................

## 3 Avant de deviner de quoi parle le texte, complétez les 5 phrases ci-dessous à l'aide des prépositions suivantes:

*in – from – into – by – of*

**1.** It is made .................. flowers, fruit, roots, pods and beans, wood, moss, lichen, leaves or resin.

**2.** The raw material is turned .............. a concentrated solution through distillation or other means.

**3.** The packaging is often made .................. glass.

**4.** It is often made .................. the south of France.

**5.** It can be made .................. Givenchy, Dior and other fragrance creators.

It is ..........................................................................

## 4 Transformez ces phrases directes en phrases indirectes.

**1.** "I'm afraid you aren't suitable for the position."

He said ..........................................................................

**2.** "I will show you the workshop later."

He said ..........................................................................

**3.** "You cannot talk to the operators while they are working."

He said ..........................................................................

**4.** "Don't go into the research lab."

She told ..........................................................................

**5.** "I am going to explain later."

She told ..........................................................................

**6.** "Have you got any questions?"

He asked me ..........................................................................

**7.** "I will look after the paperwork myself."

He said ..........................................................................

**8.** "You must have a medical."

He told me ..........................................................................

**9.** "When can you start?"

He asked me ..........................................................................

**10.** "I have to give 3 month's notice."

I explained ..........................................................................

## CORRIGÉS

**1.** 1. The advert is put in the local paper. 2. The advert is read by potential applicants. 3. The HR manager is called by the people who are interested. 4. A CV and cover letter are requested. 5. An appointment is fixed for an interview. 6. Several applicants are interviewed. 7. A shortlist is drawn up by the personnel assistant. 8. The applicants are interviewed by the C.E.O. 9. The successful applicant is offered the job. 10. The offer is accepted by the applicant and a contract is signed.
**2.** 1. The in-house applications are treated first. 2. All the applications have been filed (by the personnel assistant). 3. Is the French engineer going to be taken on? 4. Training is promised with the job (by the H.R. Manager). 5. The foreman was not replaced when he retired last year. 6. The operators are / get awarded a productivity bonus if the results are good (by the director). 7. The working hours should be changed.... 8. The application form has not been computerized yet. 9. Will the recruiting system be standardized in the future? 10. The sales manager got / was fired last week....
**3.** 1. from 2. into 3. of 4. in 5. by / it is perfume
**4.** 1. He said he was afraid I wasn't suitable for the position. 2. He said he would show me / us the workshop later 3. He said I couldn't talk to the operators while they were working. 4. She told me not to go into the research lab. 5. She told me she was going to explain later. 6. He asked me if I had any questions. 7. He said he would look after the paperwork himself. 8. He told me I had to have a medical. 9. He asked me when I could start. 10. I explained that I had to give 3 months' notice.

# Les causatifs

**Comparez !**

*She filled in the application form.*
*She had the application form filled in (by the assistant).*

## Emploi des causatifs

C'est le "faire faire" en français. On ne fait pas l'action soi-même, mais on en porte la responsabilité. Les principaux verbes causatifs sont *have, make, let*.

**1.** Si l'objet direct du verbe causatif est à l'origine de l'action :

| Sujet | Verbe causatif | Objet direct (personne) | Base verbale | Sens |
|---|---|---|---|---|
| *He* | *had* | *the applicant* | *write a sample email* | Donner la responsabilité à quelqu'un de faire quelque chose |
| *I'll* | *have* | *my assistant* | *draw up the contract tomorrow* | Demander à quelqu'un de faire quelque chose |
| *She* | *made* | *the candidate* | *speak English* | Obligation |
| *The rail strike* | *made* | *me* | *late for the interview* | Action involontaire |
| *Being on a shortlist* | *makes* | *him* | *nervous* | Sentiments – Notez l'adjectif à la place du verbe |
| *He* | *lets* | *the interviewers* | *do as they like* | Permettre |

Notez que :
***Will*** ou ***would*** suivi par le causatif ***have*** exprime un désir ou une volonté :
*I **won't have** the applicants queuing up outside my office.*
(Voir annexe 2 pour d'autres astuces avec *make* et la différence entre *make* et *do*.)

Pour d'autres verbes (*get, allow, cause, force, get, order, tell, want…*)

| Sujet | Verbe causatif | Objet direct (chose/personne) | Infinitif (avec *to*) |
|---|---|---|---|
| *We* | *got* | *the head hunter* | *to choose just 3 candidates* |
| *The job centre* | *told* | *him* | *to go for the interview* |
| *The competition* | *caused* | *the company* | *to close down* |
| *They* | *will allow* | *trainees* | *to go home early on Friday* |

**2.** Si l'objet direct subit l'action du verbe causatif :

| Sujet | Verbe causatif | Objet direct (chose) | Participe passé |
|---|---|---|---|
| *The applicant* | *will need* | *her contract* | *signed a.s.a.p.* |
| *Could you* | *get* | *the cover letter* | *finished by tomorrow?* |
| *The H.R. manager* | *wants* | *the interviews* | *organised next week* |
| *Sarah* | *had* | *her CV* | *written by a specialist* |

# Le subjonctif

**Comparez !**

*I would like you to fill out all your personal details.*
*It is recommended that you fill out all your personal details.*

## Emploi du subjonctif

Le subjonctif est associé avec les phrases suivantes (la liste n'est pas exhaustive).
*To advise / ask / command / demand / desire / insist / propose / recommend / request / suggest / urge (…) that…*
*It's a good idea / a bad idea / best / crucial / desirable / essential / imperative / important / necessary / recommended / required / requested / right / urgent / vital / wrong (…) that…*
→ *It is essential that* ***you be*** *on time for the interview;*
→ *He insisted that* ***she (should) understand*** *the conditions before she signed.*

| Sujet | Expression | Objet | base verbale | |
|---|---|---|---|---|
| *She* | *suggested that* | *I* | *request* | *on-the-job training* |
| *It* | *is best that* | *you* | *take* | *your time to fill in the document* |

D'autres expressions avec le subjonctif.
*Ring them up now lest* ***you don't get*** *time later.*
*Whether* ***it be*** *a good or bad thing, you need the job.*
***Be*** *that as it may.*
*Far be it from me to judge, but I don't think you* ***have taken*** *enough* ***care*** *with your CV.*
*If need* ***be****, you can ask for training once you've got the job.*
***Come*** *what may your job is safe for the time being.*
*Suffice it to say your salary* ***is*** *within the guidelines.*

**1.** *Should* dans une forme subjonctif

- *That + should +* infinitif.

*We think* ***that you should improve*** *your language skills.*

- *That + should + be +* comparatif.

*He thinks Sophie's cover letter* ***should be shorter****.*

- Reporting: *that + should + advise, ask, bed, command, demand, intend, instruct, order, request, require, stipulate, warn.*

*He was warned* ***that he shouldn't refuse*** *an appointment if he wanted the job.*

• *Reaction* (souvent négatif) : ***be + amazed, disappointed, sad, surprised, worried***… + ***that***.
*She* ***was surprised that*** *they should want to know her height on the application form.*

## L'infinitif d'intention

**Comparez !**

*He will telephone for an appointment.*
*He will telephone to fix an appointment.*
*She is going to PLP to have an interview tomorrow.*

### Emploi de l'infinitif d'intention

| | Preposition | infinitive | Noun |
|---|---|---|---|
| *She is going to PLP* | *for* | | *an interview tomorrow* |
| *She is going to PLP* | | *to have* | *an interview tomorrow* |

## Négatives piégeuses

Certains mots en anglais (*hardly, nowhere, neither*…) sont des « négatives ».
Ne faites pas une double négation !

*He has hardly ever held down a job.*
→ ~~*He has hardly never held down a job.*~~

*We haven't ever seen the new C.E.O.*
→ ~~*We haven't never seen the new C.E.O.*~~

*No-one likes his way of interviewing.*
→ ~~*No-one doesn't like his way of interviewing.*~~

*There is nowhere I like better than the office.*
→ ~~*There isn't nowhere I like better than my office.*~~

*It is necessary not to waste too much time.*
→ ~~*It is necessary to don't waste too much time.*~~

*Neither of the applicants is very suitable.*
→ ~~*Neither of the applicants isn't very suitable.*~~

*Neither John nor Bill filled in the application form.*
→ ~~*Neither John nor Bill didn't fill in the application form.*~~

## 1 Choisissez la bonne réponse.

**1.** My father .................. wear a skirt for the interview.
**A.** made me to
**B.** made me

**2.** Could you let me .................. your answer within the next couple of days?
**A.** to have
**B.** have

**3.** I will need .................. your application delivered by Monday.
**A.** to have
**B.** have

**4.** Could you get him .......................... me tomorrow?
**A.** to call
**B.** call

**5.** I'll have my secretary .................. your contract this afternoon.
**A.** send
**B.** sent

**6.** My father will not allow me .................. for the job in the bar.
**A.** apply
**B.** to apply

**7.** I'm still not sure about the job, and they want me .................. right away.
**A.** to sign
**B.** signed

**8.** We had the job advert .................. on the website last week.
**A.** put
**B.** to put

**9.** The interviewer's personal questions made him to be angry
**A.** to be angry
**B.** angry

**10.** I need you .................. the computer tests ready before they all arrive.
**A.** to get
**B.** get

## 2 Mettez le verbe entre parenthèses à la forme subjonctif – ou une autre.

**1.** I insist that he (come) ............. for a third interview.

**2.** Would you like him (come) .................. tomorrow?

**3.** When he (come) .................., please show him straight into my office.

**4.** Do you need applicants (have) .................. a personality test?

**5.** Could you tell me if he (have) .................. any experience?

**6.** They require that all applicants (have) .................. a clean drivers licence.

**7.** We highly recommend that you (be) .................. aware of the terms.

**8.** Do you think it's necessary that we (check) .................. the applicants' records?

**9.** They asked us (bring) .................. all the necessary paperwork.

**10.** I suggest that you (remove) .................. your earings before you see the manager.

## 3 Trouvez l'erreur et corrigez-la.

**1.** I'm going to the HR office for to get the applicants' files.

..................................................................................

..................................................................................

..................................................................................

..................................................................................

**2.** She has hardly never worked in her life!

..................................................................................

..................................................................................

..................................................................................

..................................................................................

**3.** It is highly recommended that you to decide on your days off before you sign.

..................................................................................

..................................................................................

..................................................................................

..................................................................................

..................................................................................

**4.** The student will need his work experience agreement to be validated before he starts.

..................................................................................

..................................................................................

..................................................................................

..................................................................................

..................................................................................

**5.** The story he told last night about the interview really make me laugh!

..................................................................................

..................................................................................

..................................................................................

..................................................................................

..................................................................................

**6.** I'll have the 3 shortlisted applicants to come and see you in the morning.

..................................................................................

..................................................................................

..................................................................................

..................................................................................

..................................................................................

**7.** Something tells me that neither of the interviewers doesn't want me for the job.

..................................................................................

..................................................................................

..................................................................................

..................................................................................

..................................................................................

**8.** Will your future boss let you to leave work early on Friday afternoons so we can miss the rush hour traffic?

..................................................................................

..................................................................................

..................................................................................

..................................................................................

..................................................................................

**9.** He went the whole way to New York for have the interview.

..................................................................................

..................................................................................

..................................................................................

..................................................................................

..................................................................................

**10.** I'm always telling him that he work harder so he can get a good job.

..................................................................................

..................................................................................

..................................................................................

..................................................................................

..................................................................................

## 4 Mettez le mot qui convient dans la phrase.

*allow – ever – get – have – insist – made – make – nobody – required – to*

**1.** We'll .................. the lawyer check through the small print.

**2.** He's gone to see the HR manager, .................. ask for more training.

**3.** .................. really wants to be promoted to that position.

**4.** We could .................. him to agree to a lower salary with higher commission.

**5.** They will .................. us to work a 4-day week if we want.

**6.** That person at the job centre is so nice. She does .................. me laugh!

**7.** She hasn't .................. been for an interview before.

**8.** The company .................. her sign the confidentiality clause, against her will really.

**9.** It's .................. that you take an English exam to prove your language skills.

**10.** I .................. that you listen to my advice about job seeking.

## 5 Choisissez la bonne réponse dans cette conversation.

Jo: Where are you going?

Mike: I'm off to London **(1)** to / for to get a job!

Jo: Oh yes. And where are you going to find that?

Mike: The woman at the job centre suggested I **(2)** go / to go and see people.

Jo: So who are you going to see?

Mike: Well, she **(3)** had / have her assistant type up a list of suitable companies.

Jo: Do you think they'll see you just like that? They **(4)** hardly never / hardly ever do that.

Mike: I'll just have to **(5)** make / made them see me.

Jo: They probably won't even **(6)** let / to let you come into the building!

Mike: Just you wait and see, I'll **(7)** make / to make you eat your words!

2 days later…

Jo: So, how did the job interviews go?

Mike: Well, I called the job centre and got them **(8)** to advise / advise me on where to go first. They recommended I **(9)** go / to go to MIS Ltd. as they had jobs on offer. They said it was vital that I **(10)** am / be on time as the boss is a stickler for punctuality.

Jo: Go on. What happened?

Mike: Well, they **(11)** had / to have me fill in an application form, then I had a short interview and after they told me **(12)** wait / to wait in the lobby. I went off **(13)** for / to have a cup of coffee, got back 10 minutes later and…

Jo: You are **(14)** making / having me stressed!

Mike: … they said that neither of the other two candidates **(15)** wasn't / was right for the job and offered the job to me!!

## 6 Complétez la phrase avec le mot qui convient.

**1.** They ......... ever offer a job on the first interview.

**2.** You must stop sitting around. You really have to ......... yourself a job!

**3.** As an exception we ......... our employees to wear casual clothes on public holidays.

**4.** Please don't worry, I'll ......... my doctor send you a certificate on Monday.

**5.** Be that as it ........., you still have to sign the dotted line.

### CORRIGÉS

**1.** 1. B 2. B 3. A 4. A 5. A 6. B 7. A 8. A 9. B 10. A
**2.** 1. come 2. to come 3. comes 4. to have 5. has 6. have 7. be 8. check 9. to bring 10. remove
**3.** 1. I'm going to the HR office to get the applicants' files. 2. She has hardly ever worked in her life! 3. It is highly recommended that you decide on your days off before you sign. 4. The student will need his work experience agreement validated before he starts. 5. The story he told last night about the interview really made me laugh! 6. I'll have the 3 shortlisted applicants come and see you in the morning. 7. Something tells me that neither of the interviewers wants me for the job. 8. Will your future boss let you leave work early on friday afternoons so we can miss the rush hour traffic? 9. He went the whole way to New York to have the interview. 10. I'm always telling him to work harder so he can get a good job.
**4.** 1. have 2. to 3. nobody 4. get 5. allow 6. make 7. ever 8. made 9. required 10. insist
**5.** 1. to 2. go 3. had 4. hardly ever 5. make 6. let 7. make 8. to advise 9. go 10. be 11. had 12. to wait 13. to 14. making 15. was
**6.** 1. hardly 2. get 3. allow 4. have 5. may

JOB SEEKING

## 1 À partir des indices, formulez une question.

Score : ..... / 6

1. Get – on-the-job training – we ..........
2. "N'est-ce pas" – be good – the take home pay ..........
3. Have to work – you – unsocial hours ..........
4. There – pension scheme – is ..........
5. Be interested – part time job – would – you ..........
6. Flexitime – can – work ..........

## 2 Entourez l'erreur et corrigez-la !

Score : ..... / 10

1. Those are interesting, aren't it? ..........
2. Who did receive a phone call from Tom? ..........
3. For who are you writing that report? ..........
4. I don't think that job looks very good. So don't I ..........
5. He doesn't get to work on time, doesn't he? ..........
6. Could you tell me what was your last job? ..........
7. They demanded that we to try on the uniform. ..........
8. "I don't think he's got the job." "Hasn't you?" ..........
9. I am suitable for the job, I am not? ..........
10. Why you don't ask for a training course? ..........

## 3 Entourez la bonne réponse.

Score : ..... / 8

| | | |
|---|---|---|
| **1.** "You're not still job-hunting, are you?" | **a)** Yes, I am. | **b)** No, I aren't. |
| **2.** "My son will be the best." | **a)** He will? | **b)** Will he? |
| **3.** "Which of you went to the interview?" | **a)** Did he. Mark. | **b)** He did. Mark (did). |
| **4.** "Nobody applied for the job." | **a)** Didn't they? | **b)** Didn't he? |
| **5.** "That's a strange covering letter." | **a)** Is that? | **b)** Is it? |
| **6.** "Why are you doing that for her?" | **a)** She wants it done | **b)** She wants it be done |
| **7.** "Why are you going out?" | **a)** To find a job | **b)** For to find a job |
| **8.** "Why did you agree to a 50-hour week?" | **a)** He to make me | **b)** He made me |

## 4 Dans chacune des listes suivantes, entourez la / les bonne(s) réponse(s)

Score : ..... / 6

1. Me too – he too – she too
2. Would you mind to tell – if I ask – if I asked
3. Haven't we meet – met – meeting
4. Hardly anybody – nobody – any

**5.** Neither – nor – not either

**6.** I'm late, am I – aren't I – am I not

**7.** Don't do that, will – won't – shall you

**8.** Neither of the job offers wasn't – weren't – were – was

## 5 Mettez le texte suivant à la voix passive.

**Score : ..... / 10**

Ask a specialist to write your CV and collect up information. Then, sort the different elements and put them in reverse order. Give a description of your personality, then add other elements. Mention skills, then re-check the spelling. Finish off the layout, and birth of a new CV!

.......................................................................................................................................................

.......................................................................................................................................................

.......................................................................................................................................................

.......................................................................................................................................................

## 6 Rapporter l'entretien téléphonique suivant.

**Score : ..... / 10**

**1.** He – ask – "why are you calling?" **2.** I – tell – "I'm looking for a job." **3.** I – say – "I want to speak to the H.R. manager." **4.** He – tell – "I'll put you through." **5.** She – say – "I have seen your letter." **6.** She – tell – "you don't have enough skills." **7.** I – answer – "I am going to learn English." **8.** She – say – "I can't see how you can do the job." **9.** She – suggest – "why don't you try something else." **10.** She – tell – "don't call us, we'll call you".

.......................................................................................................................................................

.......................................................................................................................................................

.......................................................................................................................................................

.......................................................................................................................................................

.......................................................................................................................................................

**Score total : ..... / 50**

### CORRIGÉS

**1.** 1. Do we get on-the-job training? 2. The take home pay is good, isn't it? 3. Do you have to work unsocial hours? 4. Is there a pension scheme? 5. Would you be interested in a part time job? 6. Can you work flexitime?
**2.** 1. Those are interesting, aren't they? 2. Who received a phone call from Tom? 3. Who are you writing that report for? / For whom are you writing the report? 4. I don't think that job looks very good. Neither do I. 5. He doesn't get to work on time, does he? 6. Could you tell me what your last job was? 7. They demanded that we try on the uniform. 8. I don't think he's got the job. Don't you? / Hasn't he? 9. I am suitable for the job, aren't I? 10. Why don't you ask for a training course?
**3.** 1. A 2. B 3. B 4. A 5. B 6. A 7. A 8. B
**4.** 1. Me too 2. If I asked 3. Met 4. Anybody – any 5. On peut garder les trois ! 6. Aren't I? 7. Will 8. Was
**5.** A specialist is asked to write your CV and information is collected up. Then the different elements are sorted and they are put in reverse order. A description of your personality is given, then other elements are added. Skills are mentioned then the spelling is re-checked. The layout is finished off and a new CV is born!
**6.** 1. He asked why I was calling. 2. I told him I was looking for a job. 3. I said that I wanted to speak to the H.R. manager. 4. He told me he would put me through. 5. She said she had seen my letter. 6. She told me I didn't have enough skills. 7. I answered that I was going to learn to speak English! 8. She said she couldn't see how I could do the job. 9. She suggested I tried something else. 10. Finally, she told me not to call them, (that) they would call me.

# 6 Les noms



## Le pluriel des noms

### Pluriels réguliers et pluriels irréguliers

**1.** En général, on ajoute un –*s* pour marquer le pluriel.

*1 Leaflet → 3 leaflets*
*Mr & Mrs Dupont → the Duponts*
*a poster → 3 posters*
*stock-keeping unit → SKUs*

**!** Notez les modifications orthographiques pour les noms se terminant par :

| -s/-sh/-ch/-x/-z/-o | une consonne + y | -fou / -fe |
|---|---|---|
| *box → boxes* | *supply → supplies* | *shelf → shelves* |

**2.** Certains pluriels sont irréguliers.

*a man / woman → 3 men / women*
*1 penny → 3 pence*
*an analysis → 3 analyses*
*an erratum → 3 errata*
*1 person → 3 people*
*1 foot → 3 feet*
*a hypothesis → 3 hypotheses*
*a criterium → 3 criteria*

### Des noms pluriels ou singuliers ?

**1.** Sont singuliers, certains mots se terminant en *-ics*.

*Politics is an interesting subject.*
→ La politique est un sujet intéressant.

*Economics is complicated.*
→ L'économie est complexe.

**2.** Sont singuliers et/ou pluriels, certains mots se terminant en –*s*.

*a means of promotion*
→ un moyen de promotion

*several means of promotion*
→ plusieurs moyens de promotion

*a glassworks*
→ une verrerie

*some glassworks*
→ des verreries

Certains mots singuliers sont utilisés avec un verbe au pluriel (comme un groupe de personnes) : *The police have captured the culprit.* Mais : *The policeman is on the watch.*

**3.** Sont pluriels, les articles constitués de deux parties identiques.

*scissors = a pair of scissors* *jeans = a pair of jeans*

**4.** Sont généralement suivis d'un verbe au pluriel (en anglais britannique), les noms singuliers évoquant un groupe de personnes. (En anglais américain, ils sont suivis d'un verbe au singulier).

*The company / SMC Inc. are thinking of launching the product next month.*
→ L'entreprise / SMC Inc. pense lancer le produit le mois prochain.

*The committee have decided to increase the advertising budget.*
→ Le comité a décidé d'accroître le budget publicité.

*The marketing team want to do more market research.*
→ L'équipe marketing veut faire plus de recherches de marché.

**5.** Sont suivies d'un verbe au singulier, les sommes d'argent, les distances, les durées.

*Fifty thousand Euros seems not much to pay for a catch line these days.*
→ Cinquante mille euros semblent peu pour créer un slogan accrocheur de nos jours.

*500 kilometres is too far to go for a trade fair.*
→ Faire 500 kilomètres est un trop long trajet pour aller à un salon.

*Six years was a long time to penetrate the market.*
→ C'était trop long de pénétrer le marché en six ans.

# Les noms dénombrables et indénombrables

## Des noms dénombrables ou indénombrables

Un nom peut être dénombrable ("*countable*" = C) ou indénombrable ("*uncountable*" = U). Est généralement indénombrable, ce que l'on ne peut pas compter : liquides, aliments, matières, couleurs, sports, etc.

| Countables | | Uncountables | |
|---|---|---|---|
| *a / an*<br>*2 or 3*<br>*some* (= quelques) | *suitcase*<br>*Euros*<br>*machines* | *some*<br>(= du, de la, des) | *luggage*<br>*money*<br>*machinery* |

↳ Le verbe est, selon le cas, au singulier ou au pluriel.
*A suitcase is in the car.*
*Four Euros are in the bag.*

↳ Le verbe est toujours au singulier : un indénombrable ne prend jamais de -s.
*Some luggage is in the car.*
*Some money is in the bag.*

Il y a des catégories de noms indénombrables tel que :
– les matériels : *plastic, silver, wood, gold*…
– les langues : *French, Italian, Dutch*
– les activités humaines : *tennis, geography*…
– la nourriture : *tea, coffee, wine, milk*…
– les couleurs : *red, orange, green*…
– les idées abstraites : *love, death, life*…

### Les principaux noms anglais indénombrables

*accommodation, air, applause, assistance, advertising, advice, baggage, behaviour, bread, business, chaos, camping, cash, courage, cutlery, chess, clothing, crockery, conduct, damage, dancing, dirt, dust, employment, equipment, evidence, electricity, fun, furniture, first aid, hardware, harm, health, homework, housing, information, insurance, imagination, luck, leisure, litter, luggage, machinery, mud, money, music, news, nonsense, permission, parking, pay, photography, progress, poetry, pollution, produce, publicity, research, rubbish, safety, scenery, shopping, sightseeing, sunshine, software, traffic, transport, travel (sea, air…), underwear, unemployment, violence, weather, work*

## Des noms dénombrables et indénombrables

Certains mots peuvent être à la fois dénombrables et indénombrables : *a paper* (C) (= a newspaper) / paper (U), a competition (C) / competition (U), a time (C) / time (U), etc.
*Have a good time at the trade fair.* → *I haven't got time to finish it.*

Par ailleurs, un nom indénombrable peut devenir dénombrable à condition de :

- lui attribuer une quantité.
*Information* (U) → *a piece of information* (C)  *Tea* (U) → *a cup of tea* (C)

- utiliser un nom composé.
*Software* (U) → *a software program* (C)  *Research* (U) → *a research project* (C)

## 1 Mettez les groupes nominaux suivants au pluriel.

| Singular | Plural |
|---|---|
| 1. a generic product | .............................. |
| 2. a product range | .............................. |
| 3. a market in a foreign country | .............................. |
| 4. a market survey | .............................. |
| 5. a stage in the product life cycle | .............................. |
| 6. the service life of our product | .............................. |
| 7. a game designed for a child | .............................. |
| 8. market strategy | .............................. |

## 2 Les noms ci-dessous sont-ils suivis d'un verbe au singulier ou au pluriel ? Les deux sont parfois possibles !

1. the police ....................................
2. electronics ....................................
3. species ....................................
4. the staff ....................................
5. series ....................................
6. the audience ....................................
7. a pair of glasses / glasses ....................................
8. firm ....................................
9. people ....................................
10. JMM Plc. ....................................

## 3 Dans les règles de grammaire suivantes, barrez ce qui est incorrect.

1. With a countable noun, use a / an / 2-3-… / some.
2. With an uncountable noun, use a / an / 2-3-… / some.
3. With a countable noun, the verb is single / plural.
4. With an uncountable noun, the verb is single / plural.
5. It is / is not possible to make an uncountable noun, countable.

## 4 Pour chacun des noms, écrivez le déterminant qui convient. Ensuite faites des paires de mots semblables.

| | a / an / some | pair |
|---|---|---|
| 1. coin | .............................. | ............ |
| 2. work | .............................. | ............ |
| 3. item | .............................. | ............ |
| 4. job | .............................. | ............ |
| 5. machinery | .............................. | ............ |
| 6. cash | .............................. | ............ |
| 7. task | .............................. | ............ |
| 8. machine | .............................. | ............ |
| 9. goods | .............................. | ............ |
| 10. unemployment | .............................. | ............ |

## 5 À l'aide de la liste de mots ci-dessous, transformez les noms indénombrables en noms dénombrables.

*forecast – slice – piece – bag – bit – cup*

1. shopping a ....................................................
2. advice a ....................................................
3. information a ....................................................
4. coffee a ....................................................
5. toast a ....................................................
6. weather a ....................................................

## 6 Entourez l'erreur et corrigez-la !

1. The company has branchs in several towns.

.......................................................................................

2. The informations about the product were very interesting.

.......................................................................................

3. The shops where factorys sell their goods directly are called factory outlets.

.......................................................................................

4. You pay for advertising but publicity are free.

.......................................................................................

5. The salespersons were very helpful.

.......................................................................................

6. Our new product is selling well – business are good.

.......................................................................................

7. Their EDLP (every day low price) product is a trousers.

.......................................................................................

8. We need to invest in a market research.

.......................................................................................

## 7 Complétez les phrases suivantes par *a*, *an* ou *some*.

1. We have .......................... research to do for this new market.

2. They want to open .......................... retail outlet in the new shopping centre.

3. If we are lucky, we'll get .......................... free publicity in the local newspapers.

4. We try to reach .......................... broad cross section of consumers.

5. We're going to have .......................... work to do to build an identity for the product.

6. It is hard to think up good ideas for .......................... advertising campaign.

7. That bad article in the press did .......................... harm to our reputation.

8. I think we should do .......................... prime time advertising on the television.

## 8 Complétez les phrases à l'aide des mots ci-dessous qui conviennent.

*a good time / good time – a competition / competition – experiences / experience – a paper / paper – a noise / noise – a room / room*

1. I think we should put a small ad in .......................... .

2. There isn't .......................... in the brochure to put any more information.

3. We'll have to work hard, we are facing a lot of .......................... .

4. I hope you have .......................... at the trade fair.

5. I don't like that jingle, it makes too much .......................... .

6. He had some interesting .......................... when he was selling door-to-door.

7. We shall have to order more .......................... to print those catalogues.

8. Could you please reserve .......................... at the king's head hotel for the launch.

## CORRIGÉS

**1.** 1. Generic products 2. Product ranges 3. Markets in foreign countries 4. Market surveys 5. Stages in product life cycles 6. The service lives of our products 7. Games designed for children 8. Market strategies
**2.** 1. Plural 2. Singular 3. Singular / plural 4. Plural 5. Singular / plural 6. Plural 7. Singular / plural 8. Plural 9. Plural 10. Plural
**3.** 1. With a countable noun, use a /an / 2-3-... / Some (correct!). 2. With an uncountable noun, use some. 3. With a countable noun, the verb is single / plural (correct!). 4. With an uncountable noun, the verb is single. 5. It is possible to make an uncountable noun, countable.
**4.** 1. a 2. some 3. an 4. a 5. some 6. some 7. a 8. a 9. some 10. some. Pairs: 1-6 ; 2-7 ; 3-9 ; 4-10 ; 5-8
**5.** 1. A bag of shopping (attn. A bag for shopping = a shopping bag – compound noun!). 2. A bit of advice 3. A piece of information 4. A cup of coffee (one can also say "a coffee"). 5. A slice of toast 6. A weather forecast
**6.** 1. The company has branches in several towns. 2. The information about the product was very interesting. 3. The shops where factories sell their goods directly are called factory outlets. 4. You pay for advertising but publicity is free 5. The salespeople were very helpful. 6. Our new product is selling well – business is good. 7. Their EDLP (every day low price) product is a pair of trousers. 8. We need to invest in market research.
**7.** 1. some 2. a 3. some 4. a 5. some 6. an 7. some 8. some
**8.** 1. a paper 2. room 3. competition 4. a good time 5. noise 6. experiences 7. paper 8. a room

MARKETING

# Le génitif (dit aussi « cas possessif »)

Le génitif exprime généralement un rapport de possession ou de parenté entre deux éléments.
*Whose computer has the best software?*
*John's (computer).*

## Formation du génitif

| Marque du génitif | Formation du génitif | Exemples |
|---|---|---|
| 's<br>ou<br>' | nom singulier + 's<br>nom pluriel + '<br>nom pluriel irrégulier + 's | *The* ***assistant's*** *mobile phone.*<br>*The* ***assistants'*** *mobile phones.*<br>*The* ***salesmen's*** *meeting.* |

↳ Le possesseur (personne ou animal) est placé en première position.
Le nom qui suit la marque du génitif peut être supprimé s'il a été préalablement mentionné.
*Who's file is this? Mary's*

Les objets ne peuvent pas posséder en anglais – il faut avoir recours au *of*.
*the packaging of the product*
Ou changer le nom en adjectif et créer un nom composé.
*the product packaging*

! Si une même chose est possédée par deux personnes, le 's s'accole au second nom.
*Bill and Ben's e-business* → L'entreprise est partagée.
*Bill's and Ben's e-businesses* → Ils ont chacun la leur.

## Autres emplois du génitif

Le génitif s'applique aussi :

**1.** À des institutions ou à des groupes de personnes ('s ou *of*).
*the company's products* — *the products of the company*

**2.** À l'expression du temps (*yesterday, next month*, ...) et de la durée.
*Yesterday's meeting was very boring, tomorrow's should be better.*
*You'll have about a five minutes' wait for the fax to arrive.*

La durée peut aussi être exprimée par un adjectif composé.
*You'll have about a five-minute wait for the fax to arrive.*

**3.** À l'expression du lieu, pour traduire le français « chez ».
*The baker's* → *The baker's shop* — *At my mother's* → *My mother's house*

### Les emplois de *of*

*Of* s'emploie :
- Quand le groupe nominal est très long.
*What is the name of the customer who wanted some information about our goods?*
- Pour les choses et les idées (on peut aussi utiliser un nom composé).
*The address of the office*
- Après *the beginning / end / top / bottom / front / back / middle / side...*
*The middle of the letter is too long.*

# Les noms composés



**Comparez !**

*Forecast sales* → les ventes prévues
*A sales forecast* → une prévision des ventes

## Quel est le mot principal ?

**1.** Un nom composé est généralement constitué de deux éléments séparés par un trait d'union, par un simple espace (choix le plus simple en cas de doute) ou au contraire réunis en un seul mot.
*check-out / check out / checkout*

**2.** Quand il y a plus de deux éléments, on utilise souvent un acronyme.
*Point of Sale (POS)*
*Every Day Low Price (EDLP)*

**3.** Dans un nom composé, le ou les premiers éléments jouent le rôle d'adjectif(s).
*luncheon voucher*
*book voucher*
*gift voucher*
*cash voucher*

C'est donc le dernier élément, le nom principal, qui porte la marque du pluriel.
*A reply coupon* → *reply coupons*

**Exception** La marque du pluriel est aussi portée par le premier élément quand celui-ci correspond à:

- *man, woman* ou *child*
*women workers*
- un nom indénombrable
*a customs officer*
- une des activités d'une institution, d'une entreprise, d'un département, etc.
*sales department*

## Comment construire un nom composé ?

**1.** Nom + nom
*brand image* | *trade name*
*niche market* | *export drive*

**2.** V-*ing* + nom / nom + v-*ing*
*a meeting room* | *a marketing manager*
*risk-taking* | *cost-cutting*

**3.** Nom + *phrasal verb*
*a market breakthrough* | *a price mark-down / up*

**4.** Préposition + nom
*a backlog of orders* | *a middleman*

## 1 Exprimez la possession en utilisant le génitif ou *of*.

Ex. ▶ The supplier who makes the packaging – his phone number.
→ The phone number of the supplier who makes the packaging

**1.** The tender which comes from the supplier.

..........................................................................

..........................................................................

**2.** The office shared by Joe and Jill.

..........................................................................

..........................................................................

**3.** The sales figures from last year.

..........................................................................

..........................................................................

**4.** Wool which comes from a lamb.

..........................................................................

..........................................................................

**5.** The reservations which are for the women.

..........................................................................

..........................................................................

**6.** The USB keys which belong to Mark and to Simon.

..........................................................................

..........................................................................

**7.** Work which will take ten weeks.

..........................................................................

..........................................................................

**8.** The invoices which belong to the customers.

..........................................................................

..........................................................................

**9.** On the page, at the bottom.

..........................................................................

..........................................................................

**10.** The shop which belongs to the grocer.

..........................................................................

..........................................................................

## 2 À l'aide des indications entre parenthèses, traduisez les phrases suivantes.

**1.** L'ordinateur de la femme de mon collègue.
(computer – wife – colleague)

..........................................................................

..........................................................................

**2.** Le portable de la belle-sœur de mon frère.
(laptop – sister-in-law – brother)

..........................................................................

..........................................................................

**3.** Le logiciel du fournisseur de ma filiale.
(software – supplier – subsidiary)

..........................................................................

..........................................................................

**4.** La souris de l'assistant de leur patron.
(mouse – assistant – boss)

..........................................................................

..........................................................................

**5.** Le clavier du manager de leur chef d'équipe.
(keyboard – manager – foreman)

..........................................................................

..........................................................................

## 3 À l'aide des mots proposés, formez un nom composé qui s'applique à chacune des définitions suivantes.

*price – fair – mail-order – word – increase/mark-up – price – selling – marketing – product – price – workers – trade – office – sales – selling/sales – processing – life-span – department – contract – wholesale*

**1.** The price for goods you buy wholesale.

..........................................................................

..........................................................................

**2.** The price for which you sell your goods.

..........................................................................

..........................................................................

**3.** The department which deals with marketing.

..........................................................................

**4.** A contract for sales.

..........................................................................

5. Selling goods using mail order.

..........................................................................................

6. The people who work in offices.

..........................................................................................

7. Using a computer to "process" words.

..........................................................................................

8. An increase in prices.

..........................................................................................

9. How long a product will last on the market.

..........................................................................................

10. Where you can show your products.

..........................................................................................

## 4 À partir des mots soulignés, formez si possible des noms composés.

1. A bottle which doesn't necessarily have champagne in it.

..........................................................................................

2. A bottle containing champagne.

..........................................................................................

3. Milk which comes from a cow.

..........................................................................................

4. Information you put in the computer.

..........................................................................................

5. The counter where you check in at a hotel or airport.

..........................................................................................

6. A shop used by a butcher.

..........................................................................................

## 5 Reformulez à partir des mots soulignés.

1. The place (company/person) where your supplier is.

..........................................................................................

2. The trade fair which is next week.

..........................................................................................

3. The new general manager of the company.

..........................................................................................

..........................................................................................

4. A ten-week campaign.

..........................................................................................

5. The buying power of the consumers.

..........................................................................................

..........................................................................................

6. The environment strategy of the city.

..........................................................................................

..........................................................................................

## 6 Entourez la bonne réponse.

1. There'll be a ten month's / ten months' delay before we complete the mailing list.
2. I really like the slogan for cow's / cow milk.
3. Could you check through ABC / ABCs and PLB / PLB's contracts?
4. I suppose we could all meet at the customer / customer's.
5. Next year's / next years' teaser campaign must be wittier.
6. The children's / childrens' toy market is worth looking into.

## CORRIGÉS

**1.** 1. The supplier's tender. 2. Joe and Jill's office. (one office shared) 3. Last year's sales figures. (time expression) 4. Lamb's wool. (taken from a lamb) 5. The women's reservations. (irregular plural) 6. Mark's and Simon's USB keys. (two USB keys) 7. Ten weeks' work. (length of time) 8. The customers' invoices. (plural) 9. The bottom of the page. (position) 10. The grocer's shop.
**2.** 1. My colleague's wife's computer. 2. My brother's sister-in-law's laptop. 3. My subsidiary's supplier's software. 4. Their boss's assistant's mouse. 5. The foreman's manager's keyboard.
**3.** 1. A wholesale price. 2. A selling/sales price. 3. The marketing department. 4. A sales contract. 5. Mail-order selling. 6. Office workers. 7. Word processing. 8. A price increase/mark up. 9. Product life-span. 10. A trade-fair.
**4.** 1. A champagne bottle. 2. A bottle of champagne. 3. Cow's milk. 4. Computer input. 5. A check-in counter. 6. A butcher's shop.
**5.** 1. My supplier's. 2. Next week's trade fair. 3. The company's new general manager. 4. Ten week's campaign. 5. The consumers' buying power. 6. The city's environment strategy.
**6.** 1. Ten months' 2. Cow's 3. ABC's and PLB's 4. Customer's 5. Next year's 6. Children's

## 1 Entourez la bonne réponse.

Score : ..... / 10

1. Six months is / are a long time for a market survey.
2. The salespeople / sales persons really like the new product.
3. Use this / these scissors to cut up the leaflet.
4. The firm is / are marketing custom-made products.
5. Good publicity would be to have a series / some series of articles in the paper.
6. The police has / have distributed handbills about the "neighbourhood watch" campaign.
7. Ten thousand Euros is / are a lot to spend on an advertising campaign.
8. Electronics is / are a fast-growing market.
9. We have noticed three erratum / errata on your leaflet.
10. The staff want / wants to improve our company image.

## 2 Entourez la bonne réponse.

Score : ..... / 10

1. Competition is / are important to stimulate business.
2. Is / Are the papers full of interesting promotions today?
3. Hard work never harm / harms anyone.
4. Tins is / are used to pack the goods.
5. The accommodation they offer is / are pretty small.
6. The works is / are located in a town near London.
7. Time is / are short, we must finish the proposal today.
8. There isn't / aren't room for the prices on that page of the catalogue.
9. Experience of the market is / are important in our job.
10. A lot of knowledge is / are needed to promote a product well.

## 3 Entourez l'erreur et corrigez-la !

Score : ..... / 10

1. Researches are done to find the target customer. ..........................................................................
2. A music enhances a T.V. advertisement. ..........................................................................
3. We could have a fun with a new publicity stunt. ..........................................................................
4. I think we should put that advert on at a prime time. ..........................................................................
5. The adman got an applause after he showed his new idea. ..........................................................................
6. That T.V. spot are complete nonsense! ..........................................................................
7. Our targeting is based on a leisure, not a work and a job. ..........................................................................
8. Litter and pollution is the subjects of a lot of advertising films. ..........................................................................
9. The tooling for the new prototype are defective. ..........................................................................
10. I think I need an assistance with the new campaign. ..........................................................................

## 4 Créez un nom composé à l'aide des mots soulignés.

Score : ... / 10

1. People who hunt for bargains. ..........
2. An acknowledgement of an order. ..........
3. The price of your goods for retail selling. ..........
4. The list of people you will mail your catalogue to. ..........
5. The point which makes your goods sell well. ..........
6. A market which is geared towards a special niche of people. ..........
7. If you look on a pie chart, you can see the share of the market you have, and the percentage.
..........
8. A store where there are many departments. ..........
9. A store where you serve yourself. ..........
10. A survey to study the market. ..........

## 5 Reliez les termes français à leur traduction.

Score : ..... / 10

| | | |
|---|---|---|
| **1.** les légumes provenant d'une ferme | **a)** • | • **c)** farm vegetables |
| une ferme produisant des légumes | **b)** • | • **d)** a vegetable farm |
| **2.** un produit de qualité | **a)** • | • **c)** a quality product |
| la qualité des produits | **b)** • | • **d)** product quality |
| **3.** une vitrine | **a)** • | • **c)** a window display |
| le contenu d'une vitrine | **b)** • | • **d)** a display window |
| **4.** une agence de publicité | **a)** • | • **c)** an advertising agency |
| la publicité par agence | **b)** • | • **d)** agency advertising |
| **5.** un essai de produit sur le marché | **a)** • | • **c)** a test market |
| un marché ciblé pour essayer un produit | **b)** • | • **d)** a market test |
| **6.** la fin d'un produit | **a)** • | • **c)** an end product |
| le produit fini | **b)** • | • **d)** a product end |
| **7.** un soldeur | **a)** • | • **c)** a discount store |
| une remise de magasin | **b)** • | • **d)** a store discount |
| **8.** le marché des magazines | **a)** • | • **c)** a trade magazine |
| un magazine commercial | **b)** • | • **d)** the magazine trade |
| **9.** des problèmes avec des clients | **a)** • | • **c)** customer problems |
| des clients à problème | **b)** • | • **d)** problem customers |
| **10.** une qualité normale | **a)** • | • **c)** a quality standard |
| une norme de qualité | **b)** • | • **d)** standard quality |

**Score total : ..... / 50**

### CORRIGÉS

**1.** 1. is 2. salespeople 3. these 4. are 5. a series 6. have 7. is 8. is 9. errata 10. want
**2.** 1. is (U) 2. Are (C) 3. harms (U) 4. are (C) 5. is (U) 6. are (U) 7. is (u) 8. isn't (U) 9. is (U) 10. is (U)
**3.** 1. research is 2. Music 3. fun / some fun 4. at prime time 5. some applause 6. is 7. on leisure, not work 8. litter and pollution are 9. tooling ... is 10. some assistance
**4.** 1. Bargain hunters 2. Order acknowledgement 3. Retail price 4. Mailing list 5. Selling point 6. Niche market 7. Market share 8. Department store 9. Self-service 10. Market survey
**5.** 1. a-c / b-d 2. a-c / b-d 3. a-d / b-c 4. a-c / b-d 5. a-d / b-c 6. a-d / b-c 7. a-c / b-d 8. a-d / b-c 9. a-c / b-d 10. a-d / b-c

# 7 Les articles et quantificateurs



## L'article indéfini *a / an*

### Forme de l'article indéfini : *a* ou *an*

On emploie :

• *a* devant les consonnes et le *u-* exprimé
*a factory visit* *a university*

• *an* devant les voyelles et le *h-* non-exprimé
*an industry* *an hour*

### Emploi de l'article indéfini *a / an*

On emploie l'article indéfini *a / an* :

• lorsque l'objet dont on parle est indéfini, qu'on le présente pour la première fois.
→ *a new schedule*

• devant les noms de métiers.
→ *She's a technician. He's an engineer.*

• après les exclamatifs *what* et *such*.
→ *What an exciting new process! Such a marvellous invention!*

• avec *quite* et *rather* (« plutôt »).
→ *Quite an inventive research team. Rather a / a rather bad solution.*

• dans les expressions de temps et de mesure.
→ *Once a week, 50 miles an hour / 10 Euros a kilo*

## L'article défini *the* et l'absence d'article

### L'article défini *the*

On emploie l'article défini *the* pour :

• quelque chose de spécifique.
→ *They have a wide range of products but the products are not on the market yet.*

• une chose unique.
→ *the earth, the moon*

• les océans, rivières, mers, canaux.
→ *the Pacific, the Suez Canal*

• les chaînes de montagnes, archipels.
→ *the Alps, the Bahamas* (mais une île ou montagne individuelle ne prend pas d'article : *Madeira, Mount Etna*)

• les hôtels, restaurants, organisations.
→ *the Ritz Hotel, the BBC*

• les points cardinaux.
→ *the north*

• les instruments de musique.
→ *the piano, the guitar*

- les entités, les espèces animales et végétales (EXCEPTION *man* = l'espèce humaine, et *woman*.)
→ *the Euro, the bear, the tulip*
- les inventions.
→ *the radio, the television, the Internet* EXCEPTION Si vous parlez de l'appareil de la télévision / radio : *The book is on the television*.)
- les noms incluant *of*.
→ *the Chamber of Commerce*
- les noms de familles au pluriel.
→ *the Smiths*
- les journaux.
→ *The Times, The Guardian* (mais *Time magazine*)
- un groupe de personnes (*the* + adjectif).
→ *the unemployed, the wealthy*
- l'abstrait (*the* + adjectif).
→ *the intangible*
- les comparatifs d'égalité et les superlatifs.
→ *the best item, the same*

## L'absence d'article, dit « article zéro » (ø)

Il y a absence d'article ou article zéro pour :

- généraliser.
→ *Customers are demanding.*
- les noms indénombrables pour généraliser.
→ *Metal, sugar, Spanish, green…*
- les noms désignant les repas.
→ *Breakfast is at 8 am.*
- les noms suivis d'un numéro.
→ *The demonstration is in room 51.*
- les activités humaines.
→ *working, history, tennis*
- les planètes.
→ *Venus, Mars* (EXCEPTION *The earth, the sun, the moon*)
- les idées abstraites.
→ *love, life, death…*
- les jours de la semaine.
→ *Monday, Tuesday…* (EXCEPTION *at the weekend*)
- les magazines *Newsweek, Vogue* (EXCEPTION *the* est déjà dans le titre *The Economist.*)
- *most*.
→ *Most people enjoy window shopping.* (EXCEPTION si vous spécifiez : *Most of the people in the town enjoy window shopping.*)
- les maladies → *cancer, Aids* EXCEPTION *the flu, the mumps, the measles, the plague – a cold*
- les lieux familiers *work, home, bed, space, school, prison, hospital, university, church*
→ *She's at work.* (EXCEPTION Si vous parlez d'une chose spécifique : *The hospital* (l'immeuble) *is being renovated. The work is complicated.*)

• les noms de lieux : continents, pays, villes, squares, parcs, lacs, rues, etc. (EXCEPTION les États fédéraux) → *Asia, France, Paris, Times Square, Hyde Park, Lake Geneva, Sixth Avenue, The United States, the UAE…, The High Street – GB ; Main Street USA, The Vatican.*)

• les titres → *Mr / Mrs / Miss / Ms Smith, Doctor*

• les noms de sociétés et espaces baptisés du nom de leur fondateur.
→ *Lloyds Bank, St Paul's Cathedral, Ford, MacDonald*

Pour rendre une « généralité » spécifique :

• le pronom relatif (*who, whom, that, which, whose*).
→ *Emails take up a lot of time. The emails that she sends take up a lot of time.*

• une préposition.
→ *He is the love of my life.*

• un adjectif ne rend pas un nom spécifique.
→ *Efficient, user-friendly mobile phones are best sellers.*

## Les quantificateurs indéfinis *some* et *any*

*Some* et *any* expriment l'idée d'une quantité indéterminée : employés devant des noms dénombrables pluriels et devant des noms indénombrables, ils se traduisent par « quelques » ou « du, de la, des ».

| | Countables | Uncountables |
|---|---|---|
| Phrases affirmatives | *There are some computers (2 or 3,* sens : quelques*)* | *There is some software.* (sens : du, de la, des) |
| Phrases négatives | *There aren't any computers.* | *There isn't any software.* |
| Phrases interrogatives | *Are there any computers?* | *Is there any software?* |

↳ En règle générale, on utilise *some* dans les phrases affirmatives, *not any* dans les phrases négatives et *any* dans les phrases interrogatives.

Cependant :

**1.** On utilise *any* dans une phrase affirmative :

• Dans le sens de « n'importe »
*You can use any packaging you like.* *We could put the pallets anywhere.*

• Avec une nuance négative
*They improve the product without any R&D.* *Hardly anyone came.*

• Après *if* (ou une nuance de *if*)
*If you have any designs, show me.* *I apologise for any misunderstanding.*

**2.** On utilise *some* dans une phrase interrogative quand on suppose la réponse positive.
*Would you like some toast?* *Have you got some advice for me?*

(Contrairement à la question ouverte *Have you got any advice for me?*)

Ces mêmes règles s'appliquent pour *somebody / someone* (« quelqu'un »), *something* (« quelque chose »), *somewhere* (« quelque part »).
*There isn't anyone I trust more than you.*

**!** Si par rapport au verbe, ces composés se comportent comme des singuliers, on leur attribue cependant les pronoms et adjectifs pluriels *they / them / their.*
*Someone has left their business card.* *Did you see them?*

INDUSTRY

## 1 Complétez les phrases suivantes par *a* ou *an*.

1. The cost of the raw material is £24.00 .... kilo.
2. We have to think up .... European industrial approach.
3. He has been .... active methods manager.
4. What .... original idea!
5. What do you do? I'm .... operator on the machines.
6. The product test should take .... hour.
7. We will have the product brainstorming in .... hotel.
8. Altering the image of the product is quite .... gamble.

## 2 Avec ou sans *the* ? Dans chacune des listes suivantes, entourez l'intrus.

1. Washington – Germany – Middle east – Spain
2. same commission – dollar – board of trade – university
3. 10th floor – room 21 – flight BA201 – item 62
4. Ms Jones – Browns – Doctor Wells – Lord Smith
5. suppliers – salespeople – company president – customers
6. South – Georges V Hotel – Barclays bank – Mediterranean
7. unemployed – elderly – rich – man
8. work – hospital on the corner – space – school

## 3 Complétez les phrases suivantes par *a, an, some, any*.

1. We need to find ..................... idea to improve our storage.
2. ..................... products are in drums, others in bags.
3. There isn't ..................... space left for our raw materials, we'll have to expand.
4. There aren't ..................... pallets to put the boxes on.
5. Is there ..................... fork lift truck available to move these goods?
6. There were ..................... reject supplies, not many.
7. Will there be ..................... changes to the racks?
8. Would you like ..................... help in working out the new layout?

## 4 Complétez le dialogue en utilisant les mots de la liste ci-dessous.

*any – anyone – anything – anywhere – some – any – some – anything – any – anything – some – someone*

Boss: Good morning. Have you got **(1)** ..................... news about the shortage of raw material?

Assistant: Yes, we have found **(2)** ..................... alternative suppliers but there aren't **(3)** ..................... contracts drawn up for now.

Boss: Are there **(4)** ..................... possibilities of delivery next week?

Assistant: I'm counting on it! We shall send **(5)** ..................... requests this afternoon, and then we hope **(6)** ..................... will say they can deliver.

Boss: Would you like **(7)** ..................... help with calculating the quantities?

Assistant: Yes, that's a good idea. Is there **(8)** ..................... available to run the computer program through?

Boss: I think Bill could handle that. Let me know if **(9)** ..................... can be delivered in time, if not, we'll have to put the pressure on.

Assistant: Thank you. I don't know **(10)** ..................... else to turn.

Boss: Have you got **(11)** ..................... else to tell me?

Assistant: No, I don't think there's **(12)** ..................... at all.

## 5 Entourez l'erreur et corrigez-la !

1. Hardly nobody is really quality conscious.

..........................................................................................

..........................................................................................

..........................................................................................

**2.** Somebody gave us her brochure, it was shoddy.

..................................................................................

..................................................................................

..................................................................................

**3.** Would you like any advice to improve your quality management?

..................................................................................

..................................................................................

..................................................................................

**4.** If you do some spot checks, remember to write the batch number.

..................................................................................

..................................................................................

..................................................................................

**5.** We must do anything to correct the defects.

..................................................................................

..................................................................................

..................................................................................

**6.** It is flawless. It hasn't got some flaws.

..................................................................................

..................................................................................

..................................................................................

**7.** If nothing is disposable, it means it can be thrown away.

..................................................................................

..................................................................................

..................................................................................

**8.** There isn't nothing we can do about the wear and tear.

..................................................................................

..................................................................................

..................................................................................

**9.** Who can assess the product. Somebody – that's what self-inspection is about.

..................................................................................

..................................................................................

..................................................................................

**10.** Could you find anywhere to pin up the quality dashboards? Yes, of course.

..................................................................................

..................................................................................

..................................................................................

## 6 Complétez les phrases suivantes par *a*, *an*, *the*, *ø*, *some* ou *any*.

**1.** I think that he's .................. technician.

**2.** Did the operator clear .................. space we need to store the spare parts?

**3.** It's rather .............. old-fashioned workshop, isn't it?

**4.** Shall we make .................. more prototypes?

**5.** Let's tidy up the place – .................. C.E.O. is coming round any minute now!

**6.** .................. operators are threatening to strike about the overtime problem.

**7.** That machine is meant to be working at a rate of 500 pieces .................. hour.

**8.** What is the problem with .................. machine number 4?

**9.** What .................. amazing thing – we've been working over capacity for 5 days now!

**10.** If you need .................. more casual workers, let the foreman know.

**11.** Can you get ................ pallets from the warehouse?

**12.** What time do the workers have ................. lunch?

**13.** It doesn't matter which part you use – .................. of them will do.

**14.** I think it would be a good idea to take on ................. new methods engineer to improve our production flow.

## 7 Entourez la bonne réponse.

Bill: So, you think that we should set up the / a new factory to increase our capacity?

John: Yes, we should try to find an / a turnkey plant.

Bill: Whereabouts? We don't want to go to a manufacturing town just anywhere / somewhere.

John: Well, first of all, we want to go somewhere / anywhere with no social unrest.

Bill: Good point. On top of that, the / a labour force has to include some / any skilled workers so we don't waste too much time on training.

John: At the beginning, we don't want to take on any / some casual labour either – it's very expensive.

Bill: Maybe we should try looking at a place where there have been the / some plant shut-downs – you know, where the / some working classes are having a bad time at the moment.

John: You mean an / the unemployment black spot?

Bill: Yes, look here, the / ø area 41 would seem to have some / any good subsidies and competitive conditions to encourage ø / the investors.

John: Right, let's get in touch with the / a local authorities and see if they can do something / anything for us.

Bill: Do you know the name of a / the person responsible for that area? It would be better to contact a / ø someone in the know.

John: I should be able to find out, I received a / some brochures the other day promoting an / the area. Let me have a look. They should be able to tell us if there are any / some industrial estates which are being developed.

Bill: We'll need to go somewhere with a / ø special equipment because we produce hazardous products. As well as checking out if there is the / ø water and a / some power supply. There's also the question of plant manager – can you think of anyone / someone suitable?

John: How about Simon Small – he's a / the manufacturing manager for now.

## 8 Choisissez la bonne réponse.

**1.** Laura cannot concentrate in the morning because her daughter doesn't sleep .............. .

**a)** the night **b)** at night

**2.** The plant was moved somewhere ............. of San Francisco.

**a)** south **b)** the south

**3.** What's the exchange rate against ..............?

**a)** pound **b)** the pound

**4.** He's a social worker, and spends a lot of time with .............. .

**a)** unemployed **b)** the unemployed

**5.** Did you hear that poor Robert caught ............. and missed the conference?

**a)** flu **b)** the flu

**6.** Production scheduling is in ............., just along the corridor.

**a)** the room 5 **b)** room 5

**7.** He's been given a promotion and he's moving to .............. .

**a)** The Philippines **b)** Philippines

**8.** "It's 6.30 and the shift started an hour ago. Where's Peter?" "He's still ............."

**a)** in bed **b)** in the bed

**9.** According to recent statistics ............. is the most visited country in the world.

**a)** The France **b)** France

**10.** Young people these days appear to be fascinated by .............. .

**a)** history **b)** the history

## CORRIGÉS

**1.** 1. a 2. a 3. an 4. an 5. an 6. an 7. a 8. a
**2.** 1. Middle east (the) 2. university (ø) 3. 10th floor (the) 4. Browns (the) 5. Company president (the) 6. Barclays bank (ø) 7. man (ø) 8. hospital on the corner (the)
**3.** 1. an 2. some 3. any 4. any 5. a 6. some 7. any 8. some
**4.** 1. any 2. some 3. any 4. any 5. some 6. someone 7. some 8. anyone 9. anything 10. anywhere 11. anything 12. anything
**5.** 1. hardly anybody 2. their brochure 3. some advice 4. any spot checks 5. something to correct 6. any flaws 7. if something 8. there isn't anything 9. anybody 10. could you find somewhere
**6.** 1. a 2. the 3. an 4. some 5. the 6. the 7. a 8. ø 9. an 10. any 11. some 12. ø 13. any 14. a
**7.** a – a – anywhere – somewhere – the – some – any – some – the – an – ø – some – ø – the – anything – the – ø – some – the – any – ø – ø – a – anyone (not sure if the aswer will be "yes") / some (if you think the answer should be "yes") – a
**8.** 1. b – 2. a – 3. b – 4. b – 5. b – 6. b – 7. a – 8. a – 9. b – 10. a

# Autres quantificateurs indéfinis

## De « trop » à « aucun »

| Countable | Both | Uncountable | + / – / ? sentences | |
|---|---|---|---|---|
| *Too many* | | *Too much* | | Trop |
| *So many* | | *So much* | | Tellement de |
| | *A lot / lots of* | | + (Possible dans les phrases négatives) | Beaucoup de |
| | *Plenty of* | | + | Plein de |
| *Many* | | *Much* | (Rarement dans les phrases +) | Beaucoup de |
| *How many…* | | *How much…* | ? | Combien |
| | *Enough* | | | Assez |
| | *Some* | | Sens différent C/U | Quelques (C) / du, de la, des (U) |
| *Not many* | | *Not much* | – (Not a lot) | Pas beaucoup |
| *A few* | | *A little* | – | Un peu |
| *Few* | | *Little* | Avec une nuance négative | Peu |
| | *No / None (of)* | | Verbe + | Aucun |

### Much / many

• *Much* et *many* s'utilisent surtout aux formes négatives et interrogatives.

*Do you need much casual labour?* *There aren't many machine supervisors here.*

• *Much* et *many* s'emploient aussi avec *too* (« trop de »), *so* (« tant de »), *as … as* (« autant que ») et le pronom exclamatif ou interrogatif *how*.

***How many** technicians have you got?* *There is **too much** time off.*

*Quality has got **as many workers as** methods.* *There is **so much** waste.*

• *Too* peut aussi être suivi par un adjectif :

*It's (much) too late to call them now.*

• *A lot of / lots of* et *plenty of*

*A lot of*, *lots of* et *plenty of* s'utilisent surtout dans les phrases affirmatives.

→ *We have **a lot of** / **lots of** semi-skilled workers. There is **plenty of** work in hand.*

### Enough

*Enough* se place devant un nom ou après un adjectif ou un adverbe.

*Have they got **enough raw** material?* *He doesn't work **quickly enough**!*

### A little / a few

*A little* et *a few* désignent une petite quantité. L'idée est cependant généralement positive.

*There is **a little** technological progress.* *We have **a few** robotized machines.*

### Little / few

*Little, few, only a little* et *only a few* expriment une idée plutôt négative.
*There is (very) little we can do about the level of noise in the workshop.*
*There are only a few good manufacturers around here.*

### No / none / none of

*No, none* et *none of* s'utilisent dans des phrases affirmatives, avec un verbe au singulier ou au pluriel selon le nom. Le verbe est à l'affirmatif. *No* est suivi d'un nom, alors que *none* est utilisé seul.

*There is no light industry in the town.* — *None of the waste is recycled.*
*How many firm orders have you got?"* — *"None".*

## De « tous » à « ni l'un ni l'autre »

| Uncountable | Countable pl. | Countable sg. | |
|---|---|---|---|
| *All* | | | Tous, tout |
| | *Both* | | Les deux |
| *Whole* | | | Entier |
| | | *Every* | Chaque |
| | | *Each* | Chacun |
| | | *Either* | L'un ou l'autre |
| | | *Neither* | Aucun des deux |

### All

- Pour généraliser → ***All*** *operators do overtime.* ***All*** *advice is welcome.*
- Pour être plus précis

*All / most / half of the… / half of it / us / you / them*
→ *All of the machines have broken down.*
→ *Half of them are much too old.*

- Lorsque l'on parle d'une durée, pas d'article.

→ *We'll be working on the prototypes* ***all week****.*

EXCEPTION *The production stoppage lasted most of the week.*

### Both

! Pas de *the* avant *both*
→ *Both plants are out of date.*
→ *Both (of) these schedules are workable.*
→ *Both the operator and the foreman are new.*

- Le *of* est facultif avec *the / these / those / my / your / Fred's*

→ ***Both (of) those*** *forklifts need to be serviced.*

- Le *of* est nécessaire avec *us / you / them.*

→ ***Both of them*** *want to work overtime this weekend.*

- Verbe au pluriel avec *both… and …*

→ ***Both methods and R&D*** *want to be involved in the project*

## Each

Le verbe est au singulier. → *Each machine has a different rate.*

*One* est facultatif. → *Each (one) is different. Each of our operators is well trained.*

**!** Notez la différence entre *every* (ensemble du groupe) et *each* (élément particulier).

## Every

Le verbe est au singulier. → *Every visitor to the plant must sign in.*

*One* est obligatoire
*Do you look at the quality graphs? Yes, every one.*
*Every one of our final products is checked.*

*Every* est utilisé pour exprimer la fréquence.
→ *They give new indicators **every month**.*

**!** Notez la différence entre *everyone (= person)* et *every one (= person / thing)*.

Pour individualiser parmi un groupe – *each of / every one of.*
→ ***Each of** the following changes would work. **Every one** of those tools will do.*

Notez que l'on peut combiner les deux.
→ ***Each and everyone** one of you is capable of finishing on time.*

## Either / neither (of)

• Pour parler de deux choses.
***Either** box will do, it doesn't matter which.*
*Can you work in the paint or the steel workshop? **Either** (of them).*

• Verbe affirmatif avec neither pour éviter un double négatif.
***Neither** tool **is** the right one for us. I mean that both are no good.*

• *Of* est obligatoire avec *neither / either of + us / you / them…*
***Neither of** the samples is / are good enough.*
*Either … or … / Neither … nor …*
*The flow is **neither** efficient **nor** cost-effective.*

• Si *neither* est au début de la phrase, le verbe est au pluriel.
***Neither** Jane nor Tom work in methods.*
*Who did the maintenance? – **Either** Fred or Simon.*

• *Either* peut sous-entendre un ton menaçant.
***Either** you finish the work, or I'll find another operator.*

## Whole

• Nom au singulier avec *a / the / my … + whole*
*I have never worked so hard in **my whole life** / **the whole of my life**!*

• *Whole* (au sens de complet)
*We need **the whole** process file, not just half of it.*

## 1 À partir des indices en italique, faites une phrase en utilisant le quantificateur qui convient.

no / none (of) – (not) much – (not) many – (a) few – (a) little – some – a lot of – plenty (of)

Ex. ▶ More than 200 people did the Kaizen training.
*A lot of / lots of people did the Kaizen training.*

**1.** *We need a certain amount (not a lot) more money for our advertising budget.*

We need ............................................................................
............................................................................
............................................................................

**2.** *What amount do you need?*

............................................................................
............................................................................

**3.** *We have more than enough time to plan our production.*

We have ............................................................................
............................................................................
............................................................................

**4.** *He has thought of 3 or 4 ideas for a patent.*

He has thought of ............................................................................
............................................................................
............................................................................

**5.** *There are only 5 people on the Saturday shift – that's not a lot.*

There are ............................................................................
............................................................................
............................................................................

**6.** *There is an unspecified amount of manufacturers who refuse to make wasteful throwaways.*

There are ............................................................................
............................................................................
............................................................................

**7.** *Only 2 operators put their ideas in the "ideas box".*

............................................................................
............................................................................
............................................................................

**8.** *What quantity of sub-contracted parts are you going to order?*

............................................................................
............................................................................
............................................................................

**9.** *There isn't a lot of information about the new paint workshop.*

There isn't ............................................................................
............................................................................
............................................................................

**10.** *There is inadequate space for the conveyor.*

There is ............................................................................
............................................................................
............................................................................

**11.** *There is an unspecified amount of evidence that output was low this month.*

There is ............................................................................
............................................................................
............................................................................

**12.** *There are only 2 high technology industries in the whole area.*

There are ............................................................................
............................................................................
............................................................................

## 2 En vous référant aux données chiffrées entre parenthèses, complétez les phrases par le quantificateur qui convient.

Ex. ▶ Car factories (0%) : ***no / none of*** the car factories made a profit.

**1.** Paper mills (0%) : How many did good business in the paper mill sector? ..............................

**2.** Chemical industries (2%) : ........................ business was done by out-sourcing.

**3.** Glassworks (2%) : ........................ items were made in July.

**4.** Factory outlets (4%): There was .............................. money made in the factory outlets.

**5.** Textile factories (4%): .......................... orders were taken by the textile factories.

**6.** Service industries (6%): ........................... cash was earned in the service industries.

**7.** Steel industry (6%): .............................. goods were delivered from the steel plant.

**8.** Brickworks (40%): The brickworks had .................... satisfying results.

**9.** Foundries (55%): ................................ goods were produced during the month.

**10.** Public works (60%): ...................... people ordered public works to be done.

## 3 Entourez l'erreur et corrigez-la !

**1.** The both (of) your products are innovative.

..........................................................................................

..........................................................................................

..........................................................................................

**2.** Working must suit both of workers and managers.

..........................................................................................

..........................................................................................

..........................................................................................

**3.** Both warehousing organization and cleanliness is are important.

..........................................................................................

..........................................................................................

..........................................................................................

**4.** Which product do you prefer? The both of them.

..........................................................................................

..........................................................................................

..........................................................................................

**5.** Which do you like best – working the day or the night shift? The both.

..........................................................................................

..........................................................................................

..........................................................................................

## 4 Entourez la bonne réponse.

**1.** We shall need the all / whole set of documents before we can deliver.

**2.** Every / each of our invoices is double-checked.

**3.** I have never met such a rude delivery man in my all / whole career!

**4.** You can buy the goods either / neither wholesale or retail – you choose.

**5.** We take cash-on-delivery or cash with order. Neither / either of them are acceptable.

**6.** We cannot accept your terms. Either / neither the lead time, or / nor the Incoterms are good enough.

**7.** We have met everyone / every one of our delivery deadlines.

**8.** We do our invoicing each / every monday.

## 5 Entourez la bonne réponse.

**1.** The after sales service calls back 50% their clients.

**a)** half of
**b)** the half
**c)** half (of)

**2.** 75% you will agree, we need to handle customer complaints better.

**a)** most of
**b)** most (of)
**c)** the most

**3.** The machine maintenance took ... week

**a)** most of
**b)** most of the
**c)** most

**4.** 75% service industries give a quick after sales response.

**a)** most (of)
**b)** most of
**c)** most

**5.** 50% the customers complained about the level of service.

**a)** half (of)
**b)** half of
**c)** the half

**6.** 100% them provide services.

**a)** all (of)
**b)** all of
**c)** the all

**7.** We waited ... month for a response to our complaint.

**a)** all of
**b)** all of the
**c)** all

**8.** 100% public utilities offer service jobs.

**a)** all (of)
**b)** all of
**c)** all

## 6 Complétez les phrases suivantes par *no, nothing, none, nowhere, no-one...*

**1.** The operators have ............................... work to do at the moment.

**2.** We have tried everything but there is ...................... to put the printing machine, there just isn't room.

**3.** The apprentice has learnt ...................... this week.

**4.** ............... wants to work on the bending machine – it's too noisy.

**5.** We looked for some spare packaging – it's a problem – there is ........................... .

**6.** Is there ............................... we can do to increase the production flow?

**7.** ............................... wants to take responsibility for the waste reduction campaign.

**8.** How much new tooling has been ordered this month? ................................... .

## 7 Complétez les phrases avec le mot qui convient.

*all – both – enough – enough – few – little – many – much – none – whole*

**1.** Don't you think .......... methods and R&D should be involved in the project?

**2.** If we have too .......... information we just won't know where to start!

**3.** How .......... direct workers do you need to start the pilot run?

**4.** There isn't .......... space in the workshop to add a new work station.

**5.** There are .......... assembly lines with such a short lead time. We are exceptional!

**6.** We still have a .......... time if you want to inspect the finished products.

**7.** We double check that .......... the material we need is at the work station.

**8.** Can you imagine? The .......... project has been stopped because of lack of financing.

**9.** "How many new workers have you taken on recently?" "........."

**10.** The team is efficient .........., but they don't seem to be up to schedule. We need to make some improvements.

**CORRIGÉS**

**1.** 1. We need a little more money for our advertising budget. 2. How much? 3. We have plenty of time to plan our production. 4. He has thought of a few ideas for a patent. 5. There are not many people on the saturday shift. 6. There are some manufacturers who refuse to make wasteful throwaways. 7. Few operators put their ideas in the "ideas box". 8. How many sub-contracted parts are you going to order? 9. There isn't much information about the new paint workshop. 10. There is little space for the conveyor. 11. There is some evidence that output was low this month. 12. There are few high technology industries in the whole area.
**2.** 1. None. 2. Little 3. Few 4. A little 5. A few 6. Not much 7. Not many 8. some 9. A lot of 10. Plenty of
**3.** 1. the 2. of 3. is 4. the 5. the
**4.** 1. whole 2. each of our 3. whole 4. either 5. either 6. neither... nor 7. every one 8. every
**5.** 1. c 2. a 3. b 4. c 5. a 6. b 7. c 8. c
**6.** 1. no 2. nowhere 3. nothing 4. no-one / nobody 5. none 6. nothing 7. no-one / nobody 8. none
**7.** 1. both 2. much 3. many 4. enough 5. few 6. little 7. all 8. whole 9. None 10. enough

## 1 Entourez la bonne réponse.

Score : ..... / 10

1. What do you do? I'm a / an / ø engineer.
2. We sell a lot of goods in a / an / the / ø Middle east.
3. The new factory should be good news for a / an / the / ø unemployed.
4. A / An / The / Ø R&D department at PLC Inc. is working on a new project.
5. Generally speaking, a / an / the / ø production flow is now JITP.
6. Our production subsidiaries are located in a / an / the / ø north of Italy.
7. Have you seen a / an / the / ø obsolete machinery over there?
8. You can see the item on a / an / the / ø page 25 of our catalogue.
9. The factory re-organization was quite a / an / the / ø good idea.
10. We sell our goods for €20 a / an / the / ø kilo.

## 2 Entourez l'erreur et corrigez-la !

Score : ..... / 10

1. There are some work to be done on clearing out this factory.
2. I'm sorry for some inconvenience, but it's got to be done.
3. Please don't leave your rubbish just somewhere.
4. There isn't nobody to supervise the cleaning operation.
5. Would you like any help from the methods department?
6. Are there a shelves to store small parts on?
7. Somebody has left his packed lunch on the conveyor belt.
8. Hardly someone wears the compulsory protective gloves.
9. If you have some more ideas, could you tell the foreman?
10. Now that we have a new factory, we need to find any business!

## 3 Comment dire... ? Entourez la ou les bonnes réponses.

Score : ..... / 10

| | | |
|---|---|---|
| 1. The whole day. | a) all day | b) every day |
| 2. The two things in a choice of two | a) the both | b) both (of them) |
| 3. Not one or the other. | a) neither ... nor | b) either ... or |
| 4. A complete range of goods. | a) whole | b) all |
| 5. To say how often something happens. | a) each week | b) every week |
| 6. To talk about a choice where both are possible. | a) neither (of) | b) either (of) |
| 7. To talk about sales in general. | a) sales | b) the sales |
| 8. To talk about 50% of a group. | a) half(of) the group | b) the half group |
| 9. To talk about an individual within a group. | a) each | b) every |
| 10. To talk about a majority | a) most | b) the most |

## 4 Complétez les phrases par les mots suivants : Score : ..... / 8

*a little – anywhere – few – not many – how much – none – some – any*

**1.** I need help with the design. Would you like .............................. advice?

**2.** Where should we put up the dashboards? .............................. .

**3.** I need some more money for the methods dept. ..............................?

**4.** How many defects did you find? .............................. . That's good – 0 defect!

**5.** The figures look bad. How many orders have you got? ..............................

**6.** How many people came to the factory open day? .............................. . Oh dear.

**7.** Did you get some information about the buyer? .............................. .

**8.** Did you pick up some samples for me? No, there weren't .............................. .

## 5 Complétez le dialogue par les mots suivants. Score : ..... / 6

*every – all (of) – neither... nor – all – each – both (of them) – every*

**A:** What did you think of the factory visit?

**B:** Not too bad – (1) .................................... operator knew their job – there was self-inspection at (2) .................................... workstation.

**A:** Yes, I noticed. Did you see (3) .................................... the infra-red safety measures too?

**B:** Impressive! Also there were two apprentices. (4) .................................. were being well-trained.

**A:** However, (5) .................................. the tooling .................................. the machinery appeared very well looked-after.

**B:** Nonetheless, I wouldn't mind working in a factory like that (6) ................... day .................. day!

## 6 Reliez le début et la fin des phrases. Score : ..... / 6

| | |
|---|---|
| Many / some / none of our sub-assemblies **1.** • | • **A.** still made by hand. |
| Luckily, we don't have any **2.** • | • **B.** are out-sourced to local workshops |
| Not a lot of / not much **3.** • | • **C.** recycling goes on, if I were to be honest. |
| How many by-products do we make? **4.** • | • **D.** – what are they supposed to do? |
| Many / some / no components are **5.** • | • **E.** None! None at all! |
| There are no work orders for the workers **6.** • | • **F.** hazardous products in the factory. |

**Score total : ..... / 50**

**CORRIGÉS**

**1.** 1. an 2. the 3. the 4. The 5. ø 6. the 7. the 8. ø 9. a 10. a – **2.** 1. there is 2. any inconvenience 3. just anywhere 4. isn't anybody 5. some help 6. any/no shelves 7. their packed lunch 8. hardly anyone 9. if you have any 10. some business – **3.** 1. all day 2. both (of them) 3. neither... nor 4. whole 5. every 6. either (of) 7. sales 8. half(of) 9. each 10. most – **4.** 1. some 2. Anywhere 3. How much? 4. None 5. Few/not many 6. Not many / few 7. A little 8. any – **5.** 1. each 2. every 3. all / all of 4. both of them 5. neither... nor 6. all – every (« toute la journée, tous les jours ») – **6.** 1. B 2. F 3. C 4. E 5. A 6. D

# 8 Les pronoms

COMMUNICATING

## Les pronoms personnels

| | Pronoms personnels | |
|---|---|---|
| | sujets | Objets |
| Singulier<br>1re personne<br>2e personne<br>3e personne<br>Pluriel<br>1re personne<br>2e personne<br>3e personne | *I* (je)<br>*you* (tu)<br>*he* (il) – *she* (elle) – *it* (neutre)<br><br>*we* (vous)<br>*you* (vous)<br>*they* (ils / elles) | *me* (moi)<br>*you* (toi)<br>*him* (lui) *her* (elle) *it* (neutre)<br><br>*us* (nous)<br>*you* (vous)<br>*them* (eux / elles) |
| Place dans la phrase | Avant le verbe ou l'auxiliaire, sauf à la forme interrogative.<br>*We send reminders every day.*<br>*Do they accept orders by fax?* | Après le verbe et/ou les prépositions.<br>*Give the e-mail to us.*<br>*She can answer them.* |

Inexistante en français, la forme *it* (neutre) renvoie aux objets et aux animaux, sauf quand il existe un lien affectif particulier.
*We have a cat – she's very sweet.* (Et pour les *hommes*) : *She's a wonderful car/boat!*

Contrairement au français, l'anglais ne fait jamais de redondance de sujets avec reprise par un pronom personnel.
*My boss and I / we like the Internet.* ~~*My boss and I, we ...*~~

## Les pronoms réfléchis et réciproques

### Pronoms réfléchis

*myself – yourself – himself/herself/itself – ourselves – yourselves – themselves*

On emploie les pronoms réfléchis :

**1.** Lorsque le sujet agit sur lui-même (je me..., tu te...).
*I blame **myself** for the mistake in the letter.*
*Look after **yourselves**!*

**2.** Lorsque l'on veut insister sur la personne ou la chose.
*I wrote the report (by) **myself**.*
*The letter **itself** isn't very important, but the contents are.*

**Verbes non réfléchis**

*Complain* (se plaindre), *concentrate* (se concentrer), *get up* (se lever), *lie down* (s'allonger), *relax* (se plaindre), *remember* (se souvenir), *sit down* (s'asseoir), *wake up* (se réveiller), etc.

### Pronoms réciproques

*each other – one another*

On emploie les pronoms réciproques *each other* et *one another* pour exprimer une interaction entre deux ou plusieurs personnes.
*John and Jane write to **each other** / **one another**.*
*My boss and I have known **each other** / **one another** for a long time.*

# Les pronoms relatifs

## Comparez !

*The supplier, who is based in Liverpool, has sent us a fax.*
L'information soulignée est nécessaire pour savoir de qui / quoi on parle.

*The letter, which was sent yesterday, still hasn't arrived.*
L'information soulignée est complémentaire mais pas essentielle. Dans ce cas, on utilise le pronom relatif *which* plutôt que *that* pour un objet inanimé.

Le choix du pronom relatif dépend :

| 1. de la nature de son antécédent | | 2. de sa fonction dans la proposition relative |
|---|---|---|
| **Animé (un être humain, un animal...)** | **Inanimé (un objet, une idée...)** | |
| *who* ou *that*<br>*The man who / that wrote the letter.* | *which* ou *that*<br>*The computer which / that is in his office.* | sujet |
| *who(m)* ou *that* ou *ø*<br>*The man who / that / ø I am looking for.*<br>*The man for whom I am looking.* | *which* ou *that* ou *ø*<br>*The program which / that / ø he is trying.* | objet |
| *whose*<br>*The man whose book you borrowed.* | *of which*<br>*4 offers of which 2 are feasible.* | génitif |
| *where* – *when* ou *ø* – *why* ou *ø*<br>*They work in the town where he was born.*<br>*Do you remember the time (when) there were no e-mails?*<br>*The reason (why) I'm calling is to follow-up my letter.* | | circonstanciel<br>– lieu<br>– temps<br>– cause |

↳ La forme *whom* du relatif a tendance à disparaître.
À l'oral, *that* est souvent utilisé à la place de *who*, *whom* et *which*. Les relatifs objets et circonstanciels sont aussi souvent omis.
Généralement, on utilise *that* dans une proposition relative essentielle, et *which* dans une proposition relative non-essentielle (séparée du reste de la phrase par des virgules).
Si le verbe est accolé à une préposition, n'oubliez pas la préposition.
*Do you know the customer (who) Simon wrote **to**?*

**!** Notez les constructions suivantes :
- Préposition + *whom / which: with whom, to whom, about whom, about which, without which*
*My mobile phone, **without which** I am completely lost, has been stolen.*
- Quantité + *of* + *who(m) / which: most / all / none / neither / either / some / many / much / a few / both / half / each / one...*
*The demonstrators, a few **of whom** were under twenty, were demanding higher pensions.*
- *Whoever / whatever / whichever / whenever / wherever: = any person / thing / time / place.*
*Just take **whichever** you prefer. **Whoever** volunteers will get a bonus.*

Les expressions de temps :
*I arrived at 7 pm, by **which time** / **point** the office was closed.*
→ Le temps que j'arrive à 19 heures, le bureau était fermé.

## 1 Dans chacune des listes suivantes, entourez l'intrus.

**1.** I – you – his – we

**2.** they – her – us – them

**3.** it – you – she

**4.** yourself – ourselves – each other

**5.** somebody – them – anybody – everybody – nobody

## 2 Complétez la phrase par le pronom personnel qui convient.

**1.** ......... shall send you a confirmation later in the day.

**2.** That's Tom's copy – give it to ......... .

**3.** She's called Sarah Bligh. Would you like ......... e-mail address?

**4.** I need that fax. Please give ......... to ......... .

**5.** New customers! ......... found our company on the Internet.

**6.** ......... has been using my computer! I told him not to before.

**7.** We need our customers, and they need ......... .

**8.** Where is the mailing list? I can't find ......... .

**9.** Did ......... send an order acknowledgement?

**10.** Where are the leaflets? I send ......... out.

## 3 Complétez la phrase par le pronom réfléchi ou réciproque qui convient.

**1.** He wrote the computer program ........................ .

**2.** If you two are driving all the way to head office, look after ........................ .

**3.** Bill and I enjoyed ........................ at the conference.

**4.** She's determined to fill in the spreadsheet all by ........................ .

**5.** I wonder why they are looking so pleased with .......... ................ they have just got a huge order!

**6.** I try to put ........................ in his position, and imagine what it's like to be the boss.

**7.** How long have you and the supplier known ........................?

**8.** Did you cut ........................ on that envelope?

**9.** They send ........................ updates every day.

## 4 Complétez ces phrases en utilisant un des pronoms proposés.

**1.** Simon is so boring. He's always complaining ......... .

**a)** himself **b)** ø **c)** him

**2.** We regularly send faxes to ......... .

**a)** each other **b)** ourselves **c)** us

**3.** She made the phone call in English all by ......... .

**a)** ø **b)** her **c)** herself

**4.** If you want to look at the specifications, just help ......... .

**a)** each other **b)** yourself **c)** you

**5.** Don't disturb – she's concentrating ......... hard on the report.

**a)** ø **b)** herself **c)** her

**6.** It's a wonderful catalogue. They did all the layout ......... .

**a)** them **b)** each other **c)** themselves

**7.** I'm sorry for the mistake in the contract. I blame ......... entirely.

**a)** myself **b)** me **c)** ø

**8.** We need to talk about this. Can we meet .........?

**a)** ourselves **b)** ø **c)** us

## 5 Le pronom relatif est nécessaire (quand il est sujet) ou facultatif (quand il est objet). Classez les phrases dans la colonne qui convient.

**1.** I need a copy of the letter that you wrote last week.

**2.** Could you ring back the person who called this morning.

**3.** I can't find the e-mail address which you gave me yesterday.

**4.** She gave the message to Mr Smith who will ring you later.

**5.** This is the person who he met at the trade fair in Frankfurt.

6. What's the name of the man whose e-mail address starts with boyo small.....?

| Pronom relatif nécessaire | Pronom relatif facultatif |
|---|---|
| | |

## 6 Réunissez les deux phrases proposées en une seule, en utilisant le pronom relatif qui convient.

1. I would like to speak to a person. He wrote the letter.

.................................................................................

.................................................................................

2. You wanted a report. Here it is.

.................................................................................

.................................................................................

3. I spoke to somebody. Her boss was busy.

.................................................................................

.................................................................................

4. The office was not very tidy. We met there.

.................................................................................

.................................................................................

5. You couldn't type. Can you remember the time?

.................................................................................

.................................................................................

6. Let me introduce you to a woman. She created the website.

.................................................................................

.................................................................................

7. He wants to speak to me. Do you know the reason?

.................................................................................

.................................................................................

8. We ordered the goods. Can you tell me the day?

.................................................................................

.................................................................................

## 7 Entourez l'erreur et corrigez-la !

1. He had been working hard on the report so he decided to relax himself.

.................................................................................

2. The person what did the road map is a bit too optimistic!

.................................................................................

3. We've got a letter of complaint from the customer – them are very angry about the delivery delays.

.................................................................................

4. We send invitations out to all our customers, the most of which refused!

.................................................................................

5. Could you both deal with the inquiries by yourselfs?

.................................................................................

6. That supplier always delivers late – did you send he a reminder?

.................................................................................

7. We got an order from the man visited the factory last week.

.................................................................................

8. We have been doing business with ourselves for a very long time now.

.................................................................................

**CORRIGÉS**

**1.** 1. his (object pronoun) 2. they (subject pronoun) 3. she (it & you are subject and object pronouns) 4. each other (reciprocal pronoun) 5. them (not an indefinite pronoun)
**2.** 1. I / we 2. him 3. her 4. it – me 5. they 6. he 7. us 8. it 9. you / they 10. them
**3.** 1. himself 2. yourselves / each other 3. ourselves 4. herself 5. themselves 6. myself 7. each other / one another 8. yourself 9. each other / one another
**4.** 1. b 2. a 3. c 4. b 5. a 6. c 7. a 8. b
**5.** Pronom relatif nécessaire : 2, 4, 6. Pronom relatif facultatif : 1, 3, 5.
**6.** 1. I would like to speak to the person who wrote the letter. (For a person, that is possible, who is better) 2. Here is the report (that / ø) you wanted. 3. I spoke to someone whose boss was busy. 4. The office where we met was not very tidy. 5. Can you remember (the time) when you couldn't type? 6. Let me introduce you to the woman who created the website. 7. Do you know the reason (why) he wants to speak to me? 8. Can you tell me the day (that / when) we ordered the goods?
**7.** 1. to relax 2. the person who 3. they are very angry 4. most of which / who / whom 5. yourselves 6. send him 7. the man who / that 8. doing business with each other

COMMUNICATING

# Les adjectifs et pronoms possessifs

## Forme des possessifs

| Adjectifs possessifs | Pronoms possessifs |
|---|---|
| *My*<br>(mon, ma, mes) | *Mine*<br>(le mien, la mienne, les miens, les miennes) |
| *Your*<br>(ton, ta, tes) | *Yours*<br>(le tien, la tienne, les tiens, les tiennes) |
| *His / Hers / Its*<br>(son, sa, ses) | *His / Hers / Its own*<br>(le sien, la sienne, les siens, les siennes) |
| *Our*<br>(notre, nos) | *Ours*<br>(le nôtre, la nôtre, les nôtres) |
| *Your*<br>(votre, vos) | *Yours*<br>(le vôtre, la vôtre, les vôtres) |
| *Their*<br>(leur, leurs) | *Theirs*<br>(le leur, la leur, les leurs) |

À la différence du français, comme les choses en anglais n'ont pas de genre, l'adjectif possessif s'accorde avec le possesseur, et non avec la chose possédée.

***Michael's** car = his car = it's **his*** ***Jane**'s car = **her** car = **it's** hers*

***The factory**'s pilot plant = **its** pilot plant = it's got **its** own pilot plant*

***John and my** computer = **our** computer = it's **ours***

***Sarah and Bill**'s printer = **their** printer = it's **theirs***

## Emploi des possessifs

Contrairement au français, l'anglais utilise l'adjectif possessif pour désigner une partie du corps (sauf dans une phrase passive ou encore si le possesseur occupe la fonction objet du verbe principal).

*She had hurt her thumb so she couldn't type quickly.*

*To say "hello", the man slapped me hard on the back.*

• Le possessif peut être renforcé par *own* pour exprimer une possession exclusive.

*He has **his own** office.* → Il a son propre bureau.

*She likes to work on **her own** / by herself when she has to think hard.*

→ Elle aime travailler toute seule quand elle doit bien réfléchir.

• Pour les pronoms indéfinis *everybody, somebody, anybody, nobody*, etc., on utilise le possessif pluriel.

*Everybody has paid **their** deposit for the hotel.*

*We need samples for the meeting. Oh good – somebody has brought **theirs**.*

! Emploi particulier, courant, du pronom possessif :

*A colleague of mine* ~~*a colleague of me*~~

• Les pronoms indéfinis (*everybody, somebody, anybody, nobody*...) sont considérés comme pluriels donc il faut bien accorder leur adjectif ou pronom possessif. Le verbe est au singulier.

*Everbody has taken **their** brochure.*

*Not everybody, someone has left **theirs** behind.*

# Les adjectifs et pronoms démonstratifs

## Forme des démonstratifs

| Distance de l'objet par rapport au locuteur | Singulier | Pluriel | Exemples |
|---|---|---|---|
| Proche | *this* | *these* | *"Good morning, this is John calling."*<br>*These faxes (here) must be answered quickly.* |
| Plus éloigné | *that* | *those* | *"Good morning, is that PLB Inc?"*<br>*Could you sign those letters (over there)?* |

## Emploi des démonstratifs

Adjectifs ou pronoms, *this / that / these / those* servent à désigner un objet ou une personne. En outre, ils peuvent être utilisés :

**1.** Avec les expressions de temps.
***This** week we must send out the reminders.*
*Do you remember **those** days when there was no Internet?*

**2.** Pour nuancer un adjectif, un adverbe ou *much / many*.
*The report I received was **this** long!* → Aussi long que ça !

**!** Dans une réponse courte, ajoutez *one / ones* au démonstratif.
*Which typeface do you prefer? That **one**.*

# *One / ones*

## *One*, pronom personnel indéfini

- On utilise le pronom personnel indéfini *one* pour traduire « on » dans l'expression d'une généralité.
***One** doesn't write an e-mail in capital letters, unless one is angry.*
- Ce pronom personnel a une forme réfléchie *oneself* et une forme au génitif *one's*.
*It is good to work for **oneself**.*
*In certain situations, one must make up **one's** mind quickly.*

## *One / ones*, pronom de remplacement

Ne s'appliquant qu'à des noms dénombrables, on utilise *one / ones* comme pronom de remplacement pour éviter la répétition.
*It's a pricey item. Have you seen **one**?*
*Which envelopes do you prefer? The white **ones**.*

COMMUNICATING

## 1 Complétez par les adjectifs et pronoms possessifs qui conviennent.

Ex. ▶ I have a huge filing cabinet.
It's ***my*** filing cabinet. It's ***mine***.

**1.** You have an efficient printer.
It's ...................... printer. It's ...................... .

**2.** Jane has a new mobile phone.
It's ...................... mobile phone. It's ...................... .

**3.** Bob has a high-tech computer.
It's ...................... computer. It's ...................... .

**4.** We share an old fax machine.
It's ...................... fax machine. It's ...................... .

**5.** You and Joe share a nice desk.
It's ...................... desk. It's ...................... .

**6.** Fred and Sarah share a telephone.
It's ...................... telephone. It's ...................... .

**7.** I have an office just for me and no-one else.
It's ...................... office.

## 2 Complétez en utilisant un des possessifs proposés.

**1.** The company cat has lost .......... collar.
**a)** his / her **b)** its

**2.** She is thinking of setting up business on .......... own.
**a)** his **b)** her

**3.** I need to send the file to a counterpart of .......... in the USA.
**a)** me **b)** mine

**4.** The computer screen makes .......... eyes hurt.
**a)** my **b)** the

**5.** I don't think anyone has returned .......... questionnaire yet, have they?
**a)** their **b)** his / her

**6.** I'll take JMB's advice, and send a request to a supplier of .......... .
**a)** them **b)** theirs

## 3 Suivant les indications entre parenthèses, complétez les phrases ci-dessous par le mot qui convient.

*one's – this – one – one's – on his own – their – her own – of mine – one*

Ex. ▶ Would you like a pen? No thank you, I don't need ***one*** (the pen).

**1.** He likes to add up figures .................... (alone).

**2.** Could you look over .................... spreadsheet? (The spreadsheet I have here in my hand.)

**3.** I'll put you in touch with a business contact .................... (A business contact I have.)

**4.** .................... does .................... best. (As a general rule.)

**5.** She does .................... computer programming. (She does it herself.)

**6.** One likes to be satisfied with .................... work. (As a general rule, the work one does oneself.)

**7.** I would like another ...................., please. (You want one more.)

**8.** Everyone paid .................... bills before the due date. (The bills which belonged to them.)

## 4 Entourez l'erreur et corrigez-la !

**1.** This filing cabinet over there is enormous.
..............................................................................

**2.** Our new storage facilities are better than the old one.
..............................................................................

**3.** These supplies in that corner should be on shelves.
..............................................................................

**4.** Take a look here, this goods aren't packed properly.
..............................................................................

**5.** May I introduce himself? I am the procurement officer, Simon.
..............................................................................

**6.** This batch of headed paper is finished, we need an other ones.
..............................................................................

**7.** The stock-taking was better than the ones last year.

....................................................................................

**8.** We have a shortage of those pens and pencils here.

....................................................................................

**9.** Next week we will run out of this ones over there completely.

....................................................................................

**10.** The control of office supplies has improved after those training program.

....................................................................................

## 5 Complétez le dialogue à l'aide des mots suivants.

*this – ones – my – these – those – that – yours – our – mine – one – this – theirs*

Boss: You've been checking the quality of documents leaving the office. Take a look at (1) .................... (2) .................... here.

Joe: I didn't write that one – it's not (3) .................... .

Boss: (4) .................... is not a reason – you are responsible. The assistants think that (5) .................... are double-checked for them. (6) .................... is just an example of what is wrong.

Joe: But (7) .................... that you have there are the (8) .................... that were not sent. (9) .................... I have in my hand are the right copies.

Boss: It is very important for (10) .................... company image, you know.

Joe: I have been working hard on this; my reputation is at stake, not (11) .................... .

Boss: Please have a new copy on (12) .................... desk by tomorrow morning!

## 6 Entourez la bonne réponse.

**1.** Here are some tips to improve yours / your e-mails.

**2.** An irish counterpart of mine / me always uses "smileys" – don't overdo it.

**3.** Someone I know makes his / their lines too long.

**4.** If your computer is old, like mine / my, you don't want to receive large files too often.

**5.** Don't worry, our / ours is very state of the art, and we have broadband.

**6.** These / those days, communicating with the Internet is getting easier and easier.

## 7 Reliez le début et la fin de phrase.

| | | | |
|---|---|---|---|
| It's not mine so | **1.** • | • **A.** | much nicer than theirs. |
| The one over there, yes, | **2.** • | • **B.** | their tools up-dated. |
| This belongs to me | **3.** • | • **C.** | it must be yours |
| We think that our letterhead is | **4.** • | • **D.** | should know one's competitors. |
| Does Joe or Jill own this? | **5.** • | • **E.** | It's my laptop. |
| Come here and look at. | **6.** • | • **F.** | Is it his or hers? |
| The I.T. department have had | **7.** • | • **G.** | that supplier of yours? |
| The C.E.O. always says one | **8.** • | • **H.** | software like ours. |
| We would highly recommend you use | **9.** • | • **I.** | this letter – it's a joke! |
| Could you give me the contact details of | **10.** • | • **J.** | I mean that one. |
| This looks like our new suppliers quote. | **11.** • | • **K.** | No we don't, I can do it on my own. |
| We need help to re-do our invoices. | **12.** • | • **L.** | It's mine, I'm looking forward to the conference. |

## CORRIGÉS

**1.** 1. your / yours 2. her / hers 3. his / his 4. our / ours 5. your / yours 6. their / theirs 7. my own
**2.** 1. a 2. b 3. b 4. a 5. a 6. b
**3.** 1. on his own 2. this 3. of mine 4. one – one's 5. her own 6. one's 7. one 8. their
**4.** 1. That filing cabinet over there is enormous. 2. Our new storage facilities are better than the old ones. 3. Those supplies in that corner should be on shelves. 4. Take a look here, these goods aren't packed properly. 5. May I introduce myself? I am the procurement officer, Simon. 6. This batch of headed paper is finished, we need another one. 7. The stock-taking was better than the one last year. 8. We have a shortage of these pens and pencils here. 9. Next week we will run out of those ones over there completely. 10. The control of office supplies has improved after that training program.
**5.** 1. this 2. one 3. mine 4. that 5. theirs 6. this 7. those 8. ones 9. these 10. our 11. yours 12. my
**6.** 1. your 2. mine 3. their 4. mine 5. ours 6. these
**7.** 1. C 2. J 3. E 4. A 5. F 6. I 7. B 8. D 9. H 10. G 11. M 12. K

COMMUNICATING

## 1 Complétez le texte suivant par le pronom personnel sujet ou objet qui convient.

**Score : ..... / 18**

Dear Sir or Madam,

**(1)** ............................ regret to inform **(2)** ........................... that the product is no longer available but **(3)** ........................ has been superseded by another one. I believe your purchaser is Mary Coward. Would **(4)** ............................ like **(5)** ............................ to send **(6)** ............................ some samples? Otherwise, **(7)** ............................ have a new salesman and **(8)** ............................ will be in Paris on Monday with some samples. **(9)** .......................... can bring **(10)** .......................... with **(11)** ............................ other customers have seen our new product and **(12)** ............................ are very pleased with **(13)** ......................... . If **(14)** ........................... should require any further information, please do not hesitate to contact **(15)** ......................... .

You can reach **(16)** ........................ personally on 06.61.39.84.82. **(17)** ............................ look forward to hearing from **(18)** ............................ .

## 2 Retrouvez pour chacune des phrases le mot qui convient parmi la liste suivante.

**Score : ..... / 8**

*a road map – our brochure – computer skills – a letter of application – a postcard – an agreement / a contract – a spreadsheet – a social media*

**1.** People use it to share news with one another.

**2.** I managed to fill in the columns of figures all by myself!

**3.** He wrote it himself and sent it to the personnel officer.

**4.** They did all the legal work themselves when they loaned the machines.

**5.** If you need information about our products, please help yourself.

**6.** It is best to work out how to use the software (by) oneself.

**7.** They send them to each other when they go on holiday.

**8.** Let's schedule the product development ourselves and send them a chart.

## 3 Complétez les phrases par le pronom relatif qui convient.

**Score : ..... / 10**

**1.** I am writing to apply for the position ............................ was advertised in the Daily Mull this morning.

**2.** Following your letter, ............................ I received this morning, I am sending you some samples.

**3.** I regret to inform you that the person ..................... company produces the spare parts has retired.

**4.** Following the meeting, ............................ we discussed our terms of sale, I would be grateful if you could send me the agreement as soon as possible.

**5.** What do you say to someone ............................ is going for an interview? "Good luck"!

**6., 7.** Further to my call on Monday, in ............................ the person to ............................ I spoke promised to ring back immediately – and didn't, I would like written confirmation of the delivery dates of our goods.

**8.** We enclose details of the new additions to our range, ............................ are more affordable, yet in keeping with our high quality standards.

**9.** The reason ............................ I'm writing is to invite you to our booth at the trade fair in June.

**10.** Unable to get an answer by telephone, I am writing to get in contact with the person .......... .................. is responsible for purchasing.

## 4 Entourez l'erreur et corrigez-la!

**Score : ..... / 6**

1. My colleague and me, we prefer sending e-mails to sending letters.
2. To avoid mistakes in the future, you must read the information back to yourselves.
3. Nobody has updated his production forecast although we asked for the figures last week!
4. Have you sent a copy of the production flow chart to the person which came for the audit?
5. I must get in touch with a friend of them about my work experience.
6. Can you imagine, Peter even has her own company car these days.

## 5 Reliez le début et la fin de dialogue.

**Score : ..... / 8**

| | | | |
|---|---|---|---|
| What kind of mouse do you prefer to use? | **1.** • | • **A.** | The best is to work it out oneself. |
| What is the small long thing over there? | **2.** • | • **B.** | I'm not too sure myself. |
| Look at the things I've got here on my e-mail! | **3.** • | • **C.** | These are e-mail addresses. |
| With a search engine, you have to understand how to ask the right question. | **4.** • | • **D.** | That's a USB key. |
| It's difficult to understand all this software. | **5.** • | • **E.** | I didn't realize it was all that complicated |
| When are we going to get broadband? | **6.** • | • **F.** | The infra-red ones. |
| What are those thing you've got there "do", "at", "com" .....? | **7.** • | • **G.** | Those are "emoticoms" – to show – one's mood. |
| Do you think you'll ever understand? | **8.** • | • **H.** | This month, I hope. |

**Score total : ..... / 50**

### CORRIGÉS

**1.** 1. I / we 2. you 3. it 4. she 5. me / us 6. her 7. I / we 8. he 9. he 10. them 11. him 12. they 13. it 14. you 15. me / us 16. me 17. I / we 18. you
**2.** 1. social media 2. a spreadsheet 3. a letter of application 4. an agreement / a contract 5. our brochure 6. computer skills 7. a postcard 8. a road map
**3.** 1. which 2. which 3. whose 4. where 5. who 6. 7. which – whom 8. which 9. why / that / ø 10. who
**4.** 1. and I 2. back to each other 3. their production forecast 4. the person who 5. a friend of theirs 6. his own
**5.** 1. f 2. d 3. g 4. e 5. a 6. h 7. c 8. b

# 9 Les adjectifs et les adverbes



## Les adjectifs

Contrairement au français, les adjectifs en anglais ne s'accordent pas.
*The new computer* *The new computers*

### Formation des adjectifs

• On peut créer un adjectif à partir d'un nom en ajoutant un des suffixes suivants : *-ful, -less, -ish, -like, -y, -ed, -ing*
*Skilful, harmless, yellowish, businesslike, wealthy, interested, boring*

! L'adjectif avec le participe présent (*-ing*) et l'adjectif participe passé (*-ed* ou verbe irrégulier) sont employés pour exprimer des idées différentes.
Cause : *The idea is fascinating. She's an amazing person.*
Effet / réaction : *We are all fascinated. They were amazed by what she had to say.*

• Ces participes peuvent aussi être utilisés comme subordonnées descriptives :
*The woman standing over there is our product manager.*
*(The woman who is standing over there…)*
*The cheeses made in France are delicious.*
*(The cheeses which are made…)*

### Place de l'adjectif dans la phrase

Généralement, les adjectifs se placent :

**1.** Avant le nom qu'ils qualifient.
*The tired commuter*

EXCEPTION Les adjectifs en *-ible* / *-able*, lorsqu'ils sont associés avec *first, last, only* ou un superlatif, se placent immédiatement après le nom.
*It is an offer available for a month only. It is the best offer possible.*

Lorsque le nom est précédé de deux adjectifs qualificatifs, mettez soit une virgule soit *and* entre les deux adjectifs (mais obligatoirement *and* s'il s'agit de deux couleurs).
*A beautiful and interesting item* *A beautiful, interesting item*
*A blue and red shop sign* ~~*A blue, red shop sign*~~

**2.** Après un verbe d'état (*appear, be, feel, get, look, seem, smell, sound, taste*)
*That looks interesting.* *The product got out-of-date.*

EXCEPTION Les adjectifs servant à classifier (*digital, main, only, whole,* etc.) ou à souligner (*absolute, complete, mere,* etc.) ne se placent jamais après un verbe d'état, mais toujours avant un nom.
*A digital camera* ~~*The camera is digital*~~
*An absolute failure* ~~*The failure was absolute*~~

Les "*a adjectives*" (*afraid, alight, alike, alive, alone, ashamed, asleep, awake, aware*), ainsi que les adjectifs « de santé et de bien-être » (*content, fine, glad, ill, poorly, sorry, (un)sure, upset, (un) well*) se placent toujours après un verbe d'état, et jamais avant un nom.
*They are similar products.*
*The products are alike.*

**3.** Selon un ordre particulier : l'opinion est suivie des faits, eux-mêmes classés dans un ordre hiérarchique bien établi.

| Opinion | Size | Shape | Age | Colour | Pattern | Origin | Made of | Type | Noun |
|---|---|---|---|---|---|---|---|---|---|
| *A nice* | *large* | *oval* | *old* | *yellow* | *striped* | *French* | *China* | *personalised* | *plate.* |
| *A pretty* | *small* | *round* | *modern* | *blue* | *flowery* | *Italian* | *plastic* | *unbreakable* | *glass.* |
| *An awful* | *huge* | *square* | *new* | *red&pink* | *spotted* | *American* | *cotton* | *T* | *shirt.* |

**4.** Après un adverbe de degré.
Il existe les adjectifs gradables que l'on peut associer avec les mots « *very…* » et les adjectifs non-gradables qui expriment déjà quelque chose de fort, et que l'on ne peut associer qu'à un adverbe très fort. Voici quelques exemples :

| | |
|---|---|
| **Adverbe associé :** *extremely, deeply, hugely, immensely, really, very, pretty, fairly, quite, rather, reasonably, slightly…* | **Adjectifs gradables ("nuancables"):** *colourful, efficient, happy, old, small, etc.* |
| **Adverbe associé :** *absolutely, completely, entirely, really, simply, totally, utterly, pretty, quite…* | **Adjectifs non-gradables ("non-nuancables"):** *amazing, ghastly, incredible, wonderful, useless…* |

*That was an **extremely (very) good** presentation.*
*They have brought out a **totally amazing** invention.*

**5.** Les chiffres : le nombre devient un adjectif, donc pas de « s » sur les chiffres.
→ *Four hundred thousand dollars.*
Adjectif + *to* + infinitif : *The user manual is **easy to understand**.*

# Les adverbes

## Formation des adverbes

**1.** En règle générale, les adverbes se forment à partir de l'adjectif auquel on ajoute le suffixe *–ly*.
***Quick → quickly***

EXCEPTIONS
Pour les adjectifs qui se terminent en *-y* : *heavy → heavily*
Pour les adjectifs qui se terminent en *-ic* : *basic → basically*
Pour les adjectifs qui se terminent en *-e* : *complete → completely*

**2.** Les adjectifs qui se terminent par –ly (*friendly, lively, elderly, lonely, lovely,* etc.) nécessitent d'avoir recours à une phrase adverbiale.
*He's a silly man. → He works in a silly way.*

**3.** Certains adjectifs sont irréguliers.
*good → well*

**4.** *Hard, fast, late, early* et *monthly* sont à la fois adjectifs et adverbes.

! Ne confondez pas : *hard* (dur) et *hardly* (à peine / presque pas) :
*He works very **hard**.* *I can **hardly** wait, I'm so excited!*

## Place de l'adverbe dans la phrase

**1.** Les adverbes de manière et de lieu
Ils se placent après le verbe ou, s'il y en a un, après l'objet direct mais jamais entre le verbe et l'objet direct !
*He doesn't work **hard**.*
*She speaks English **very** well.*

**!** L'adverbe de manière se place avant l'adverbe de lieu.
*It was a good restaurant: we ate **well** there.*

**2.** Les adverbes de temps
Ils se placent en fin de phrase (cas général) ou au début (pour accentuer).
*They went to a trade fair in Paris **last week**.*
***Last month** we had record sales.*

**3.** Les adverbes de fréquences (*already, always, ever, never, (not) often, rarely, seldom, sometimes, still, usually*, etc.)
Ils se placent avant le verbe mais après l'auxiliaire (donc après *be*).
*They have **never** worked on Saturday.*
*He is **always** early for work.*

**4.** Les adverbes de degré (*more, nearly, totally, very*, etc.)
Ils se placent immédiatement avant le verbe, l'adjectif ou l'adverbe qu'ils nuancent.
→ *Your idea is **totally** unacceptable!*

**5.** Les prépositions adverbiales (*in, out, up, down, over, back, forward*, etc.)
Elles se placent en début de phrase, suivies par le verbe puis le sujet, à moins que le sujet soit un pronom.
***In** came Tom.*
***In** he came.*

**6.** Utilisez un adverbe pour donner une nuance au verbe principal.
→ *I don't **quite** see what you mean.*

**7.** Adverbe + adverbe pour donner plus de nuance.
→ *She types **incredibly quickly**.*

**8.** Pour donner un sens restrictif ou négatif *then, only when, only in this way, scarcely, scarcely ... when, seldom, so neither, or* en début de phrase, avec inversion du sujet.
***On no account** must this switch be touched.*

EXCEPTIONS

• *Used to* : l'adverbe se place avant *used to*.
*She **never** used to like business lunches.*
*My son **always** used to ring once a day.*

• *Have to* : l'adverbe se place avant l'auxiliaire modal.
*We **hardly** ever have to send a reminder.*
*You will **always** have to be on time.*

## 1 Donnez le contraire des adjectifs soulignés.

1. a reliable machine — ***unreliable***
2. a hard-working salesman ........................
3. an easy-to-use robot ........................
4. high-quality goods ........................
5. an invaluable piece of jewellery ........................
6. a light plastic ........................
7. a silent appliance ........................
8. a weak link ........................

## 2 Qualifiez chacun des objets en mettant dans l'ordre qui convient les adjectifs suivants.

**1. Network:** european / digital / new / worldwide / best-ever / and completely hassle-free.

..........................................................................................
..........................................................................................
..........................................................................................
..........................................................................................
..........................................................................................
..........................................................................................

**2. Car:** king-sized / hybrid / American / brand-new / environment-friendly / with multi-function leather steering wheel.

..........................................................................................
..........................................................................................
..........................................................................................
..........................................................................................
..........................................................................................
..........................................................................................

**3. Packaging:** small / plastic / British / high-quality / colourful / give your goods a state-of-the art image.

..........................................................................................
..........................................................................................
..........................................................................................
..........................................................................................
..........................................................................................
..........................................................................................



**4. Cottage:** timber-framed / charming / 17th century / 5-bedroomed / Welsh / with far-reaching views.

..........................................................................................
..........................................................................................
..........................................................................................
..........................................................................................
..........................................................................................
..........................................................................................

## 3 Complétez chacune des phrases par l'adjectif qui convient, en vous aidant des indices entre parenthèses.

*long – big / large – wide / broad / deep – heavy – high / tall*

1. How .................. is it? (a building)
2. How .................. is it? (a bridge)
3. How .................. is it? (a road)
4. How .................. is it? (a piece of cheese)
5. How .................. is it? (a box)
6. How .................. is it? (a swimming pool)

## 4 Complétez chaque phrase par le mot qui convient après lui avoir ajouté *-ed* ou *-ing*.

Ex. ▶ Interest
The product presentation was ***interesting***.
He was ***interested*** in the presentation.

1. Satisfy

The marketing department were ................................ because the results of our latest customer survey were ................................ .

2. Amuse

Making toys for businessmen can be an ........................ .......... job – even the director seemed ........................ ......... when he saw the new R&D project.

3. Astonish

I was ................................ when I saw how much logistics had improved – in fact, all the changes in the factory were ................................ .

**4.** Exhaust

However, the lean manufacturing training was completely ................................ and the participants were quite ................................ .

**5.** Disappoint

They only offered a 2% discount – that's ................................ – the supply chain manager will be ................................ .

**5** **Nuancez chaque adjectif en utilisant l'un des adverbes suivants. Aidez-vous des indices entre parenthèse : + = faible, ++ = moyen, +++ = fort**

*absolutely – totally – really / pretty – slightly – completely – rather*

**1.** It's a (+++) ................................ invaluable tailored solution to your packaging needs.

**2.** I do think that's a (++) ................................ common marketing strategy – think of something different!

**3.** It is a (++) ................................ cheap item compared with the competition.

**4.** It's a (+) ................................ more eye-catching advert than the last one – not much.

**5.** It's an (+++) ................................ awful idea to launch that product now – the market is saturated.

**6.** The only thing I can say, is that it's a (+++) ................................ useless household appliance!

**6** **À partir de l'adjectif donné, formez l'adverbe, puis écrivez-le dans la phrase, après avoir choisi la place qui lui convient.**

**1.** Good → ................................ .

The goods sold ................................ in the new shop ................................ .

**2.** Very efficient → ................................ .

The new procurement department ................................ runs ................................ .

**3.** Loud → ................................ .

You don't need to ................................ speak ................................ , I can hear you all right.

**4.** Economic → ................................ .

................................ speaking ................................ we are doing the right thing to increase the selling cost.

**5.** Steady → ................................ .

The company has ................................ been ................................ growing ................................ since last year.

**6.** Rapid → ................................ .

It's a nice device, but it doesn't operate ................................ enough ................................ .

**7.** Fine → ................................ .

The machine has been ................................ tuned ................................ for 0 tolerance.

**8.** Hard → ................................ .

They have been ................................ working ................................ on that design all winter.

**7** **Entourez la bonne réponse.**

**1.** This is the last possible launch date / last launch date possible.

**2.** The foodstuff in that shop smells bad / badly smells.

**3.** They are marketing an American enormous car / enormous American car.

**4.** Their inventions are always / always are very innovative.

**6.** They are using pink, green / pink and green colours in their catalogue.

**7.** I understand quite / quite understand that you prefer the latest model.

**8.** The product just isn't good enough / enough good.

**8** **Choisissez la bonne réponse.**

**1.** We're lucky; .... spend money on promoting our products.

**a)** we hardly ever have to **b)** we have to hardly ever

**2.** It was very .... to get all the specifications included in the product.

**a)** hardly **b)** hard

**3.** Customers will .... be able to tell that this is just an upgrade.

**a)** hardly **b)** hard

**4.** The new idea the marketing department have come up with is .... .

**a)** totally unworkable **b)** unworkable totally

**5.** Seldom .... such a user-friendly computer.

**a)** have I seen **b)** I have seen

**6.** The product .... sell so well.

**a)** used never to **b)** never used to

**7.** We are surprised by how .... the new product is selling.

**a)** good **b)** well

**8.** NPI (New Product Introduction) is .... .

a) remarkably efficiently **b)** remarkably efficient

**9.** It is .... to launch the new product.

**a)** nearly time **b)** time nearly

**10.** Customers are .... disappointed by PLC's products.

**a)** hardly ever **b)** hardly never

## 9 Choisissez le mot qu'il faut pour la conversation.

Bob: Morning John! How are you?

John: **(1)** Well / Good thank you. We are working **(2)** frantically / frantic to get **(3)** on time our new smartphone out / our new smartphone out on time.

Bob: So you're **(4)** immensely / completely busy at the moment then?

John: Right. On top of which, the customer decided he wanted **(5)** pink and orange / pink, orange packaging at the last minute!

Bob: So you must be a bit **(6)** tired / tiring at the moment. Products **(7)** always have to / have to always come out on the market on time too.

John: On top of which, I'm getting to bed **(8)** too lately / too late with all the launch parties too!

Bob: Well all I can say is that the publicity campaign was **(9)** really / real good!

John: Thanks. The whole point is that **(10)** the customers are aware / we have aware customers.

Bob: I think you've achieved that. I'll be off now. Good luck with everything.

## CORRIGÉS

**1.** 1. unreliable 2. lazy 3. hard-to-use 4. low-quality 5. worthless 6. heavy/dark 7. noisy 8. strong

**2.** 1. The best-ever, wordwide, new, european digital network – and completely hassle-free. 2. An environment-friendly, king-sized, brand-new american hybrid car with multi-function leather steering wheel. 3. High-quality, small, colourful, british, plastic packaging – give your goods a state-of-the-art image. 4. A charming, 5-bedroomed, 17th century, welsh, timber-framed cottage with far-reaching views.

**3.** 1. How high / tall is it? 2. How wide / broad is it?

**4.** 1. satisfied – satisfying 2. amusing –amused 3. astonished – astonishing 4. exhausting-exhausted 5. disappointing – disappointed.

**5.** 1. It's a completely invaluable tailored solution to your packaging needs. 2. I do think that's a rather common marketing strategy think – think of something different! 3. It is a really / pretty cheap item compared with the competition. 4. It's a slightly more eye-catching advert than the last one. 5. It's an absolutely awful idea to launch that product now the market is saturated. 6. The only thing I can say, is that it's a totally useless household appliance!

**6.** 1. The goods sold well in the new shop. 2. The new procurement department runs very efficiently. 3. You don't need to speak loudly, I can hear you all right. 4. Economically speaking we are doing the right thing to increase the selling cost. 5. The company has been growing steadily since last year. 6. It's a nice device, but it doesn't operate rapidly enough. 7. The machine has been finely tuned for 0 tolerance. 8. They have been working hard on that design all winter.

**7.** 1. last launch date possible 2. smells bad 3. enormous american car 4. hard 5. are always 6. pink and green 7. quite understand 8. good enough

**8.** 1. a – 2. b – 3. a – 4. a – 5. a – 6. b – 7. b – 8. b – 9. a – 10. a

**9.** 1. Well (Some people would answer "good", which is grammatically incorrect) – 2. frantically 3. our new smartphone out on time. 4. immensely 5. pink and orange 6. tired (As a consequence, he could also be "tiring"! 7. always have to 8. too late 9. really 10. the customers are aware

# Le comparatif et le superlatif

## Le comparatif

**1.** « Plus… que » : le comparatif de supériorité

| Adjectifs/adverbes | Comparatif |
|---|---|
| 1 syllabe / 2 syllabes en *-y*, *-er -ow*, *-le*<br>*late* | *-er … than* (pour comparer 2 éléments)<br>*later than* |
| 2 syllabes et plus<br>*efficiently* | *more … than*<br>*more efficiently than* |

↳ Pour certains adjectifs de 2 syllabes (*clever, narrow, quiet, simple, shallow*, etc.), on peut utiliser indifféremment l'une ou l'autre forme.
*The new machine is **quieter** / **more quiet** than the old one.*

**2.** « Moins … que » : le comparatif d'infériorité
Quel que soit le nombre de syllabes, l'adjectif / l'adverbe est précédé de *less* et suivi de *than*.
→ *He is less fluent in English **than I am**.* *He is no less fluent in English **than me**.*

**3.** « Aussi … que » : le comparative d'égalité
• Pour établir une équivalence, il est possible d'utiliser :
*the same* + nom + *as* ou *as* + adj. / adv. + *as* (et ne pas ~~*than*~~ !)
*The table is **the same** height as the desk.* *The table is **as** high **as** the desk.*

**!** Dans un comparatif d'égalité, l'article se place entre l'adjectif et le nom.
*It's as good **a** time as any to launch the product.*

• À la forme négative, on peut avoir : ***not as** / **so… as*** (= *less … than*)
*It is **not** selling **as** well **as** we thought it would.*
*It **isn't as** good a bargain **as** we had hoped for.*

• *Almost / nearly as* + adjectif + *as* (presque) :
*The store manager is not **nearly as good as** we thought he would be.*

• *Just as* + adjectif + *as* (tout aussi que) :
*The project is **just as stimulating as** the last one.*

• *Twice / half as … (as …)* → Deux fois plus / moitié moins (que) …
*Three times as big / small (as …)* → Trois fois plus grand / petit (que) …

**4.** « De plus en plus…, de moins en moins… » : le double comparatif
L'emploi d'un double comparatif sert à exprimer une progression.
→ *It is getting **harder and harder** to find a good sales outlet.*

**5.** « Plus… plus…, plus… moins, etc. » : *the* + comparatif
*The* + comparatif permet d'exprimer une double progression avec un lien de cause à effet.
→ ***The cheaper** the product, the more likely it is to sell.*

### Pour nuancer la comparaison

Pour nuancer la comparaison mettez *slightly / hardly / a little / a bit / somewhat / much / a lot / far / a great deal…* devant le comparatif.
*It is a great deal lighter than we thought. It is **hardly worth** trying.*

De même avec *even* :
*The product is **even better than** we had hoped.*

Any / no + comparatif :
*The new table computer is **no better** than the former one.* (verbe à l'affirmatif)
*We can't wait **any longer** for the new product to be launched.* (verbe au négatif)

! Notez l'utilisation du pronom sujet accompagné du verbe ou du pronom objet seul.
*He is no better at marketing **than I am / than me (than we are / than us)**.*

## Le superlatif

**1.** « Le plus… » : le superlatif de supériorité

| Adjectifs / adverbes | Superlatif |
|---|---|
| *1 syllabe / 2 syllabes en -y, -er, -ow, -le*<br>*late* | *the -est*<br>*the latest* |
| *2 syllabes et plus*<br>*efficiently* | *the most*<br>*the most efficiently* |

*Most* + adjectif = *very* → *Their techniques are most / very interesting.*

**2.** « Le moins… » : le superlatif d'infériorité
Quel que soit le nombre de syllabes, l'adjectif / l'adverbe est précédé de *the least*.
→ *That is **the least** eye-catching package I have ever seen.*

**3.** Complément de l'adjectif

- On emploie *in* pour un lieu ou un groupe, *of* pour le temps.

*He's far **the best salesman in** our team.* *This is one of **the best results of** the year.*

- *One of the* + superlatif + nom au pluriel (souvent avec le *present perfect*)

→ *This is **one of the best offers** on the market.*

! Pas de *the* après le génitif ou l'adjectif possessif.
*She's the shop's worst salesperson.* *It's our prettiest window display.*

## Formations irregulières

| Adjectifs / adverbes | Comparatif | Superlatif |
|---|---|---|
| *good / well* | *better … than* | *the best* |
| *bad* | *worse … than* | *the worst* |
| *far* | *farther / further … than* | *the farthest / furthest* |
| *old* | *older / elder … than* | *the oldest / eldest* |
| *much / many* | *more … than* | *the most* |
| *little / few* | *less (U) than / fewer (C)* | *the least (U) / the fewest (C)* |

! *Further* peut aussi signifier « plus de ». → *Have you had further news about the complaint?*

# Les adjectifs composés

Les adjectifs composés permettent de condenser une longue phrase. Ils sont invariables, comme les adjectifs simples.
*a sales contrat with five pages* = *a five-page sales contrat*
*a company which is ten years old* = *a ten-year old company*

## Comment construire un adjectif composé ?

Pensez : 1 + 2 = 3 (1 et 2 lié par un trait d'union) :
(1) *cutting* + (2) *edge* = (3) *technology*.
L'adjectif (1) décrit (2). 1 et 2 ensemble décrivent (3)

| Formation des adjectifs composés | Exemples |
|---|---|
| adjectif + nom | *a* ***three-hour*** *meeting* |
| nom + adjectif | *a* ***user-friendly*** *computer* |
| adjectif + nom *-ed* | *a* ***small-minded*** *manager* |
| adj. / adv. / nom + participe passé | *a* ***self-employed*** *consultant*<br>*a* ***well-known*** *brand*<br>***computer-assisted*** *design (CAD)* |
| adj. / adv. / nom + V-*ing* | *a* ***slow-moving*** *article*<br>*a* ***long-lasting*** *product*<br>*a* ***labour-saving*** *device* |
| verbe + nom | *a* ***tell-tale*** *mark* |
| auxiliaire + verbe | *a* ***would-be*** *manager* |

PRODUCTS



## 1 Formez les comparatifs et les superlatifs des adjectifs et adverbes suivants.

| | Adjective/ adverb | Comparative | Superlative |
|---|---|---|---|
| 1. | easy | | |
| 2. | down-market | | |
| 3. | good | | |
| 4. | wide | | |
| 5. | quietly | | |
| 6. | bad | | |
| 7. | simple | | |
| 8. | wet | | |
| 9. | little / few | | |
| 10. | hard | | |

## 2 Complétez les phrases par un comparatif ou un superlatif.

**1.** Our ski resort had a (great) ............................ influx of tourists than ever before.

**2.** That package tour has (efficient) ............................ travel infrastructures than the other one.

**3.** I would suggest the atacama desert in chile, it's (quiet) ............................ place around.

**4.** The tourist market doesn't look too good, but it could get (good) ............................ / (bad) ............................

**5.** The (smart) ............................ place to stay is the Explora, a luxurious hotel in the town centre.

**6.** That seaside resort was (crowded) ............................ place I've ever been to.

**7.** You usually suffer (little) ............................ from jetlag travelling West to East.

**8.** It is one of the (remote) ............................ and (little explored) ............................ places in the world.

**9.** The cut-price operators are not always a lot (cheap) ............................ than the upmarket ones.

**10.** One of the (popular) ............................ expeditions is to the Valley of the Moon.

**11.** The tour operator in the high street offers (good) ............................ value for money around.

**12.** Sightseeing and shopping in the local markets is much (exhausting) ............................ than sitting on the beach all day long.

## 3 Complétez les phrases avec les mots suivants.

*more... more... – the least – more... less... cheaper... greater... – more... better... – less... less...*

**1.** The .................... work I do today, the .................... I do tomorrow.

**2.** There are .................... and .................... openings for our product.

**3.** The ............................ cost-effective it is, the ............................ .

**4.** The market is getting .................... and .................... competitive.

**5.** That's one of .................... informative meetings I've ever been to.

**6.** The .................... your costs, the .................... your margin.

## 4 Entourez l'erreur et corrigez-la !

**1.** The market share is the same than last year.

..............................................................................................

..............................................................................................

..............................................................................................

**2.** Do you think you could get back to me as sooner as possible?

..............................................................................................

..............................................................................................

..............................................................................................

**3.** The new production line is twice more streamlined than the old one.

..............................................................................

..............................................................................

..............................................................................

**4.** The metal alloy from the new supplier is not as strong so the former one.

..............................................................................

..............................................................................

..............................................................................

**5.** Your sales director sounds almost so bad-tempered as mine!

..............................................................................

..............................................................................

..............................................................................

**6.** PMB PLC. doesn't have as good reputation as JMB Inc.

..............................................................................

..............................................................................

..............................................................................

**7.** The foreign market is just important as the domestic market.

..............................................................................

..............................................................................

..............................................................................

**8.** They haven't got many customers any more – maybe only as little as ten.

..............................................................................

..............................................................................

..............................................................................

## 5 Construisez un adjectif composé à partir des indices en italique.

**1.** *A trade fair which lasts four days.*

..............................................................................

..............................................................................

..............................................................................

**2.** *A note worth twenty euros.*

..............................................................................

..............................................................................

..............................................................................

**3.** An accountant who has been well trained.

..............................................................................

..............................................................................

..............................................................................

**4.** A product which has been badly designed.

..............................................................................

..............................................................................

..............................................................................

**5.** An assistant who works hard.

..............................................................................

..............................................................................

..............................................................................

**6.** A bid which you put in at the last minute.

..............................................................................

..............................................................................

..............................................................................

**7.** The lastest technology which "cuts the edge".

..............................................................................

..............................................................................

..............................................................................

**8.** A strike where you sit down.

..............................................................................

..............................................................................

..............................................................................

**9.** A person who uses their left hand.

..............................................................................

..............................................................................

..............................................................................

**10.** A cover which you can see through.

..............................................................................

..............................................................................

..............................................................................

## 6 Complétez les phrases par un comparatif ou un superlatif, selon le contexte, en utilisant les adjectifs et les adverbes ci-dessous.

*same – fast – good – reliable – important – much – tough – little – bad – fast – simple – fast – far*

**1.** It is .................... appliance we have ever had – it never breaks down.

**2.** Customer satisfaction is .................... a high selling price.

**3.** The new device is better there are only 3 parts – in the old device there were 10. There are .................... in the old device.

**4.** These two items are identical this one is just .................... the other one!

**5.** This machine is very quick – it can produce 500 items per second. It is .................... on the market.

**6.** The product quality is not very good. I'm sure you can design something .................... that.

**7.** I think we should look .................... into the complaints about our product defects.

**8.** At least the instructions for this device are not complicated – they are .................... than the last ones.

**9.** The competition we are getting from importers of foreign goods is getting .................... & .................... .

**10.** You get .................... satisfaction from seeing your product in every shelf and in every shop window.

**11.** The design of their new product is really not very attractive – they couldn't have done it .................... .

**12.** For most customers, .................... effort they have to make to understand how a product works, the better life is!

## 7 Retrouvez la réponse à la question.

**Questions**

**1.** Why did you choose one brand instead of the other? .....
**2.** Can't you write up a better marketing blurb than that? .....
**3.** How many people do you think we should invite to the launch party? .....
**4.** What is the downside of that input device? .....
**5.** What is the size of the smallest smartphone you know? .....
**6.** When would you like to see the first samples? .....
**7.** What's so special about that product design? .....
**8.** Why do you think the "green" foodstuff is selling so badly? .....
**9.** Did you realize that over 50% of consumers think that a brand's social network page is more important than their website? .....
**10.** We're really struggling to enter the market on the other side of the planet. .....

**Réponses**

**A.** The more the merrier.
**B.** It's a particularly cutting-edge and easy-to-use device.
**C.** XYZ is known to be much more efficient.
**D.** That's most interesting; we must use that information for our next campaign.
**E.** I agree, it's getting tougher and tougher to break into the Far Eastern market.
**F.** Today if possible, we really cannot wait any longer.
**G.** It's the best I can do.
**H.** It's not nearly as user-friendly as the other keyboard.
**I.** It's in the least attractive packaging I've ever seen.
**J.** I've no idea, but at least half as big as yours!

## CORRIGÉS

**1.** 1. easier (than) – the easiest 2. more down-market (than) – the most down-market 3. better (than) – the best 4. wider (than) – the widest 5. more quietly (than) / quieter than – the most quiet / the quietest 6. worse (than) – the worst 7. more simple / simpler (than) – the most simple / the simplest 8. wetter than – the wettest 9. less / fewer (than) – the least / the fewest 10. harder (than) – the hardest

**2.** 1. c – greater 2. c – more efficient 3. s – the quietest / the most quiet 4. c – better / worse 5. s – smartest 6. s – the most crowded 7. c – less 8. s – remotest – least explored 9. c – cheaper 10. s – most popular 11. s – the best 12. c – more exhausting

**3.** 1. The more work I do today, the less I do tomorrow. 2. There are less and less / more and more openings for our product. 3. The more cost-effective it is, the better . 4. The market is getting more and more / less and less competitive. 5. That's one of the least informative meeting I've ever been to. 6. The cheaper your costs, the greater your margin.

**4.** 1. The market share is the same as last year. 2. Do you think you could get back to me as soon as possible? 3. The new production line is twice as streamlined as the old one. 4. The metal alloy from the new supplier is not as strong as the former one. 5. Your sales director sounds almost as bad-tempered as mine! 6. PMB PLC doesn't have as good a reputation as JMB Inc. 7. The foreign market is just as important as the domestic market. 8. They haven't got many customers any more – maybe only as few as ten.

**5.** 1. A four-day trade fair. 2. A twenty-euro note. 3. A well-trained accountant. 4. A badly-designed product. 5. A hard-working assistant. 6. A last-minute bid. 7. Cutting-edge technology. 8. A sit-down strike. 9. A left-handed person. 10. A see-through cover.

**6.** 1. the most reliable 2. more important than. 3. not as many as / less than 4. the same as 5. the fastest 6. better than 7. further 8. simpler / more simple 9. tougher – tougher 10. the most 11. worse 12. the least

**7.** 1. C – 2. G – 3. A – 4. H – 5. J – 6. F – 7. B – 8. I – 9. D – 10. E

PRODUCTS

## 1 Placez les adjectifs entre parenthèses à la place qui convient.

**Score : ..... / 8**

**1.** The ......................... C.E.O. is ......................... of the problem with the contract. (aware)

**2.** The ......................... assistant ......................... is ......................... .(overworked / underpaid)

**3.** The ...................... advantage ...................... of the new product is the fact that it ................. is ......................... . (main / adaptable)

**4.** We sell our products in an ......................... market ......................... . (unstable)

**5.** This is the first ......................... launch date ......................... . (possible)

**6.** The ......................... items ......................... in France are not the same as those in the UK. (sold)

**7.** The ......................... trend ......................... is towards quality not low-cost. (underlying)

**8.** He ......................... seems ......................... I think we can offer him the job. (responsible)

## 2 Complétez les phrases après avoir choisi les comparatifs ou les superlatifs appropriés.

**Score : ..... / 14**

*the most efficient – best offer – more reliable – the most important factor – shorter – much cheaper – more regularly any more – no better – easily – better delivery – bigger quantities – more timely – less expensive freight*

Seller : You realise we have one of **(1)** ......................... after-sales services in the sector and the competitor's product is **(2)** ......................... than ours.

Buyer : Yes, I agree, but we need appliances which are **(3)** ......................... than yours, than we don't need after sales! Anyway, delivery lead times are **(4)** ......................... for us.

Seller : It is difficult for us to make our lead times **(5)** ......................... however, our transport costs are **(6)** ......................... than the competition.

Buyer : Can you guarantee me **(7)** ...................... deadlines, **(8)** ...................... costs and a discount if we order **(9)** .........................?

Seller : We should be able to manage that **(10)** ......................... in return, we expect your payments to be **(11)** ......................... and for you to put in your orders **(12)** ......................... .

Buyer : I'll check with the office about that – is that your **(13)** .........................?

Seller : That's right, but I can't wait **(14)** ...................... for your answer, other customers are queuing up.

## 3 Entourez la bonne réponse.

**Score : ..... / 16**

Looks **(1)** well / good, doesn't it? But rest assured, the "cook-all" is **(2)** more / most than a **(3)** pretty / prettily face. Amongst its **(4)** practicaler / more practical assets are a **(5)** mainly programmable / programmable main oven and a **(6)** conventional / convention top oven. The **(7)** new gas / gas new hob has four burners, and a **(8)** toughened-glasses / toughened-glass lid which **(9)** safety / security purposes incorporates our unique **(10)** cooking-safe / safe-cooking system – the **(11)** most safe / safest on the market. **(12)** Both / the both ovens also benefit from (13) self-cleaning systems

/ systems self-cleaning. The controls are **(14)** as easy-to-use than / as easy-to-use as they are stylish. A dual fuel or an **(15)** all-electric / all-electrics version are also available. For a brochure showing our **(16)** full / fully range of goods please call (0044) 1622 745 891.



## 4 Récrivez les phrases suivantes en utilisant un adjectif composé à partir des éléments soulignés.

**Score : ..... / 6**

**1.** It would certainly appear to be a company driven by performance.

..........................................................................................................................

**2.** They have a reputation for selling goods which last a long time.

..........................................................................................................................

**3.** It has become a retail company which is not the first but the second in size (large) in the country.

..........................................................................................................................

**4.** His salary has reached a sum made up of seven figures.

..........................................................................................................................

**5.** Have you heard of "Likus" – it's a discount chain which is growing fast?

..........................................................................................................................

**6.** They have finally decided to close down their store which is 133-years-old.

..........................................................................................................................

## 5 Traduisez les mots entre parenthèses.

**Score : ..... / 6**

**1.** The (meilleur) ......................... things come in little packages.

**2.** A (bon) ......................... name is better (que) ......................... riches.

**3.** The (plus) ......................... the (plus joyeux) ......................... .

**4.** (Le dernier) ......................... but not (le moins) ......................... .

**5.** (Mieux [vaut] tard que jamais) ......................... late (que) ......................... never.

**6.** (Plus) ......................... haste, (moins) ......................... speed.

**Score total : ..... / 50**

### CORRIGÉS

**1. 1.** The C.E.O. is aware of the contract. **2.** The overworked assistant is underpaid. **3.** The main advantage of the new product is the fact that it is adaptable. **4.** We sell our products in an unstable market. **5.** This is the first launch date possible. **6.** The items sold in France are not the same as those in the UK. **7.** The underlying trend is towards quality not low-cost. **8** He seems responsible, I think we can offer him the job. – **2. 1.** the most efficient **2.** no better **3.** more reliable **4.** the most important factor **5.** shorter **6.** much cheaper **7.** better delivery **8.** less expensive freight **9.** bigger quantities **10.** easily **11.** more timely **12.** more regulary **13.** best offer **14.** any more – **3. 1.** good **2.** more **3.** pretty **4.** more practical **5.** programmable main **6.** conventional top **7.** new gas **8** toughened-glass **9.** safety **10.** safe-cooking **11.** safest **12.** both **13.** self-cleaning systems **14.** as easy-to-use as **15.** all electric. **16.** full – **4. 1.** A performance-driven company. **2.** Long-lasting goods. **3.** He second-largest retail company. **4.** A seven-figure sum. **5.** A fast-growing discount chain. **6.** 133-years-old store. – **5. 1.** The best things come in little packages. **2.** A good name is better than riches. **3.** The more the merrier. **4.** (The) last but not (the) least. **5.** Better late than never. **6.** More haste, less speed.

# Les prépositions



## Les prépositions de temps

### 1. Un moment / une date

| |
|---|
| *at, in, on, ago, on time, in time, after, before, by, past, as soon as, by the time* |

***At (around/about)*** *10 o'clock, lunchtime, Christmas, the weekend, night...*
***In*** *half-an-hour, the morning, July, 2013...*
***On*** *Monday, Easter day, a birthday, February 28th, ...*
*He left 5 hours* ***ago****.*

***ago*** + **prétérit** = « il y a » (~~*there is 5 hours ago*~~)
*The train left* ***on time****.* → à l'heure
*Be at the airport* ***in time*** *for the baggage checks.* → dans les temps
*11 o'clock is* ***after*** *10 o'clock but 9 o'clock is* ***before*** *10 o'clock.* → après … avant
*You should check-in* ***by*** *9.00.* → pas plus tard que
*It's time to leave for the airport, it's* ***past*** *8 o'clock.* → passé
*I'll book the tickets* ***as soon as*** *I have the dates.* → dès que
***By the time*** *we get to the station, the train will have gone.* → d'ici à ce que

### 2. La durée

| |
|---|
| *for, since, during, while, throughout, until, within, from…to, between* |

*We travelled for 5 hours.* → pendant 5 heures
*How long have you been here? For 10 minutes. Since 2 o'clock.*

*For / since* + present perfect = « depuis »
Contrairement à *since*, *for* se trouve souvent avant un quantificateur.

**!** Ici nous utilisons le prétérit malgré *since*.
*It seems like ages since we saw you.* ~~*It seems like ages since we have seen you.*~~
*The phone rang a lot* ***during*** *the trip* → pendant le voyage
***While*** *we were travelling, the phone rang.* → pendant que nous voyagions
*He slept* ***throughout*** *the flight.* → pendant toute la durée du voyage
*The travel agency is open* ***until (/till)*** *6 pm.* → jusqu'à
*Please pay for your tickets* ***within*** *a fortnight* → sous
***From*** *Monday* ***to*** */* ***(until)*** *Friday.* → de … à
*The travel agency is closed* ***between*** *Christmas and the New Year* → entre

### 3. La continuité / le changement d'une situation

| |
|---|
| *still, no longer, yet, already, in the end, at last, as from* |

*He* ***still*** *hasn't come out of the meeting. Is he still in the meeting?*
→ situation inchangée (*still* se place en milieu de phrase)
*He hasn't left the meeting* ***yet****. Has he left the meeting* ***yet****?*
→ situation d'attente (*yet* se place en fin de phrase)
*He is* ***no longer*** */ (isn't any longer) in a meeting.* → situation changée
*He is* ***already*** *out of the meeting.* → situation anticipée (*already* se place en milieu de phrase)
Pour information, aux États-Unis certains utilisent le prétérit avec *just, yet, already*.
***In the end*** *he gave up waiting and went home* → Finalement
*We've been waiting for ages, I'm glad that you're here* ***at last****!* → Enfin
***As from*** *now I shall always travel first class.* → À partir de

# Les prépositions de lieu et de mouvement

## Pour (se) situer dans l'espace et pour indiquer un mouvement

| | | | | | |
|---|---|---|---|---|---|
| *AT* (à – Statique) | + | *He's at work.* | *TOWARDS* (vers) (1) | → + | *Go towards the church.* |
| *TO* (à – Dynamique) | → | *Go to the office.* | *UP/DOWN* (en haut, en bas) | ↗ ↘ | *Drive up/down the hill.* |
| *FROM* (de) | + → | *From London to Paris.* | *BY* (à côté de) | + + | *It's by the ring road.* |
| *ON* (sur) | ○ on — | *Ride on the beach on a bike.* | *NEXT TO / BESIDE* (à côté de) | + + | *Do sit next to me.* |
| *ON TOP OF* (statique) | ○ on ═ | *On top of the pile.* | *NEAR* (près de) | + + | *I live near the factory.* |
| *ONTO* (sur) (dynamique) | ↘ — | *Get onto the bus.* | *PAST* (au-delà de) | → □ | *Go past the town hall.* |
| *OFF* (de) | ↗ — | *Take your shoes off the table.* | *BEYOND* (au-delà de) | → □ | *Don't go beyond the limits.* |
| *IN* (dans) | [+] | *He is in the bath right now.* | *AWAY* (from) (éloigné (de)) | + → | *The works are away from town.* |
| *INTO* (dans) | → [+] | *Get into the taxi before it rains.* | *FAR AWAY* (from) (très éloigné (de)) | + ↘ | *He's far away from here.* |
| *OUT OF* (de) | □→ | *Get the milk out of the fridge.* | *AGAINST* (contre) | /\| | *Lean your bike against the wall.* |
| *INSIDE* (à l'intérieur de) | [+] | *Come inside, it's cosy.* | *BETWEEN* (entre) | + // + | *It's between the two trees.* |
| *OUTSIDE* (dehors) | + □ | *Outside it's so icy.* | *AMONG* (parmi) *AMONGST* | + / + + + + | *The cat among the pigeons.* |
| *UNDER* (sous) *UNDERNEATH* *BENEATH* | — □ | *Put your case under the bed.* | (A)ROUND (autour (de)) | ⟲ | *Go (a)round the roundabout.* |
| *OVER* (sur/par-dessus) | → □ | *Go over the bridge.* | *AHEAD* (devant) | + → | *Road work ahead.* |
| *ABOVE** (au-dessus) | □ — | *They live above the shop.* | *IN FRONT OF* (devant) | + □ | *Park in front of the office.* |
| *BELOW** (en-dessous) | — □ | *The garage is below the flat.* | *BEHIND* (derrière) *IN BACK OF* | □ + | *Hide behind the bush.* |
| *OPPOSITE* (en face de) | + \|\| + | *It is opposite the bar.* | *ALONG* (le long de) | — → — | *Go along the road.* |
| *ACROSS* (à travers) | –\|\|→ | *Walk across the park.* | *THROUGH* (à travers) | –□→ | *Drive through the forest.* |

\+ = Statique → = dynamique * sur un plan vertical

1. aussi : *upwards, downwards, backwards, forwards*…

Un verbe suivant une préposition prend la forme « *-ing* ».

# EXERCICES



## 1 Complétez les phrases suivantes par *still, no longer, yet* ou *already*.

**1.** Have you checked-in for flight AF401 ....................?

**2.** The check-in desk isn't open .................. what shall I do?

**3.** However, some people haven't gone through customs and immigration .................... .

**4.** Has the plane for Dubai .................... left?

**5.** No, there's .................... time if you run to gate 41.

**6.** They haven't closed the departure .................... .

**7.** You must have a place for me, I booked my seat 2 months .............. .

## 2 Complétez les phrases à l'aide des prépositions de temps suivantes :

*while – during – on time – in time – at the end – in the end – at last*

**1.** He fell asleep .................... the drive to Basel.

**2.** We looked hard to find the cheapest flight ................ we decided to fly with Jetsimple.

**3.** The telephone rang three times ................ we were on the train.

**4.** What a nice surprise, the train is .................... .

**5.** It has been a long trip, but we have arrived ................ .

**6.** .................... of the rough voyage, the passengers got off the ship quickly.

**7.** We have to leave at 5 am sharp tomorrow morning, please be at the office .................... .

## 3 Complétez les phrases suivantes par *since, for* ou *ago*.

**1.** How long have you been waiting for the plane? .............. 8.30 this morning!

**2.** They travelled .............. three days without stopping.

**3.** He last went to the headquarters in Rome three years ..............

**4.** The company has been in Blois .............. 1985.

**5.** We were called to the lounge half an hour .............. .

**6.** My luggage has been held up in Moscow .............. 2 days now.

## 4 Complétez le dialogue à l'aide des prépositions de temps suivantes.

*at – in – on – from – by that time – to – before – after – by – in – until – by the time*

Client: Good morning, I'd like to rent a car **(1)** .............. Monday **(2)** .............. Thursday.

Agency: When would you like to pick it up?

Client: **(3)** .............. Monday, early **(4)** .............. the morning. Say **(5)** .............. 6 am.

Agency: Return on Thursday. You should bring the car back **(6)** .............. 6 pm.

Client: I don't know if I can be there **(7)** .............. 7 pm. Can you wait **(8)** .............. then?

Agency: We'll be shut **(9)** .............. , I'm afraid.

Client: I can only leave Paris **(10)** .............. . The meeting, at 5.30 pm, **(11)** .............. . I drive to Romorantin, it'll be too late.

Agency: I'll have to check that. Could you ring me back **(12)** .............. an hour?

## 5 Entourez la bonne réponse.

**1.** The travel agent is open within / throughout the day, but closed between / as from 12.00 and 1.00.

**2.** You can pick up the tickets past / as from tomorrow, but don't go past / as from the end of the week.

**3.** Please pay for your ticket within / between one month.

**4.** I would like confirmation of the booking as soon as / as from possible please.

**5.** As it's a long haul flight, you'll have a stopover from / to about 11 am from / to about 3 pm.

**6.** If you want to benefit from the special price tickets, you should book between / within now and the end of the month.

## 6 Complétez les phrases ci-dessous par la préposition qui convient. (Plusieurs réponses sont parfois possibles.)

**1.** It is ..................... the main building, ..................... the factory.

**2.** It is ..................... the meeting room and the canteen.

**3.** It is ..................... the first floor, ..................... showroom which is ..................... the ground floor.

**4.** ..................... the showroom, is an underground car park.

**5.** When you arrive, go directly ..................... the building.

**6.** The receptionist's desk is just ..................... you. Ring the bell because she works ..................... a screen and may not see you arrive.

**7.** You may be ..................... several applicants, so you may have to wait.

## 7 À l'aide des indices entre parenthèses, complétez le texte par les prépositions de lieu qui conviennent.

How to get (à) **(1)** ......... our factory (en provenance de) **(2)** ............ our head office. Go (sous) **(3)** ............ the bridge, (en bas) **(4)** ............ the steep slope, and turn (dans) **(5)** ............ Well Street. Come (de) **(6)** ............ Well Street and then go (à travers) **(7)** ............ the main road. Drive (le long de) **(8)** ............ the country road for about 5 kilometres. Go (en haut) **(9)** ............ the hill and then drive (au-delà de) **(10)** ............ the industrial estate – don't go (à travers) **(11)** ............ it or you'll get completely lost! At this time you are going (éloigné de) **(12)** ............ town. Go (autour de) **(13)** ............ the roundabout. You'll then get (sur) **(14)** ............ the motorway at exit 9 and get (de) **(15)** ............ again at exit 11. Pay (à) **(16)** ............ the toll and go (par-dessus) **(17)** ............ the flyover (vers) **(18)** ............ the city centre. You'll see traffic lights (devant) **(19)** ............ turn (à droite) **(20)** ............ and you cannot miss the factory on your left.

## 8 Précisez la place des chiffres du carré ci-dessous en utilisant les prépositions suivantes :

*in the middle/centre – at the top – at the bottom – on the right – on the left – bottom left – top right – in the left-hand corner*

| | | |
|---|---|---|
| 1 | 2 | 3 |
| 4 | 5 | 6 |
| 7 | 8 | 9 |

**1.** ..........................................................................

**2.** ..........................................................................

**3.** ..........................................................................

**4.** ..........................................................................

**5.** ..........................................................................

**6.** ..........................................................................

**7.** ..........................................................................

**8.** ..........................................................................

**9.** ..........................................................................

### CORRIGÉS

**1.** 1. yet 2. any longer 3. yet 4. already 5. still 6. yet
**2.** 1. during 2. in the end 3. while 4. on time 5. at last 6. at the end 7. in time
**3.** 1. since 2. for 3. ago 4. since 5. ago 6. for 7. ago
**4.** 1. from 2. to 3. on 4. in 5. at 6. by 7. before 8. until 9. by that time 10. after 11. by the time 12. in
**5.** 1. throughout – between 2. as from – past 3. within 4. as soon as 5. from 6. between
**6.** 1. in – opposite / near / by 2. between 3. on – above – on 4. below / under 5. inside / into 6. in front of – behind 7. among
**7.** 1. to 2. from 3. under 4. down 5. into 6. out of 7. across 8. along 9. up 10. past 11. through 12. (far) away from 13. around 14. onto 15. off 16. at 17. over 18. towards 19. ahead 20. right
**8.** 1. at the top on the left / top left / in the top left-hand corner 2. at the top in the middle 3. at the top on the right / top right / in the top right-hand corner 4. on the left in the middle / middle left 5. in the middle 6. on the right in the middle / middle right 7. at the bottom on the left / bottom left / in the bottom left-hand corner 8. at the bottom in the middle 9. at the bottom on the right / bottom right / in the bottom right-hand corner.

# Verbes et prépositions

**Comparez !**

***Get off** / **on** the bus at Sloane Square.*
→ Descendez du / montez dans le bus à Sloane Square.
Le verbe est suivi d'une préposition en anglais comme en français, mais ce ne sont pas les mêmes.

*We must **listen to** the announcement about the flight times.*
→ Nous devons écouter l'annonce concernant les heures de vol.
Le verbe anglais est suivi d'une préposition. Le verbe français ne l'est pas.

***Ask** the air hostess **for** more information.*
→ Demandez à l'hôtesse de l'air pour plus d'informations.
Le verbe français est suivi d'une préposition. Le verbe anglais ne l'est pas.

## Les principaux verbes anglais avec prépositions

| | |
|---|---|
| *– care (give importance to), complain, read, talk (something / someone)*<br>*– do (something about something)*<br>*– dream (topic)*<br>*– hear (be told)*<br>*– remind (someone about something – don't forget)*<br>*– think (concentrate on)*<br>*– warn* | ***+ ABOUT*** |
| *– protect* | ***+ AGAINST*** |
| *– abide* | ***+ BY*** |
| *– aim, glance, laugh, look, point, smile, stare*<br>*– shout (angry)*<br>*– throw (to hit something, often in anger)* | ***+ AT*** |
| *– account, beg, hope, long, search, wait*<br>*– apply, apologise, ask (for something)*<br>*– ask, charge, forgive, thank (someone for something)*<br>*– blame (someone / something for something)*<br>*– care (like something)*<br>*– leave (destination)*<br>*– pay (someone for someone / something)* | ***+ FOR*** |
| *– adapt (from something)*<br>*– escape, hide, part*<br>*– hear (have a phone call / letter)*<br>*– protect (someone from something)*<br>*– suffer (an illness)* | ***+ FROM*** |
| *– abide (poetical and rather archaic), believe, specialize, succeed, take part* | ***+ IN*** |
| *– break, bump, crash, cut, drive, divide, run, split, translate* | ***+ INTO*** |

| | |
|---|---|
| *– consist, die, smell<br>– accuse (someone)<br>– approve (something / someone)<br>– complain (a pain / disease)<br>– dream (imagine)<br>– hear (know about)<br>– remind (someone of something = makes you remember)<br>– think (idea / opinion)* | ***+ OF*** |
| *– comment, concentrate, depend, get, insist, live, rely, spend<br>– blame (something on someone)<br>– congratulate (someone on something)<br>– wait (someone)* | ***+ ON*** |
| *– adapt (to something)<br>– admit, agree, announce, answer, apologize, charge, describe, demonstrate, explain, listen, mention, point out, prefer, prove, report, suggest, speak, talk (someone)<br>– write (something) to (someone)<br>– apply, complain, confess, happen (someone)<br>– apologise (someone for something)<br>– introduce (someone to someone)<br>– invite (someone to something)<br>– shout (to be heard)<br>– throw (to be caught)* | ***+ TO*** |
| *– agree, charge, collide, cover, fill / fill up, part, provide, supply* | ***+ WITH*** |
| *– answer, ask, cost, deny, forgive, obey, permit, phone, refuse, remind, tell, thank (someone)<br>– change, deny, discuss, doubt, enter, guarantee, lack, play, remember, tackle (something)* | ***Pas de Preposition*** |

Dans cette liste, certaines prépositions se trouvent dans plusieurs cases. Une préposition différente modifiera le sens du verbe. La liste n'est pas exhaustive.

## Verbes à particule (*phrasal verbs*)

**Comparez !**

*He is **looking up** at the top of the Eiffel Tower.*
→ Il regarde en haut = verbe + préposition

*He **looks up** to his boss.*
→ Il respecte son patron = *phrasal verb.*

*"Mrs Jones, I don't understand this word". "**Look it up** in the dictionary".*
→ Cherchez dans une source de référence (dictionnaire, Internet…) = *phrasal verb.*

**!** La même combinaison de mots peut vouloir dire quelque chose de complètement différent.

On appelle *phrasal verbs* les verbes possédant une particule adverbiale qui modifie le sens du verbe de base.

On distingue deux catégories de *phrasal verbs* :

**1.** Les non-divisibles : l'objet se place automatiquement après la particule.
*The taxi will **call for** you at 8 am.*

**2.** Les divisibles : l'objet se place, au choix, avant ou après la particule.
*I dropped **Bill off**.* *I dropped **off Bill**.*

Lorsque l'objet est un pronom, celui-ci se place obligatoirement entre le verbe et la particule.
*I dropped **him** off.*

Mais, ne séparez pas les deux parties du *phrasal verb* :
– Si l'objet est très long ;
*He **filled in** the immigration form for the U.A.E.*
– Si le verbe est suivi d'une préposition.
*I can't **keep up** with airline prices!*

## Adjectifs et prépositions

**Comparez !**

*He was very angry at the air hostess when she spilt the coffee on his suit.*
*He was very angry about the stain on his new suit.*

| | |
|---|---|
| – *amazed, astonished, brilliant, bad / good, clever, disgusted, excellent, hopeless, shocked, surprised, terrible at (something)*<br>– *angry, annoyed at (someone)* | ***AT*** |
| – *angry, annoyed, anxious, crazy, delighted, disappointed, excited, frightened, furious, glad, happy, nervous, pleased, upset, worried, sorry, surprised about (something)* | ***ABOUT*** |
| – *impressed, upset by (someone / something)*<br>– *amazed, annoyed, astonished, delighted, disapointed, disgusted, excited, shocked, surprised, worried by (something)* | ***BY*** |
| – *sorry for (doing something)*<br>– *(feel) happy / pleased / sorry for (someone)*<br>– *famous, grateful, responsible for (something)* | ***FOR*** |
| – *absent from, different from* | ***FROM*** |
| – *disappointed in (someone) / interested, involved in (something)* | ***IN*** |
| – *afraid, ashamed, frightened, scared, terrified of (someone / something)*<br>– *kind / nice of (someone to do something)*<br>– *aware, certain, critical, envious, fond, full, glad, (in)capable, independent, jealous, proud, short, sick, sure, suspicious, tired, tolerant, typical of (someone / something)* | ***OF*** |
| – *dependent on, keen on* | ***ON*** |
| – *(be) nice / kind rude to (someone)*<br>– *similar / identical to (someone / something)*<br>– *prior to (something)*<br>– *close, engaged / married, grateful, polite / rude to (someone)* | ***TO*** |
| – *angry, annoyed, delighted, disgusted, furious, impatient, involved … with (someone)*<br>– *bored, busy, delighted, crowded, familiar, fed up, pleased, disappointed with (something),*<br>– *happy, good, impressed, satisfied, tired with (someone / something)* | ***WITH*** |

Dans cette liste, certaines prépositions se trouvent dans plusieurs cases. Une préposition différente modifiera le sens. La liste n'est pas exhaustive.

TRAVELLING AROUND

## 1 Complétez cette conversation avec les prépositions qui conviennent.

Jim : Jane, can you write an e-mail **(1)** ........................ the head office about my visit?

Jim : Also, please remind me **(2)** ........................ taking the spreadsheets, or I might forget.

Jane : All right. Could you just look **(3)** ........................ your itinerary to make sure it's not too full?

Jim : Yes, I think I remember I complained **(4)** .......... .............. that last time !

Jane : We must also ask the bank to provide you **(5)** ....... ................ some foreign currency.

Jim : Good point. Have you heard **(6)** ........................ the airline about their baggage policy ?

Jane : Oh, and Jim, don't forget that you have to apply **(7)** ........................ a visa.

Jim : Jane, I really do rely **(8)** ........................ you for your help – thank heavens you're here!

## 2 Entourez l'erreur et corrigez-la !

**1.** Remember to get from the bus at the Watershed office block.

..............................................................................

..............................................................................

**2.** Ask to the air hostess if we can get up and walk around.

..............................................................................

..............................................................................

**3.** I hope we don't have to wait the plane much longer.

..............................................................................

..............................................................................

**4.** Could you phone to the travel agent and book the ticket ?

..............................................................................

..............................................................................

**5.** I think these directions need to be translated in English.

..............................................................................

..............................................................................

**6.** Don't forget to tell to Mr Jones that we are arriving early on Monday morning.

..............................................................................

..............................................................................

## 3 Complétez les phrases à l'aide des mots choisis dans chacune des deux listes.

| Verb | Particle |
|---|---|
| check – check – fill – held – see – stop – take – turn | in – off – off – out – over – round – up – up |

**1.** Please remember to ...................... one hour before departure time.

**2.** Don't forget to ................. the car with petrol before we leave.

**3.** If you go past the warehouse, you will have gone too far, and you'll have to .................. .

**4.** Did the plane ................. on time yesterday?

**5.** The hotel rules say that you must ................. before midday.

**6.** So sorry that we're late, we were ................. by the road works.

**7.** I have to go to the station to ................. the C.E.O. this afternoon.

**8.** It's a long-haul flight, you'll have to ................. in Singapore.

## 4 Remettez dans le bon ordre les mots soulignés dans chaque phrase.

**1. a)** We have to <u>meeting off the call</u>.

..............................................................................

..............................................................................

**b)** Can't we just <u>put back it to</u> another date ?

..............................................................................

..............................................................................

**2. a)** We have a come problem against up.

..............................................................................

..............................................................................

**b)** We will have to of agreement out the back.

..............................................................................

..............................................................................

**3. a)** John organised the meeting – last up he it week set.

..............................................................................

..............................................................................

**b)** We have to forward the date of the meeting with B&B Inc. bring.

..............................................................................

..............................................................................

**4. a)** The secretary minutes took down the during the meeting.

..............................................................................

..............................................................................

**b)** Here's the report, it would be a good idea if you could look over it.

..............................................................................

..............................................................................

## 5 Associez chaque adjectif à sa préposition. Puis, utilisez-les pour compléter les phares.

| | |
|---|---|
| absent • | |
| angry • | • about |
| delighted • | • at |
| different • | • by |
| familiar • | • from |
| good • | • of |
| tired • | • with |
| typical • | |
| worried • | |

**1.** The train was very late, and the passenger got very ............................... the ticket controller.

**2.** She is ............................... the health hazards of flying a long way.

**3.** He's always on an aeroplane – he must be very ........ ........................ travelling.

**4.** I was ............................... their invitation to a conference in Washington.

**5.** It was ............................... James to book a first-class ticket.

**6.** Air travel these days is very ............................... what it was before.

**7.** You won't get lost, Bill is ............................... the town.

**8.** The manager is on business trip, he will be ............. .................. the office for 2 weeks.

## 6 Entourez la bonne réponse.

**1.** The steward on the aeroplane was rude to / at me!

**2.** They are very interested in / of opening a subsidiary abroad.

**3.** Meet sheila, she is responsible about / for booking all our travel arrangements.

**4.** I'm not very keen at / on the idea of taking the tunnel – I'd rather take the plane.

**5.** I'm furious about / by having been over-charged by the taxi driver.

**6.** This hotel is very similar at / to the one we stayed in for the London trade fair.

**7.** I'm a bit nervous of / about the flight to Dehli – I've never been on an aeroplane before.

**8.** We showed him where the factory was, and he was very grateful for / of our help.

**9.** He was disappointed by / in both the food and the service offered by the airline – he'll go with another company next time.

## 7 Ajoutez la bonne préposition (ou Ø) après le verbe ou l'adjectif.

**1.** I would like to remind .......... you that the company does not pay for business class tickets.

2. The passengers are blaming the pilot .......... the very bumpy flight.

3. We were very satisfied .......... the service on the high-speed train in China.

4. The captain threw the line .......... the man on the quayside, who caught it and tied up the ferry.

5. You do not need to shout .......... the bus driver just because there's a traffic jam. It's not his fault!

6. It was so nice ............ the hotel manager to upgrade our room.

7. The travel agency specializes .......... journeys to South Africa.

8. What do you think .......... the idea of have conference calls and no more travelling?

9. Well done James! I was very impressed .......... the way you negotiated our travelling expenses with the accounts department.

10. I would like to congratulate you .......... your skillful driving.

11. I'm afraid you'll have to pay .......... the damage to your hotel room Mr. Bull.

12. She's really scared .......... flying but has to take a plane at least once a week.

13. I guarantee .......... you that our plane will be late yet again!

14. Just because I'm the CEO, you don't have to wait .......... me hand and foot!

15. I'm sorry sir but you must abide .......... the rules and not take any liquids onto the plane.

**8 Choisissez la bonne réponse. (Référez-vous à l'annexe 4 pour plus de verbes à particule).**

1. I'm off to the station to ......... the Italian supplier.
**a)** pick out **b)** pick up **c)** pick into

2. The hotel says that we have to .......... before 6 pm. Any later and we lose our room.
**a)** check in **b)** check over **c)** check out

3. If you could just pay for my ticket, and I'll .......... when my paycheck comes in.
**a)** pay it for **b)** pay back you **c)** pay you back

4. I'm sorry we're so late but the car .......... and it took ages to get a hire car.
**a)** broke into **b)** broke up **c)** broke down

5. That travel voucher is worth a lot of money. Please don't...........
**a)** throw it away **b)** throw out it **c)** throw it over

6. Before I give you the keys, could you please .......... this form?
**a)** fill up **b)** fill in **c)** fill into

7. Do you think you could .......... at the airport at the end of the afternoon?
**a)** drop me off **b)** take me off **c)** pick me off

8. If you don't pay attention, travel expenses certainly .......... fast!
**a)** add on **b)** add out **c)** add up

9. I love flying, but I'm always rather nervous when the plane ...........
**a)** takes out **b)** takes off **c)** takes up

10. I've got dreadful jetlag. I hope it will .......... before the conference starts.
**a)** wear over **b)** wear off **c)** wear out

**CORRIGÉS**

**1.** 1. to 2. about 3. at 4. about 5. with 6. from 7. for 8. on
**2.** 1. get off the bus 2. ask the air hostess 3. wait for the plane 4. phone the travel agent 5. translated into english 6. tell Mr Jones
**3.** 1. check in 2. fill up 3. turn round 4. take off 5. check out 6. held up 7. see off 8. stop over
**4.** 1. a) call off the meeting / call the meeting off b) put it back to 2. a) come up against a problem b) back out of the agreement 3. a) he set it up last week b) to bring forward the date of the meeting with B&B Inc 4. a) took down the minutes / took the minutes down b) look it over
**5.** 1. angry at / with 2. worried about 3. tired of 4. delighted by 5. typical of 6. different from 7. familiar with 8. absent from
**6.** 1. to 2. in 3. for 4. on 5. about 6. to 7. about 8. for 9. by
**7.** 1. Ø – 2. for – 3. with – 4. to – 5. at – 6. of – 7. in – 8. of – 9. by – 10. on – 11. for – 12. of – 13. Ø – 14. on – 15. by
**8.** 1. B – 2. A – 3. C – 4. C – 5. A – 6. B (Fill out in US English) – 7. A – 8. C – 9. B – 10. B

TRAVELLING AROUND

## 1 Complétez cette description d'hôtel à l'aide d'une préposition.

Score : ..... / 8

**1.** There is a car park ................ the hotel.

**2.** The bedrooms are ................ the 3rd floor.

**3.** The business centre is ................ the fitness centre

**4.** And ................ the restaurant.

**5.** Go ..... reception to get to the meeting room.

**6.** The lifts take you ........... the 1st, 2nd and 3rd floors.

**7.** The phones are ................ the business centre.

**8.** Reception is ................ the meeting room and the lifts.

## 2 Retrouvez les prépositions qui manquent.

Score : ..... / 6

**1.** The head office is ................ 24 Smith street.

**2.** The subsidiary is ................ London.

**3.** The sales department is ................ the fourth floor.

**4.** We have several branches ................ the continent.

**5.** I'm afraid he is not here, he's ................ Italy.

**6.** The factory is ................ the corner of Apple Street and Pear Road.

## 3 À partir des données ci-dessous, répondez aux questions suivantes en utilisant une préposition.

Score : ..... / 8

*London = New York. Tuesday 26th january 2005. Flight AF801. Departure : 10.45 Arrival : 18.45 (British time). Baggage check-in at least 2 hours before departure.*
Call Freda at 18.45. Meeting point – next to passport control. For info : last visit in 2001.

**1.** Where is Bill going? ..........................................................................................

**2.** What time is his flight? ..........................................................................................

**3.** When must he check in his baggage? ..........................................................................................

**4.** How long does the flight last? ..........................................................................................

**5.** When is his flight (date)? ..........................................................................................

**6.** When must he call Freda? ..........................................................................................

**7.** Where must they meet? ..........................................................................................

**8.** He hasn't been to New York ........................................ years / .................................... 2001.

## 4 Entourez la ou les bonne(s) réponse(s).

Score : ..... / 10

**1.** This catalogue looks good, I shall send off for it / send it off for.

**2.** Here is the audit form, please fill in it / fill it in.

**3.** I don't understand why, but I just cannot get through to head office / get to head office through.

**4.** Here are the dashboards – could you hand out them / hand them out?

**5.** The lawyer has drawn up the agreement / drawn the agreement up.

**6.** Mr Been is on the line. Oh, can you put through him / put him through.

**7.** I must remember to ring back the supplier / to ring the supplier back.

**8.** Ask the accountant to go to the bank and take out some cash / take some cash out.

**9.** Could you pay back the money you borrowed from me / pay the money you borrowed from me back?

**10.** I'm sorry I can't help you now, but I have completely run out of time / run of time out.

## 5 Reliez le début et la fin de chaque phrase.

**Score : ..... / 10**

| | | | |
|---|---|---|---|
| I would like to thank you | **1.** • | • **A.** | with the service they offer. |
| I asked | **2.** • | • **B.** | for your help. |
| Do you suffer | **3.** • | • **C.** | for my passport. |
| He is quite aware | **4.** • | • **D.** | the air hostess for some coffee. |
| We are most satisfied | **5.** • | • **E.** | in our travel agent. |
| We are really disappointed | **6.** • | • **F.** | into Japanese for me? |
| I am sorry | **7.** • | • **G.** | of the advantages of taking the train. |
| What are you doing? I'm looking | **8.** • | • **H.** | for their in-flight food and service. |
| The company are famous | **9.** • | • **I.** | from jet lag? |
| Could you translate this | **10.** • | • **J.** | for being so late. |

## 6 Entourez la bonne réponse.

**Score : .... / 8**

**1.** They are annoyed about / at / with the cancellation.

**2.** When he was told about the overbooking, he shouted at / to the air hostess.

**3.** It was nice of / to them to call about the flight delays.

**4.** Thank you for reminding me about / of confirming the flight.

**5.** "It was a dreadful flight!" "I'm sorry about / for that."

**6.** He blamed the airline staff for / on losing his suitcase.

**7.** If you have any complaints, apply for / to the management.

**8.** He is frightened about / of flying.

**Score total : ..... / 50**

## CORRIGÉS

**1.** 1. in front of 2. on . 3. above 4. below 5. through 6. to 7. in 8. between
**2.** 1. at 2. in 3. on 4. on 5. in 6. at
**3.** 1. from London to New York. 2. at 10.45. 3. by / before 8.45. 4. for 8 hours. 5. on Tuesday 26th January. 6. as soon as he arrives / on arrival. 7. by / beside passport control. 8. for 4 years. / since 2001.
**4.** 1. send off for it 2. fill it in 3. get through to head office 4. hand them out 5. drawn up the agreement / drawn the agreement up 6. put him through 7. ring the supplier back / ring back the supplier 8. Both answers are possible. 9. pay back the money you borrowed from me 10. run out of time
**5.** 1. b 2. d 3. i 4. g 5. a 6. e 7. j 8. c 9. h 10. f
**6.** 1. about 2. at 3. of 4. about 5. about 6. for 7. to 8. of

Pour éviter les erreurs en anglais, il est parfois utile d'apprendre des petites « formules ».

## FOR + OBJECT + TO + VERB

| | |
|---|---|
| *It is important for a lawyer to be honest.* | → importance |
| *It is rare for a woman to be a stonemason.* | → fréquence |
| *It is easy for him to use that software.* | → difficulté / facilité |
| *It is too complicated for me to understand.* | → après "*too*" + adjectif |
| *The car isn't sporty enough for him to buy it.* | → après adjectif + "*enough*" |
| *She's waiting for the aeroplane to arrive.* | → après "*wait*" |
| *He'll arrange for your room to be upgraded.* | → après "*arrange*" |

## GET

| | |
|---|---|
| GET + NOM = obtenir | *He **got his electricity** bill this morning.* (Sens : obtenir.)<br>*I **got a cold** waiting at the bus stop.* (Sens : attraper.)<br>*Simon has **got a new job**!* (Sens : obtenir.) |
| GET + ADJECTIF = devenir | *Watch out – you're **getting fat**!* (Sens : tu es en train de grossir.)<br>*Mary and Jo are **getting married** in August.* (Sens : ils vont devenir mariés.)<br>*He **got soaked** on the boat trip.* (Sens : il est devenu trempé.) |
| GET + PRÉPOSITION = mouvement | *Hurry up and **get on** the bus before it leaves.*<br>***Get off** the train at Didcot.*<br>***Get into** the taxi quickly, we're running late.* |
| GET TO = arriver | *What time do we **get to** the station?*<br>*They **got to** the airport just in time!* |

## IT

- *It* + présent simple + *me* :

*It frightens me.* *Unemployment worries me.*

- *It's time* + prétérit : ***It's time** we **increased** our prices – our rivals did so ages ago.*
- *It's* + adjectif + sujet + *should* + base verbale :

***It's strange they should like** working the night shift. **It's nice he should want** to visit us.*

## LOOK, FEEL, TASTE, SOUND, SMELL

Ces verbes peuvent être utilisés comme « verbes de perception ». C'est l'impression que vous avez, ce n'est pas un fait.

- VERBE + ADJECTIF pour exprimer un état. Le verbe est au présent simple.

*That **looks expensive**.* *It **feels hot** in here.* *It **tastes delicious**.*
*It **sounds fascinating**.* *It **smells lovely**.*

- ***To look*** et ***to sound*** peuvent être suivis par un article + nom à la place de l'adjectif :

*It looks a good deal.* *They sound an efficient team.*

Ces verbes peuvent être suivis par *as if* ou *as though* :
*It **looks as** if they'll go bankrupt.* *You **sound as though** you're really fed up!*

• VERBE + *LIKE* pour exprimer une ressemblance. Le verbe est au présent simple.

*She **looks like** her sister.* *It **feels like** silk but it's not! It tastes like sugar but…*

*It **sounds like** a wonderful trip!* *It's a nice perfume, it **smells like** a flower.*

• En réponse à une question avec *be like*, utilisez *be*:

*What was the meeting like? It was really boring.*

*What is your boss like? He's very intelligent, but not very patient.*

• *FEEL LIKE* + *ING* pour une impression

*I'm tired. I **feel like going** on holiday.* *Do you **feel like taking** a few days off?*

## MAKE OR DO

***MAKE*** (utilisé plus souvent que *do*) (Voir aussi les causatifs, page 76)

Généralement, il a un sens plus pratique : la création ou la construction de quelque chose.

*Isabelle is making a prototype.* *Their firm is making a lot of money these days.*

Le fait d'être « bon » en quelque chose :

*He makes a good doctor.* *He would have made a good psychologist.*

On trouve aussi :

*MAKE SURE OF SOMETHING* = être sûr de… → *Make sure of optimal use of the tools.*

*MAKE SURE* + OBJET + VERBE = être sûr que… → *Make sure the computer is plugged in.*

*MAKE SURE* + OBJET + *BE* + ADJECTIF = vérifier que… → *Make sure the speaker is ready.*

*MAKE* = calcul → *£5.00 and £10.00, that makes £15.00.*

***DO***

– *Do* + nom = une activité → *He is **doing the time sheets**.*

– Pour remplacer un autre verbe → *Could you **do** the report? (do = write)*

– Pour parler du travail (intellectuel) → *Have you **done** your data update?*

– Pour parler de quelque chose de non précis

→ *What are you doing?* *He **is doing well** these days.*

*He **has done something** to the computer.*

Il est difficile de proposer une règle parfaite pour toutes les expressions utilisant *do* ou *make*. En voici quelques unes pour vous aider :

| DO | | MAKE | | |
|---|---|---|---|---|
| *the washing up (UK)* | *business* | *a mistake* | *a discovery* | *the bed* |
| *the dishes (US)* | *work* | *a profit / loss* | *money* | *a speech* |
| *a favour* | *one's best* | *a phone call* | *an appointment* | *enquiries* |
| *damage* | *with / without* | *a decision* | *a suggestion* | *a point* |
| *away with* | *an exercise* | *a comment* | *a remark* | *a complaint* |
| *good / harm* | *sport* | *an excuse* | *an exception* | *a difference* |
| *homework* | *without* | *an offer* | *a choice* | *a bid* |
| | | *an attempt* | *progress* | *demands* |
| | | *a journey* | *arrangements* | *a list / plan* |
| | | *friends* | *a joke* | *love / war* |
| | | *a noise / sound* | *a contribution* | |
| | | *a habit of doing something* | | |
| | | *a success of something* | | |

Une expression qui combine les deux ! ***Make do with*** (se contenter de).

*We don't have much food. We'll have to make do with what is left in the fridge.*

# L'ACCORD SUJET-VERBE

| Exemple | Explication |
|---|---|
| *There are some men outside who want to apply for the job.* | Pluriel irrégulier. |
| *The police have started a new recruitment campaign.* | Certains noms prennent toujours un pluriel. |
| *Safety glasses are compulsory if the job involves working with chemicals.* | Certains noms sous forme de paires (*scissors, glasses*...) sont toujours au pluriel. |
| *My colleagues and I are looking forward to the new trainee arriving.* | *And* = et (verbe au pluriel) ! Utilisez deux pronoms sujets. |
| *The boss or the employees look through the applications.* | *Or* = verbe au pluriel (à côté de "*the Smiths*" – pluriel) |
| *The employees or the C.E.O. chooses the new operative.* | *Or* = verbe au singulier (à côté de "*Mary*" – singulier) |
| *Either job offers an annual bonus/neither job offers an annual bonus.* | *Either / neither* = verbe au singulier sauf pour une interrogation avec *either of: Do either of you work overtime?* |
| *Either John or James is going to get the position.* | *Either* ... *or* = verbe au singulier |
| *Neither John nor James have suitable qualifications for the job.* | *Neither* ... *nor* = verbe au pluriel |
| *That information is very important to us.* | Verbe au singulier pour un nom indénombrable. |
| *Everybody wants job satisfaction.* | *Every / everybody / everyone / anyone / anybody / someone / no-one / nobody* = sont suivis par un verbe au singulier. |
| *Each person is responsible for their own working hours.* | *Each* = verbe au singulier |
| *The manager, but not the employees, has decided to change to flexi time.* | |
| *The employees, but not the manager, have decided to work a 35-hour week.* | Dans une phrase qui combine une partie positive et une partie négative, c'est la positive qui prime. |

# 100 VERBES IRRÉGULIERS

| | | | |
|---|---|---|---|
| *Be* | *was* | *been* | être |
| *Become* | *became* | *become* | devenir |
| *Begin* | *began* | *begun* | commencer |
| *Bend* | *bent* | *bent* | plier/courber |
| *Bet* | *bet* | *bet* | parier |
| *Break* | *broke* | *broken* | casser |
| *Bring* | *brought* | *brought* | apporter |
| *Broadcast** | *broadcast* | *broadcast* | diffuser |
| *Build* | *built* | *built* | construire |
| *Burn** | *burnt* | *burnt* | brûler |
| *Buy* | *bought* | *bought* | acheter |
| *Catch* | *caught* | *caught* | attraper |
| *Choose* | *chose* | *chosen* | choisir |
| *Come* | *came* | *come* | venir |
| *Cost* | *cost* | *cost* | coûter |
| *Cut* | *cut* | *cut* | couper |
| *Deal (with)* | *dealt* | *dealt* | s'occuper de |
| *Do* | *did* | *done* | faire |
| *Draw* | *drew* | *drawn* | dessiner |
| *Drink* | *drank* | *drunk* | boire |
| *Drive* | *drove* | *driven* | conduire |
| *Eat* | *Ate* | *eaten* | manger |
| *Fall* | *fell* | *fallen* | tomber |
| *Feel* | *felt* | *felt* | (se) sentir |
| *Fight* | *fought* | *fought* | (se) battre |
| *Find* | *found* | *found* | trouver |
| *Fly* | *flew* | *flown* | voler (avion) |
| *Forbid* | *forbade* | *forbidden* | interdire |
| *Forecast** | *forecast* | *forecast* | prévoir |
| *Forget* | *forgot* | *forgotten* | oublier |
| *Forgive* | *forgave* | *forgiven* | pardonner |
| *Freeze* | *froze* | *frozen* | geler |
| *Get* | *got* | *got* | obtenir |
| *Give* | *gave* | *given* | donner |
| *Go* | *went* | *gone* | aller |
| *Grow* | *grew* | *grown* | croître |
| *Hang* | *hung* | *hung* | pendre |
| *Have* | *had* | *had* | avoir |
| *Hear* | *heard* | *heard* | entendre |
| *Hide* | *hid* | *hidden* | (se) cacher |
| *Hit* | *hit* | *hit* | frapper |
| *Hold* | *held* | *held* | tenir |
| *Hurt* | *hurt* | *hurt* | (se) blesser |
| *Keep* | *kept* | *kept* | garder |
| *Know* | *knew* | *known* | savoir |
| *Lay* | *laid* | *laid* | poser |
| *Lead* | *led* | *led* | mener |
| *Learn** | *learnt* | *learnt* | apprendre |
| *Leave* | *left* | *left* | laisser/partir |
| *Lend* | *lent* | *lent* | prêter |
| *Let* | *let* | *let* | permettre |

# 100 VERBES IRRÉGULIERS

| | | | |
|---|---|---|---|
| *Lie* | *lay* | *lain* | être étendu |
| *Light* | *lit* | *lit* | allumer |
| *Lose* | *lost* | *lost* | perdre |
| *Make* | *made* | *made* | faire |
| *Mean* | *meant* | *meant* | vouloir dire |
| *Meet* | *met* | *met* | rencontre |
| *Pay* | *paid* | *paid* | payer |
| *Put* | *put* | *put* | mettre |
| *Quit* | *Quit* | *quit* | cesser |
| *Read* | *read* | *read* | lire |
| *Ride* | *rode* | *ridden* | aller à vélo |
| *Ring* | *rang* | *rung* | sonner |
| *Rise* | *rose* | *risen* | s'élever |
| *Run* | *ran* | *run* | courir / gérer |
| *Say* | *said* | *said* | dire |
| *See* | *saw* | *seen* | voir |
| *Sell* | *sold* | *sold* | vendre |
| *Send* | *sent* | *sent* | envoyer |
| *Set* | *set* | *set* | fixer / placer |
| *Shake* | *shook* | *shaken* | secouer |
| *Shoot* | *shot* | *shot* | tirer |
| *Show* | *showed* | *shown* | montrer |
| *Shrink* | *shrank* | *shrunk* | (se) rétrécir |
| *Shut* | *shut* | *shut* | fermer |
| *Sing* | *sang* | *sung* | chanter |
| *Sink* | *sank* | *sunk* | couler |
| *Sit* | *sat* | *sat* | être assis |
| *Sleep* | *slept* | *slept* | dormir |
| *Speak* | *spoke* | *spoken* | parler |
| *Spell** | *spelt* | *spelt* | épeler |
| *Spend* | *spent* | *spent* | dépenser |
| *Split* | *split* | *split* | fendre |
| *Spread* | *spread* | *spread* | étaler |
| *Stand* | *stood* | *stood* | être debout |
| *Steal* | *stole* | *stolen* | voler / dérober |
| *Stick* | *stuck* | *stuck* | coller |
| *Strike* | *struck* | *struck* | frapper |
| *Swim* | *swam* | *swum* | nager |
| *Take* | *took* | *taken* | prendre |
| *Teach* | *taught* | *taught* | enseigner |
| *Tear* | *tore* | *torn* | déchirer |
| *Tell* | *told* | *told* | dire / raconter |
| *Think* | *thought* | *thought* | penser |
| *Throw* | *threw* | *thrown* | jeter / lancer |
| *Understand* | *Understood* | *understood* | comprendre |
| *Wear* | *wore* | *worn* | porter |
| *Win* | *won* | *won* | gagner (jeu) |
| *Withdraw* | *withdrew* | *withdrawn* | retirer |
| *Write* | *wrote* | *written* | écrire |

* Prennent aussi une forme régulière en *-ed*.

# LES VERBES À PARTICULE

## COMMUNICATIONS

| Divisible | | Non-divisible | |
|---|---|---|---|
| *Cut off* | *disconnect (phone)* | *Get through* | *make contact (phone)* |
| *Draw up* | *write a document* | *Hang up* | *put phone down (in anger)* |
| *Fill in* | *complete a form* | *Hold / hang on* | *wait (esp. phone)* |
| *Hand out* | *distribute* | *Put in for* | *apply for* |
| *Put through* | *connect (phone)* | *Ring off* | *put the phone down* |
| *Ring back* | *phone again* | *Read over / through* | *examine quickly* |
| *Ring up* | *telephone* | *Send off / away for* | *ask for by the post* |
| *Send on* | *forward by post* | *Speak up* | *speak louder (phone)* |

## MEETINGS

| Divisible | | Non-divisible | |
|---|---|---|---|
| *Bring forward* | *advance the date* | *Back out of* | *withdraw from (agreement)* |
| *Call off* | *cancel* | *Be off* | *be cancelled* |
| *Get across* | *explain the meaning* | *Carry (go / keep) on* | *continue* |
| *Look over* | *examine carefully* | *Come up against* | *face / meet with a problem* |
| *Point out* | *draw attention to* | *Follow through* | *do something right to the end* |
| *Put back / off* | *delay (the date)* | *Look through* | *examine (document)* |
| *Set up* | *organise (a meeting)* | *Take down* | *record in writing* |
| *Take over* | *gain control* | *Think of* | *have an opinion of* |

## FINANCE

| Divisible | | Non-divisible | |
|---|---|---|---|
| *Average out* | *calculate to make an average* | *Cut down (on)* | *reduce (expenses)* |
| *Count up* | *add* | *Come into* | *receive money / property* |
| *Make out* | *write out a cheque* | *Go down* | *decrease / fall – prices, rates* |
| *Pay back* | *return money owed* | *Mount up* | *increase by addition* |
| *Put up* | *raise prices* | *Run out of* | *use all of / have no more of* |
| *Sell off* | *sell at a low price* | *Sell out of* | *sell all of one item* |
| *Take away* | *subtract* | *Take out* | *withdraw money from bank* |

## TRAVELLING

| Divisible | | Non-divisible | |
|---|---|---|---|
| *Drop off* | *take & leave someone somewhere* | *Check in* | *register (hotel, airport)* |
| *Fill up* | *make full (petrol tank)* | *Check out (of)* | *leave and pay (hotel)* |
| *Hold up* | *stop / delay traffic* | *Drop in on* | *visit unexpectedly* |
| *Pick up* | *go & collect someone / thing* | *Get off / on* | *leave / board plane, train...* |
| *Put forward* | *advance the time (watch...)* | *Set off / out* | *depart / leave on a journey* |
| *See off* | *say goodbye (at station...)* | *Stop over* | *stop to refuel etc. (plane)* |
| *Turn round* | *return & go back* | *Take off* | *leave the ground (plane)* |

## ANNEXE 4 LES VERBES À PARTICULE

| Divisible | | Non-divisible | |
|---|---|---|---|
| **THINGS** | | | |
| *Cut up* | *divide into several parts* | *Be off* | *have gone bad (eggs, etc.)* |
| *Put on / off* | *switch / turn on / off* | *Break down* | *stop working (machine)* |
| *Take off* | *undress / remove clothing* | *Check up on* | *make sure all is all right* |
| *Throw away / out* | *get rid of* | *Do away with* | *get rid of, abolish* |
| *Turn up* | *make louder* | *Follow out* | *put instructions into practice* |
| *Try on* | *put on clothes to see if they fit* | *Go out* | *stop burning, shining (light)* |
| *Try out* | *see if something works by using it* | *Go with* | *match (colour / shape...)* |
| *Wear out* | *make unusable after a lot of use* | *Wear off* | *effects disappear gradually* |
| **EMOTIONS** | | | |
| *Calm down* | *become less excited* | *Be taken aback* | *be surprised / shocked* |
| *Cheer up* | *become happier* | *Care about* | *take an interest in / love* |
| *Give up* | *stop doing – it's too difficult* | *Feel up to* | *feel capable of* |
| *Groan at* | *complain* | *Put up with* | *tolerate without complaining* |

## ANNEXE 5 LES COLLOCATIONS

Des mots qui sont fréquemment associés.

Les collocations sont composées de :

- VERBE + NOM

*Give a presentation* — *Make a decision* — *Run out of time*

- NOM + VERBE

*Snow falls* — *Rain pours* — *Ideas flow*

- VERBE + ADVERBE

*Wave frantically* — *Speak highly of* — *Remember rightly*

- VERBE + PRÉPOSITION + NOM

*Burst into tears* — *Run out of cash* — *Move into a house*

- ADJECTIF + NOM

*Regular exercise* — *Black coffee* — *Antique furniture*

- ADVERBE + ADJECTIF

*Wholly satisfied* — *Utterly stupid* — *Fully aware*

- NOM + NOM

*Bar of chocolate* — *A round of applause* — *Annual turnover*

- ADVERBE + VERBE

*Bitterly regret* — *Strongly suggest* — *Completely forget*

## ANNEXE 6 TABLEAU DES TEMPS

| PAST | PRESENT | FUTURE |
|---|---|---|
| *SIMPLE PAST*<br>*+ ED (irregular verbs)*<br>• Action et moment accompli<br>*We started the meeting when the C.E.O. arrived.* | *SIMPLE PRESENT*<br>*-s for 3rd person single*<br>• État de fait ou habitude<br>*He goes to work by car.*<br>• Expression du futur après *when, if, unless, as soons as, before, until* (sauf dans les questions directes et indirectes)<br>*When he arrives, we will start the meeting.* | *SHALL (I / we) & WILL (for the others)*<br>• Décision spontanée<br>*I'll ring you back. I won't forget.*<br>• Prédiction, estimation, calcul<br>*I think he will agree to our terms. He probably won't come tomorrow.*<br>• Simple fait (langage formel)<br>*The C.E.O. will visit next Monday.* |
| *PAST PROGRESSIVE*<br>*BE (past) + VERB -ing*<br>• Action ou événement en cours à un moment donné dans le passé<br>*We were talking when he arrived and he interrupted us.* | PRESENT PROGRESSIVE<br>BE (present) + VERB *-ing*<br>• Action en cours (à court ou long terme)<br>*I am revising my tenses.*<br>*We are developing a new project.*<br>• Événement planifié dans le futur, susceptible d'être noté dans un agenda (doit inclure une expression du futur)<br>*We are meeting the new supplier on Monday.* | BE TO<br>• Semblable à *will* (encore plus formel)<br>*The C.E.O. is to visit next Monday.* |
| *PRESENT PERFECT SIMPLE*<br>*HAVE (present) + PAST PARTICIPLE*<br>• Action commencée dans le passé et continuant jusqu'à maintenant<br>*He has been busy all day.*<br>• Action s'étant déroulée à un moment non déterminé dans le passé<br>*He has been to Paris.*<br>• Action s'étant déroulée à une période non encore achevée<br>*We have had good results this week.*<br>• Actualité récente<br>*The president has (just) arrived at the airport.* | *CONDITIONAL*<br>*(0) CONDITIONAL*<br>*SIMPLE PRESENT / SIMPLE PRESENT*<br>• Ordre, instruction<br>*If you press the button, the light goes on.* | *BE GOING TO*<br>*GOING TO + INFINITIVE*<br>• Intention<br>*James is going to employ new workers.* |
| | *(1) CONDITIONAL*<br>*SIMPLE PRESENT / FUTURE*<br>• Situation réelle<br>*If we put our prices up, we'll lose clients.* | *BE ABOUT TO*<br>• Futur proche<br>*It is about to break / it is going to break.* |
| | *(2) CONDITIONAL*<br>*SIMPLE PAST / MODAL*<br>• Situation irréelle, hypothétique<br>*If he won the lottery, he would retire.* | *FUTURE PROGRESSIVE*<br>• Action que vous serez en train de faire à un moment donné dans le futur<br>*Could I come and see you at 9 am? No, we will be having our daily meeting.* |

## ANNEXE 6 TABLEAU DES TEMPS

| | | |
|---|---|---|
| *PRESENT PERFECT PROGRESSIVE*<br>*HAVE / HAS BEEN + VERB -ing*<br>• Action commencée dans le passé et toujours en cours<br>*We have been working all day.*<br>• Résultat actuel d'une action récente<br>*She is tired now because she has been negotiating hard.* | *(3) CONDITIONAL*<br>*PAST PERFECT/MODAL PERFECT*<br>• Regret (passé)<br>*If I had known, I wouldn't have come.* | *FUTURE PERFECT*<br>• Événement accompli à un moment donné dans le futur<br>*Could I come and see you at 10 am? Yes, we will have finished our meeting.* |
| *PAST PERFECT SIMPLE*<br>*HAVE (past) + PAST PARTICIPLE*<br>• Événement antérieur à un autre dans le passé<br>*We had signed the deal before they changed their minds.* | | *FUTURE PERFECT PROGRESSIVE*<br>• Durée d'une action en train de se dérouler à un moment donné dans le futur<br>*By the time they get here, we will have been waiting for 2 hours.* |
| *PAST PERFECT PROGRESSIVE*<br>*HAD BEEN + VERB -ing*<br>• Passé, résultat d'une action ayant eu lieu dans un passé antérieur<br>*She was tired yesterday because she had been negotiating hard.* | | *FUTURE SEEN FROM THE PAST*<br>• Événement planifié mais non réalisé<br>*I was going to ring you, but...* |

## ANNEXE 7 LES MAJUSCULES

En anglais, les majuscules sont obligatoires :

• sur les titres
→ *Doctor Slater, the Prime Minister*

• sur les adjectifs de nationalité
→ *French cheese, an Italian poet.*

• sur les jours de la semaine et les mois
→ *Monday, Tuesday, May, June...* (mais ne pas sur les saisons).

• sur tous les mots d'un titre d'ouvrage (sauf les articles, conjonctions, prépositions et parfois les auxiliaires) :
→ *Pride and Prejudice.*

# LES PARTICIPES

Il y a deux sortes de participes : le présent (+*ing*) et le passé (+*ed* ou verbe irrégulier).

Ils peuvent être formés dans un verbe composé, ou employés comme un adjectif ou un nom.

| | Verbe composé | Adjectif | Nom |
|---|---|---|---|
| Participe présent | • Présent progressif<br>*He is eating breakfast.*<br>• Prétérit progressif<br>*He was worrying about the meeting.*<br>• Futur progressif<br>*We are going to New York tomorrow.*<br>*They will be sleeping at this time of night.*<br>• Futur perfect progressif<br>*He will have been waiting a long time.*<br>• Pour raccourcir une phrase active<br>*He ran the marathon singing.*<br>• Pour raccourcir une clause<br>*Looking at the beautiful scenery she felt her stress disappear.*<br>• Pour décrire "come, go, sit"<br>*They came running into the house.*<br>• Avec les verbes *feel, find, hear, listen to, notice, see, smell, watch*<br>*I heard him coming into the office.*<br>*Did you see him swimming; it's not surprising he won!* | *The whining secretary eventually got fired.*<br>*That speaker is really boring.* | Gérondif<br>*He dislikes eating in a hurry but she loves snacking at her desk.*<br>*Arnaud loves flying.*<br>*Making models out of matchsticks is a great hobby.* |
| Participe passé | • Le present perfect<br>*He has bought a new laptop computer.*<br>• Le past perfect<br>*We negotiated for ages but then found out they had already signed with someone else.*<br>• Le causatif<br>*They have had their trade secrets stolen.*<br>• Le passif<br>*The contract has now been signed.*<br>• Pour raccourcir une phrase passive<br>*Having been signed, the contract is now valid.* | *You can't work with a broken computer!*<br>*It was a good speech – the participants were very interested.*<br>• Adjectif composé<br>*A well-known artist.*<br>*A blue-eyed actor.* | |
| Participe passé + participe présent | • Present perfect progressif<br>*He's exhausted, he has been playing squash.*<br>• Past perfect progressif<br>*They had been waiting for hours when the train arrived at last.*<br>• Should have + been<br>*We should have been working this weekend but the conference has been called off.*<br>• Le "ayant fait"<br>*Having done the road map she then started on the dashboards.* | | |

# BASE VERBALE – INFINITIF OU *-ING*?

## BASE VERBALE (VERBE SANS *TO*)

• Après les auxiliaires *do, can, could, may, might, will, shall, would, should, must, had better... I have to, ought to*
*You must write the report.* *Do you use the Internet a lot?*

• Après *better not, would rather* et *why not*
*Why not give the supplier a ring?*

• Après *feel, hear, let, make, notice, see, watch* (verb + object + verb)
*He makes her work hard.* *I notice you use MRP.*

• Pour l'impératif
*Work out the figures and come back to me!*

## INFINITIF (VERBE AVEC *TO*)

• Pour traduire « à » ou « de »
*It is easy **to** understand.*

• Pour exprimer une intention
*Why did you go to Paris? **To see** a customer.*

• Dans le même ordre d'idées, *intend to/manage to* + infinitif.
*As we **managed to get** delivery on time, we **intend to launch** the product next week.*

• Après *would* + verbe d'attitude envers quelque chose (*would like, would prefer...*)
***Would** you **like** something to drink?*
*He **would hate** to work in a big city.*

• Après *ask, enable, expect, force, help, invite, need, order, remind, warn, want, persuade, promise, teach, tell...* (verb + object + *to* + verb)
*I **want you to set** the machine for 20 pieces.*
*The boss **ordered her to take** a holiday.*

• Après *ask, beg, decide, expect, forget, help, hope, learn, offer, plan, promise, refuse, want ...* (verb + *to* + verb)
*He doesn't **want to know** the figures.*
*She **refused to work** overtime.*

## *-ING*

• Dans les formes progressives
*She **is calling** a supplier right now.*

• Comme sujet
***Travelling** is part of his job.*

• Après les prépositions
***Before leaving** the office, tidy your desk.*

• Après les verbes d'attitude *can't stand, dislike, don't mind, enjoy, feel like, hate, like, love, mind...*
*He **doesn't mind working** overtime.*
*She **can't stand being** late.*

• Après les verbes *avoid, admit, consider, delay, deny, do (the), finish, give up, go on, imagine, involve, keep(on), miss, practise, put off, start, suggest, ...*
*Could you **do the filing** before lunch?*
*You should **practise speaking** English.*

• Après les expressions *can't help, it's no good, it's no use, it's (not) worth, would you mind, (to be) used to...*
→ ***I can't help thinking*** *another supplier would be better. It's no use complaining.*

## VERB + -*ING* OU *TO* + VERB

Après les verbes *advise, allow, begin, bother, continue, encourage, forbid, intend, need, prefer, regret, remember, start, try...*, on peut utiliser **verbe + *ing*** ou ***to* + verbe**.
Ceci peut changer le sens de votre phrase !

*I **remember sending** the fax.*
→ Je me souviens que j'ai envoyé le fax.

*I **remembered to send** the fax.*
→ Je me suis souvenu d'envoyer le fax. (= je n'ai pas oublié)

*They **stopped doing** the customer survey.*
→ Ils ont arrêté de faire l'enquête de satisfaction.

*They **stopped to do** the customer survey.*
→ Ils ont arrêté pour faire l'enquête de satisfaction.

# ANNEXE 10 LA PONCTUATION

Soyez attentif à la ponctuation.
*An English Professor wrote the words "A woman without her man is nothing" on the chalkboard, and then asked his students to punctuate it correctly.*
*All of the males in the class wrote:*
*"A woman, without her man, is nothing."*
*However, all the females in the class wrote:*
*"A woman: without her, man is nothing."*
*Another famous quote*
*A panda eats shoots and leaves.*
*A panda eats, shoots, and leaves.*
*Punctuation is powerful!!*

• Guillemets (« *French quotation marks* ») sont peu utilisés en anglais.
Utilisez les quotation marks "...".

• Pas d'espace avant le ":", "?", "!", et "%".

• En anglais le tiret est souvent utilisé pour remplacer : " : " /" ; "/" ..."/", "-/"(...)"

• La virgule est souvent utiliser pour séparer deux adjectifs :
*I prefer the abstract, glossy leaflet.*

• La virgule s'utilise avant la phrase indirecte :
*If I remember rightly, he said, "I don't think you ought to be doing that".*

• Adresse électronique :
peter.smith@gmail.com = peter DOT smith AT gmail DOT com
Souligner = *underscore*

# CONJONCTIONS ET MOTS DE TRANSITION

## AJOUTER UNE INFORMATION

*also / as well / too* (aussi)
*and* (et)
*besides / moreover / furthermore* (d'ailleurs / de plus)
*in addition to / what's more* (en / de plus)

## CONCLURE

*finally* (finalement / enfin)
*in conclusion* (en conclusion)
*last but not least* (enfin et surtout)
*lastly* (pour finir)
*then* (donc)
*to conclude / as a conclusion* (pour conclure)

## CONTREDIRE ET PROPOSER UNE ALTERNATIVE

*actually / as a matter of fact / in fact* (en fait)
*alternatively* (autrement)
*instead* (au lieu de)

## DONNER UN EXEMPLE

*as follows* (comme suit)
*for example / for instance* (par exemple)
*such as* (tel que)
*namely* (à savoir)

## ÉTABLIR UNE COMPARAISON

*as / like* (comme)
*in comparison* (en comparaison)
*likewise* (également)
*similarly* (pareillement)

## EXPRIMER LA CAUSE ET L'EFFET

*after all* (après tout)
*as* (comme)
*as a result / consequence / consequently* (par conséquent)
*because* (parce que)
*because of* (à cause de)
*due to / owing to* (en raison de)

*given that* (étant donné que)
*since* (puisque)
*so* (donc)
*so as to* (afin de)
*subsequently* (par la suite)
*that's why* (c'est pourquoi)
*thereby* (ainsi)
*therefore* (en conséquence)
*this means* (cela veut dire)
*thus* (donc / ainsi)

## EXPRIMER L'OPPOSITION

*all the same* (tout de même)
*although / though* (bien que)
*but* (mais)
*contrary to* (contrairement à)
*despite* (malgré)
*even so* (quand même)
*even though* (même si)
*however* (cependant)
*in / by contrast* (par contraste)
*in spite of* (en dépit de)
*instead* (au lieu de)
*nevertheless / nonetheless / yet* (néanmoins)
*on the contrary* (au contraire)
*on the one hand...on the other hand* (d'un côté..., de l'autre...)
*otherwise* (autrement)
*still* (quand même)
*whereas / while* (tandis que)
*yet* (pourtant)

## GÉNÉRALISER

*as a rule* (en règle générale)
*in general* (en général)
*in most cases* (dans la plupart des cas)
*normally* (normalement)
*on the whole / overall* (dans l'ensemble)

## POSER DES CONDITIONS

*assuming that* (supposant que)
*else* (autrement)
*if / should* (si)
*in that case* (dans ce cas)
*providing that / on condition that* (à condition de)
*unless* (à moins que)

## REFORMULER

*namely* (à savoir)
*that is to say* (c'est-à-dire)
*that means* (ce qui veut dire)

## RÉSUMER

*in brief / short* (bref)
*to sum up / to recap* (en résumé)
*in a nutshell* (bref)

## SITUER DANS LE TEMPS

*after* (that) / afterwards (après)
*at that time / then* (à ce moment là)
*at the same time* (en même temps)
*before (that)* (avant)
*finally* (finalement / enfin)
*firstly, secondly...* (premièrement, deuxièmement...)
*meanwhile* (pendant ce temps)
*soon* (bientôt)
*the former / the latter* (le premier, le dernier – sur deux éléments)

## SOULIGNER / AJOUTER UNE NUANCE

*clearly* (clairement)
*indeed* (en effet)
*naturally* (naturellement)
*of course* (bien sûr)
*obviously* (évidemment)
*to a certain extent / to some degree* (dans une certaine mesure)

# MODIFICATIONS ORTHOGRAPHIQUES

## *-y* final

- *-y* devient *-ie* devant *-s* s'il est précédé d'une consonne
*country* ⇆ *countries*
- *-y* devient *-i* :
– dans le prétérit et le participe passé des verbes réguliers
*try* ⇆ *tried*
– dans le comparatif et le superlatif des adjectifs courts
*easy* ⇆ *easier*
– devant le suffixe *-ly*
*funny* ⇆ *funnily*
- *-y* se maintient devant *-ing*
*apply* ⇆ *applying*

## *-ie* final

*-ie* devient *-y* devant *-ing*
*tie* ⇆ *tying*

## Suppression de *-e*

- dans les verbes se terminant en *-e* :
– au prétérit et au participe passé des verbes réguliers
*trace* ⇆ *traced*
– au participe présent et au gérondif
*write* ⇆ *writing*

EXCEPTION auxiliaire *be (being)* et verbes en *-ee* (*seeing*)

- dans les adjectifs se terminant en *-e* :
– au comparatif et au superlatif des adjectifs courts
*wide* ⇆ *wider*
– dans les adverbes dérivés d'adjectifs en *-able*
*sociable* ⇆ *sociably*

## Doublement de la consonne finale

- dans le comparatif et le superlatif des adjectifs courts
*big* ⇆ *bigger, biggest*

EXCEPTION Il n'y a pas doublement si l'adjectif :
– se termine en *y* ou *w*
*new* ⇆ *newest*
– se termine par deux consonnes
*long* ⇆ *longest*
- comporte une double voyelle avant la consonne finale
*cheap* ⇆ *cheapest*
- dans le participe présent, le gérondif, le prétérit et le participe passé des verbes de plusieurs syllabes dont la dernière est accentuée
*preFER* ⇆ *preferred*

# LES PRÉFIXES ET LES SUFFIXES

Ce sont des règles générales – bien sûr il existe des exceptions !

## LES PRÉFIXES

Les adjectifs qui commencent par "c" prennent "in" → *incorrect*

Les adjectifs qui commencent par "p" prennent "im" → *imperfect*

Vous ne pouvez pas utiliser de préfixe avec tous les adjectifs, mais vous pouvez souvent créer un contraire avec « un ».
→ *reliable / unreliable*

La même règle s'applique aux verbes.
→ *pack / unpack, do / undo, lock / unlock*

Un préfixe différent donne un sens différent.

*dis, un, non, im / in / ir / il* = ne pas
*inter* = commun ou ensemble
*mis* = mal
*co* = commun ou ensemble
*re* = encore ou "re"
*anti* = contre
*sub* = au-dessous
*over* = trop

## lES SUFFIXES

Certains suffixes vont avec un nom ou un adjectif, d'autres avec un verbe.

| Verbe | Adjectif | Nom | Exemples |
|---|---|---|---|
| - | - | -tion / -sion | *an extension / an infection* |
| -en | -en | | *to deepen / frozen* |
| - | - | -ness | *tiredness* |
| -ify | -fy | - | *identify* |
| - | -ful | - | *useful* |
| - | -fold | - | *threefold* |
| - | - | -ship | *leadership* |
| - | -y | - | *wealthy* |
| -ise / -ize | - | - | *emphasise / co-supervise* (En règle générale "*-ise*" en anglais GB et "*-ize*" en anglais USA. Le tout est de choisir une forme ou l'autre.) |
| - | - | -ity | *complicity* |
| - | -ish | - | *greenish* |
| -ate | - | - | *liquidate* |
| - | - | -ment | *agreement* |
| - | -ese | -ese | *Vietnamese / Pekinese (Notez que les adjectifs commencent avec un majuscule.)* |
| - | - | -ance(y) / -ency(y) | *allowance / expense / urgency* |
| - | -less | - | *useless / harmless / timeless* |
| - | -like | - | *businesslike / lifelike* |

# Vocabulaire

## Avant-propos

Cette partie du livre vous fournit le vocabulaire de base nécessaire pour réussir le TOEIC, sachant que l'examen est un ***Test of English for International Communication***, souvent utilisé par les écoles ou les entreprises pour juger votre capacité à travailler dans la langue de Shakespeare. Pour ceux qui ne sont pas concernés par l'examen TOEIC, ce livre vous donnera quelques bonnes bases lexicales du monde des affaires à l'international.

Une fois tous les exercices de cette partie réalisés, et donc le vocabulaire acquis, à vous de prendre le temps de lire (livres, journaux…), de regarder des documentaires, des conférences et des films sur Internet pour augmenter encore votre maîtrise du vocabulaire et donc améliorer votre ***word bank***.

Dans l'optique de vous aider à mémoriser le vocabulaire, les exercices sont basés sur du ***mind mapping*** (schématisation conceptuelle), dans lequel les mots sont groupés par thème et sous-thème. Prenez l'habitude de mémoriser le vocabulaire de cette manière et votre apprentissage s'en trouvera facilité.

N'oubliez pas que le fait de voir un mot trois fois (la première fois quand vous le lisez, la deuxième fois quand vous le notez dans votre cahier / tableur, la troisième fois quand vous l'utilisez), va ancrer ce mot dans votre mémoire. Profitez-en !

## Sommaire


• Pour vous mettre l'eau à la bouche 162
Nous allons commencer avec quelques exercices plus généraux qui ciblent certaines difficultés de la langue anglaise.

**1.** Jobs and companies 164

**2.** Reports and meetings 166

**3.** Marketing arrangements 168

**4.** Negotiating 170

**5.** Job seeking 173

**6.** Marketing 176

**7.** Industry 178

**8.** Written and oral communication 181

**9.** Products 184

**10.** Travelling 186

**Corrigés** 189

# Pour vous mettre l'eau à la bouche

## 1 ACRONYMS

You will come across acronyms everywhere in business English, including in the TOEIC exam. Beware: 1) many companies invent their own acronyms which can be difficult to understand! 2) "A.S.A.P." (As Soon As Possible – « dès que possible ») se prononce A-S-A-P et non comme un mot « asap ».

**Match the acronyms to their definition.**
**This is an easy exercise, to start you off and make you aware.**

| | | | |
|---|---|---|---|
| **1** E.D.L.P. | • | • | **A** Information Technology & Communication |
| **2** C.F.O. | • | • | **B** Any Other Business |
| **3** P.O.S. | • | • | **C** Every Day Low Price |
| **4** M.O.Q. | • | • | **D** Annual General Meeting |
| **5** I.T.C. | • | • | **E** Strategic Business Unit |
| **6** S.M.E. | • | • | **F** Point Of Sale |
| **7** A.G.M. | • | • | **G** Small and Medium-sized Enterprises |
| **8** N.P.I. | • | • | **H** Minimum Order Quantity |
| **9** A.O.B. | • | • | **I** Chief Financial Officer |
| **10** S.B.U. | • | • | **J** New Product Introduction |

## 2 CONFUSING WORDS

Many words in English often get mixed up, and are likely to be trick questions in the TOEIC exam. Make sure that you know the difference between them.

**Choose which of the two words goes with each definition.**

**1.** Salary / Wage
**A.** Numbers of hours worked multiplied by an hourly rate of pay.
**B.** A monthly or annual fixed sum paid for a job to be done.

**2.** Dispatch / Delivery
**A.** When goods are sent off to a destination.
**B.** When goods are taken to and left at a destination.

**3.** Stakeholder / Shareholder
**A.** A person who owns part of the capital of the business.
**B.** A person who has a concern in a business (employee, supplier…)

**4.** Office / Desk
**A.** A room in which you work.
**B.** A table (with drawers) at which you work.

**5.** Earn / Win
**A.** Money gained from working.
**B.** Money gained from betting, gambling, lotteries, etc.

**6.** Advertising / Publicity
**A.** A way of making commercial products known to the public, which you pay for.
**B.** A way of making commercial products known to the public, which is free.

**7.** Jet lag / Time difference
**A.** The difference in the time between one place and another (New York / Paris = 6 hours)
**B.** The tiredness you feel after a long flight between different time zones.

**8.** Company / Society
**A.** A commercial business, hopefully making a profit.
**B.** A non-profit organisation.

**9.** Market Research / Marketing Research
**A.** Collecting and analyzing information about a target market.
**B.** All the information needed to move goods or services from producer to consumer.

**10.** Agenda / Diary
**A.** An appointment book.
**B.** The list of points to be discussed at a meeting.

## 3 FALSE FRIENDS

These are words which exist both in English and in other languages, but not always with the same meaning. Always beware of these "false cognates". The definitions given below are the English definitions, not those perhaps in your native language. The definition of the other word is given in the answer section.

### Choose the correct word for the definition.

| | |
|---|---|
| **1.** A division of an organization which deals with a certain subject. • | • Department / Service |
| **2.** Teaching and / or learning a particular skill. • | • Stage / Training |
| **3.** Something previously existing or done. • | • Former / Old |
| **4.** To make up or invent. • | • Manufacture / Fabricate |
| **5.** The last possible date. • | • Deadline / Delay |
| **6.** The advantage got from something. • | • Profits / Benefits |
| **7.** Something happening now. • | • Actual / Current |
| **8.** A social gathering or people getting together after some time. • | • Meeting / Reunion |
| **9.** To condense into a short sentence. • | • Sum up / Resume |
| **10.** The way out of somewhere. • | • Exit / Issue |

## 4 COMMON MISTAKES

There are mistakes which come up again and again when non-natives speak English. Of course, these mistakes also come up again and again in English exams. Let's look at some examples to whet your appetite.

### Which of the two sentences is correct, A or B?

**1. A.** I am agree with your latest comment.
**B.** I agree with your latest comment.

**2. A.** I would be grateful for some informations about your hotel.
**B.** I would be grateful for some information about your hotel.

**3. A.** There were several hundreds people at the trade fair.
**B.** There were several hundred people at the trade fair.

**4. A.** The meeting will be held in the conference room on Monday.
**B.** The meeting will be held in the conference room on Monday.

**5. A.** The new finance manager is a very sympathetic person.
**B.** The new finance manager is a very nice person.

**6. A.** It depends of what the margin is really.
**B.** It depends on what the margin is really.

**7. A.** We look forward to doing business with you.
**B.** We look forward to do business with you.

**8. A.** That man gets a salary of over £14,500 a month! It's huge!
**B.** That man gets a salary of over £14.500 a month! It's huge!

**9. A.** Following a deep recession, the economical situation has begun to improve.
**B.** Following a deep recession, the economic situation has begun to improve.

**10. A.** He has decided to teach his procurement officers how to use enterprise requirement software.
**B.** He has decided to learn his procurement officers how to use enterprise requirement software.

# 1. Jobs and companies

| | |
|---|---|
| *accountant* | comptable |
| *after-sales service* | SAV |
| *bankupt / go bankrupt (to)* | en faillite |
| *board of directors* | conseil d'administration |
| *branch* | succursale |
| *C.E.O. (C.F.O. / C.I.O. ...)* | Directeur Général (/ financier / d'information) |
| *clock in / out (to)* | pointer |
| *colleague* | collègue |
| *company policy* | politique d'entreprise |
| *competitor* | concurrent |
| *counterpart* | homologue |
| *customer* | client |
| *cutback (to)* | faire des économies |
| *deal with (to)* | s'occuper de |
| *downsize (to)* | réduire (effectif ...) |
| *employee* | employé |
| *exchange rate* | taux de change |
| *found (to) / founder* | fonder / fondateur |
| *grow (to) / growth* | croître / la croissance |
| *H.R. Human Resources* | R.H. |
| *headquarters / head office* | siège social |
| *I.T.(C) Information Technology (and Communication)* | Informatique |
| *in charge of (to be)* | être responsable de |
| *invest (to) / investment* | investir / investissement |
| *locate (to)* | implanter, localiser |
| *low cost* | bas prix |
| *market share* | part de marché |
| *merge (to) / a merger* | fusionner / fusion |
| *office* | bureau (pièce) |
| *outlet* | point de vente |
| *overheads* | frais généraux |
| *P&L Profit and Loss* | compte de pertes et profits |
| *parent company* | société mère |

| | |
|---|---|
| *partnership* | partenariat |
| *payroll* | effectif, personnel |
| *premises* | locaux |
| *procurement* | approvisionnement |
| *profit* | bénéfices |
| *purchasing* | achats |
| *quality* | qualité |
| *R&D Research and Development* | recherche et développement |
| *report to (to)* | rapporter à, rendre compte à |
| *responsible for (to be)* | être responsable de |
| *retailer* | vente au détail |
| *S.B.U. (Strategic* Business Unit) | unité commerciale stratégique |
| *S.M.E. (Small and Middle-sized Enterprise)* | PME |
| *sales administration* | administration des ventes |
| *sales department* | service des ventes |
| *self-employed* | travailleur indépendant |
| *shareholder* | actionnaire |
| *shift (night)* | équipe (3x8) (de nuit) |
| *showroom* | salle d'exposition |
| *sister company* | société sœur |
| *society* | association |
| *stakeholder* | partie prenante |
| *strengthen (to)* | renforcer |
| *strike* | grève |
| *subsidiary* | filiale |
| *supplier* | fournisseur |
| *supply chain* | chaîne d'approvisionnement |
| *take over (to) / takeover* | prendre le contrôle de / OPA |
| *team* | équipe |
| *turnover* | chiffre d'affaires |
| *wholesale* | vente en gros |
| *works committee / council* | comité d'entreprise |

## ACTIVITÉS

### 5 COMPANY ORGANISATION

**Put the right word into the gap.**

*branch – headquarters – department – outlets – parent company – showroom – sister company – self-employed – service – subsidiary*

**1.** Come and visit our s.......................... so you can see the high quality of our products for yourselves.

**2.** He's his own boss because he's s ......................... ...........................

**3.** To contact your bank, see our website for the contact details of your local b.......................... .

4. The p........................... ........................... decided to outsource HR for all the firms in the group.

5. The after-sales s........................... works closely with the sales administration department.

6. The company has retail o........................... all over the country.

7. The h..........................., or head office, was moved to Zurich about 5 years ago.

8. The parent company has decided to close down the s........................... in southern Spain.

9. Our s........................... ........................... in London sends in the same monthly reports as us.

10. The quality d........................... is responsible for maintaining the highest quality standards.

## 6 THE PEOPLE INVOLVED

### Match the person / people to the definition.

1. Colleague •
2. Supplier •
3. Employee •
4. Competitor •
5. Board of Directors •
6. Works Council •
7. Counterpart •
8. Wholesaler •
9. Customer •
10. Retailer •

- • a. Someone who sells goods in bulk.
- • b. Someone who is a rival against another.
- • c. Someone who sells goods to the consumer.
- • d. Someone who provides a service or product.
- • e. A committee of employee / employer representatives.
- • f. Someone whom you work with.
- • g. Someone who buys goods or services.
- • h. Someone who works for an employer.
- • i. A group of people who govern the company.
- • j. Someone with a corresponding job / functions.

## 7 COMPANY PROFILE

### Choose the right word between the words in italics.

The company was *founded / fund* by B.B. Bother in 1946. It was a small *partnership / partner hood* but soon grew to become a limited company. The *housing / premises* were firstly *located / localized* near Birmingham, but owing to considerable *growth / growing up*, we were able to buy real estate in the center of London. The *merger / fusion* with PPL Ltd in 1953, followed by some exceptional *investissement / investment* in R&D, enabled us to *weakened / strengthen* our market position, increase our *turnover / affaires figures* tenfold, and we became highly successful.

However, we saw our *market share / market parts* decreasing and feared that we were going to go *bankruptcy / bankrupt*. We were *taken over / taken out* by Blue Brass Inc. who made a lot of changes which meant we could keep our heads above water. Many *cutbacks / cutdowns* were made: first of all from a *pay ship / payroll* aspect – teams were *downloaded / downsized* and everyone in the company now has to *clock / point* in or out. We also had to reduce our *overheads / general cost* and the procurement and *purchasing / shopping* departments improved supply chain management and found new low cost suppliers. This led to social unrest, and the night shift came out on *strike / stroke* for three weeks.

Despite all these upheavals, our company *policy / politics* has never changed, "happy workers are good workers" and "customers rule ok".

## 8 RESPONSIBILITES

### Add the right preposition to the verb. *by – for – of – to – with*

1. The accountant reports ............... the C.F.O.

2. The foreman is responsible ............... the smooth running of the assembly line.

3. The warehouseman deals ............... supplying the factory on time.

4. The marketing manager is in charge ............... sales and marketing.

5. The engineer is assisted ............... 3 technicians.

# 2. Reports and meetings

| | |
|---|---|
| *A.O.B. Any other Business* | questions diverses |
| *agenda* | ordre du jour |
| *attendees* | participant |
| *audit / auditor* | audit, vérification / auditeur |
| *bar chart* | histogramme |
| *blueprint* | plan d'architecte |
| *board meeting* | réunion du conseil d'administration |
| *brainstorm (to)* | faire du brainstorming |
| *break* | pause |
| *budget* | budget |
| *chairman / chairperson* | président |
| *conference room* | salle de conférence |
| *dashboard* | tableau de bord |
| *demonstrate (to)* | expliquer / décrire |
| *figures* | chiffres |
| *flowchart* | schéma de processus / opérations |
| *forecast (to) / forecast* | prévoir / prévision |
| *graph* | graphique |
| *issue* | problème, sujet de litige |
| *line graph / run chart* | courbe (graphique) |
| *meeting* | réunion |
| *minutes* | compte-rendu |
| *monthly* | mensuel |
| *motion* | motion |
| *notify (to)* | notifier, prévenir |
| *on time* | à l'heure |
| *organisation chart* | organigramme |
| *pie chart* | camembert (graphique) |
| *polar graph* | graphique polaire |
| *present (to)* | présenter |
| *presentation* | présentation |
| *project* | projet |
| *proxy vote* | vote par procuration |
| *quarterly* | trimestriel |
| *report* | rapport |
| *results* | résultats |
| *review meeting* | réunion d'évaluation |
| *road map* | feuille de route |
| *shelve (to)* | abandonner |
| *slump (to)* | effondrer |
| *spreadsheet* | tableur |
| *steering committee* | comité de pilotage |
| *sum up (to)* | résumer |
| *take notes (to)* | prendre des notes |
| *think tank* | groupe de réflexion |
| *trade fair* | foire / salon commercial |
| *update / update (to)* | mise / mettre à jour |
| *visuals* | supports visuels |
| *weekly meeting* | réunion hebdomadaire |
| *write up (to)* | rédiger |
| *year-to-date* | à ce jour |

## ACTIVITÉS

### 9 MEETINGS

**Complete the word puzzle with the clues.**

**Across:**

**1.** A verb which means to predict the future.
**2.** To give people warning about a meeting is to … them.
**3.** The written report of a meeting is called the … .
**4.** Numbers are also known as … .
**5.** The people who come to the meeting are called … .
**6.** and **7.** A meeting of the board of directors is called a … .
**8.** A verb which means to write down the notes.
**9.** A committee which manages the overall business of a company.
**10**. An interruption during the meeting to pause a little.
**11**. The person who runs the meeting is called a … .
**12**. A meeting which takes place every 28, 30 or 31 days is a … meeting.
**13**. "I would like to put forward a …". (A proposal or suggestion).
**14**. To give a practical exhibition and explanation of something.

**Down:** Hidden word: a room where a meeting is likely to take place.

| | | | | | | | | | | | | | | | | | |
|---|---|---|---|---|---|---|---|---|---|---|---|---|---|---|---|---|---|
| 1 | | | | | F | _ | _ | _ | C | _ | _ | _ | | | | | |
| 2 | | | | | | | | N | _ | _ | _ | _ | _ | | | | |
| 3 | | | | | | | M | _ | _ | _ | _ | _ | _ | | | | |
| 4 | | | | | | | | | F | _ | _ | _ | _ | _ | _ | | |
| 5 | | | | | | A | _ | _ | _ | _ | _ | _ | _ | _ | | | |
| 6 | | | | | | B | _ | _ | _ | _ | | | | | | | |
| 7 | | | | | | | M | _ | _ | _ | _ | _ | _ | | | | |
| 8 | | | | | T | _ | _ | _ | N | _ | _ | _ | _ | | | | |
| 9 | S | _ | _ | _ | _ | _ | _ | _ | C | _ | _ | _ | _ | _ | _ | _ | _ |
| 10 | | | | | | | B | _ | _ | _ | _ | | | | | | |
| 11 | | | | | C | _ | _ | _ | _ | _ | _ | _ | _ | _ | _ | | |
| 12 | | | | | | | | M | _ | _ | _ | _ | _ | _ | | | |
| 13 | | | | | | | | M | _ | _ | _ | _ | _ | | | | |
| 14 | | | | | | | D | _ | _ | _ | _ | _ | _ | _ | _ | _ | _ |

## 10 REPORTS AND PAPERWORK

### Match the beginning of the compound noun to the end.

**First word:** *bar – blue – dash – flow – line – organization – pie – polar – road – spread*
**Second word:** *board – chart – chart – chart – chart – graph – graph – map – print – sheet*

**1.** ........................................................ **2.** ........................................................

**3.** ........................................................ **4.** ........................................................

**5.** ........................................................ **6.** ........................................................

**7.** ........................................................ **8.** ........................................................

**9.** ........................................................ **10.** ........................................................

## 11 BRAINSTORM THE VOCABULARY

### Choose the right word to put in the gap.

**1.** We will hold this meeting every 3 months. It is a ............................ meeting.
**A.** weekly **B.** trimestrially **C.** quarterly

**2.** These are the results so far this year. In other words the ............................ results.
**A.** year-to-now **B.** year-to-date **C.** year-to-update

**3.** We have decided that we will not continue with the project. We have to ............................ it.
**A.** cupboard **B.** rack **C.** shelve

**4.** They are going to launch their new product at the ............................ in Berlin.
**A.** sales fair **B.** trade fair **C.** commercial room

**5.** Those don't appear to be the most recent figures. When were they last ............................?
**A.** updated **B.** upcoming **C.** upended

**6.** The economic situation has not been very good. This is reflected in our share price which has ........... ................ slightly.
**A.** soared **B.** freezed **C.** slumped

**7.** Who is going to volunteer to ............................ the minutes of the meeting?
**A.** write in **B.** write to **C.** write up

**8.** I am here to tell you about last year's ............................ and next year's budget.
**A.** resultants **B.** results **C.** resulting

# 3. Making arrangements

| | | | |
|---|---|---|---|
| *A.G.M.* | assemblée générale | *earlier* | plus tôt |
| *a.m. (ante meridien)* | matin | *early / late (to be)* | être en avance / en retard |
| *appointment* | rendez-vous | *fix (to)* | organiser |
| *arrange (to)* | organiser | *fortnight* | deux semaines |
| *as soon as possible* | dès que possible | *free (to be)* | être disponible |
| *available (to be)* | être disponible | *itinerary* | itinéraire |
| *away on business* | absent pour affaires | *later* | plus tard |
| *be off (to)* | être annulé | *lunch* | déjeuner |
| *booked up (to be)* | occupé, réservé | *meet (to)* | rencontrer |
| *breakfast* | petit-déjeuner | *noon / midday* | midi |
| *bring forward (to)* | faire avancer | *out of the office (to be)* | être absent du bureau |
| *busy (to be)* | être occupé | *p.m. (post meridien)* | après-midi |
| *call off (to)* | annuler | *postpone (to)* | remettre à plus tard |
| *cancel (to)* | annuler | *provide (to)* | fournir |
| *change (to)* | changer | *public (/bank) holiday* | jour férié |
| *date* | rendez-vous plutôt romantique | *put back (to)* | reporter |
| *decade* | dix ans | *put forward (to)* | avancer |
| *defer (to)* | remettre à plus tard | *put off (to)* | reporter |
| *delay (to)* | retarder | *schedule* | horaire, emploi du temps |
| *deliver (to)* | livrer | *set up (to)* | organiser |
| *delivery* | livraison | *show in (to)* | faire entrer |
| *delivery delay* | retard de livraison | *suit (to)* | convenir |
| *delivery time / period* | délai de livraison | *suitable* | convenable |
| *diary* | agenda | *tea* | goûter |
| *dinner (/ supper)* | dîner (/souper) | *tied up (to be)* | être occupé |
| *dispatch* | envoi de marchandises | *topic* | sujet, thème |
| *dispatch (to)* | envoyer des marchandises | *warning* | avertissement |

## ACTIVITÉS

### 12 COMPLETE THE CONVERSATION

**Put a suitable word into the gap.**

*A.S.A.P. – booked up – breakfast – call off – diary – fix – later – lunch – noon – out of the office – public holiday – show him in – suit – tied up – topic*

**P:** Bill, good morning. I'm calling because I'm afraid I have to .................. our meeting tomorrow. I'd like to .................. another meeting .................. so we can get to the bottom of this supplier problem.

**B:** I agree Peter. Let me just look at my .................. . What do you suggest?

**P:** Well, Monday morning would .................. me. How about you?

**B:** Sorry, Monday's a .................. in the UK, so I'll be .................. then. Can you do Tuesday?

**P:** No, I'll be .................. all day Tuesday with the bankers. I'm pretty .................. next week really. Wednesday's no good at all. Let's see… What about a .................. meeting at 8 on Thursday?

**B:** I'm supposed to be seeing the C.E.O. But I could see him .................., at .................. (then he can treat me to ..................!). He probably wants to talk about his favorite .................., streamlining the supply chain. I'll check and get back to you before the end of today.

**P:** You'll have to excuse me Bill, the auditor's just arrived. (Mrs. Jones, could you please ..................?) I'll get back to you later Bill.

**B:** Fine. I'll speak to you later.

## 13 EXPLAIN THE WORDS

**Match the words to the right description.**

**1.** DECADE / FORTNIGHT
**A.** Ten years — **B.** Two weeks

**2.** EARLY / LATE
**A.** Before the usual or expected time — **B.** After the usual or expected time

**3.** TEA / DINNER
**A.** An evening meal — **B.** A snack at around 5pm

**4.** A.M. / P.M.
**A.** The afternoon — **B.** The morning

**5.** APPOINTMENT / DATE
**A.** A possibly romantic rendez-vous — **B.** An arrangement to meet

**6.** BUSY / FREE
**A.** With a great deal to do. — **B.** Available

**7.** DELAY / DEADLINE
**A.** Something being late or postponed — **B.** The latest time for finishing something

**8.** ITINERARY / SCHEDULE
**A.** A plan for a process or procedure — **B.** A document with planned travel arrangements

**9.** I LOOK FORWARD TO MEETING / SEEING YOU
**A.** For the first time you meet someone — **B.** For when you see someone again

**10.** AWAY ON BUSINESS / OUT OF THE OFFICE
**A.** This could be just for an hour or so (or more) — **B.** You might be gone for some time

## 14 DELIVERY TIMES

**Of course delivery times are also arrangements. Add another word to the word "delivery" to make a compound noun. What is the odd-man-out in the list, and why?**

*DEADLINE – DELAY – DISPATCH – TIME / PERIOD*

DELIVERY ...................................... (Will be late)

...................................... (The final date for delivery)

...................................... (The time it takes for goods to arrive)

## 15 I THINK I NEED TO CHANGE THE APPOINTMENT

**Put the words into the appropriate category.**

*ARRANGE – BE OFF – BRING FORWARD – CALL OFF – CANCEL – DEFER – DELAY – FIX – PUT BACK – PUT FORWARD – PUT OFF – SET UP*

**1.** I must *organise* a meeting. ........................ ........................ ........................

**2.** This meeting will *not take place*. ........................ ........................ ........................

**3.** We'll have to *advance the date*. ........................ ........................

**4.** He has *postponed* the appointment. ........................ ........................ ........................

# 4. Negotiating

| | | | |
|---|---|---|---|
| *agree (to)* | être d'accord | *lawyer* | avocat |
| *agreement* | accord | *let someone know (to)* | faire savoir |
| *bribe, bribery* | pot-de-vin | *M.O.Q. (Minimum Order Quantity)* | Quantité minimum de commande |
| *certificate of origin* | certificat d'origine | *make a deal (to)* | conclure un marché |
| *check (to)* | vérifier | *offer (to) / offer* | offrir / offre |
| *clause* | clause | *open-minded* | large d'esprit |
| *come back to someone (to)* | revenir vers quelqu'un | *order* | commande |
| *competitive* | compétitif | *order acknowledgement* | accusé de réception d'une commande |
| *comply (to)* | être conforme | *part order* | commande partielle |
| *compromise* | compromis | *party (parties)* | partie |
| *conclude (to)* | conclure | *penalty clause* | clause de pénalité |
| *confirm (to)* | confirmer | *price reduction* | réduction des prix |
| *convince (to)* | convaincre | *proposal* | proposition |
| *counter-offer* | contre-proposition | *purchase order* | bon de commande |
| *customs duties* | douane | *put in a tender (to)* | faire une offre |
| *deadline* | date limite | *quality defect* | défaut de qualité |
| *deal* | affaire | *quantity discount* | remise pour achat en grande quantité |
| *deal with (to)* | s'occuper de | *review (to)* | revoir, réexaminer |
| *decrease (to)* | diminuer | *sales price* | prix de vente |
| *deliver from stock (to)* | livrer des stocks | *settle (to)* | régler |
| *deposit* | arrhes / acompte | *ship (to)* | expédier |
| *disagree (to)* | ne pas être d'accord | *sign (to)* | signer |
| *discount* | remise, rabais | *specifications* | spécifications |
| *draw up (to)* | rédiger, dresser | *stick to (to)* | maintenir, rester fidèle |
| *duty (import)* | taxe, frais de douane | *tender* | offre |
| *finalize (to)* | finaliser | *terms* | conditions |
| *freight forwarder* | transporteur | *tie up loose ends (to)* | régler les derniers détails |
| *gamble / gamble (to)* | pari /parier | *transport costs* | frais de transport |
| *go back on (to)* | revenir sur quelque chose | *withdraw (to)* | se retirer |
| *goodwill* | bonne foi | | |
| *handling charges* | frais de manutention | | |
| *increase (to)* | augmenter | | |

## ACTIVITÉS

### 16 TERMS AND CONDITIONS OF SALE (extract)

**Put an appropriate word from the list below into the gaps in the text.**

*certificate of origin – customs duties (import duties) – handling charges – order acknowledgement – purchase order – quality defects – quantity discount – return – sales price – sign – shipped – transport costs*

An order is input once we have received a **1.** ................................ by e-mail or by post. We will send an **2.** ................................ to confirm the order.

The **3.** ................................ is marked on the enclosed price list.

A 5% **4.** ................................ will be offered for any orders over 5,000 items.

Each shipment is to be accompanied by a **5.** ................................ as proof of the provenance of the goods.

**6.** ................................ are to be paid by the customer in advance of shipment.

The goods are to be **7.** ................................ Ex-Works. This means that all **8.** ................................ (trucks, trains, planes…) and **9.** ................................ (loading, unloading…) are to be covered by the purchaser.

The seller will be informed of any **10.** ................................ or other problems with the delivery, in writing within 5 days of receiving the goods.

Please **11.** ................................ (in ink) and **12.** ................................ this document to the sales department within the next 10 days to confirm your agreement to these terms and conditions.

## 17 SITTING ROUND THE NEGOTIATING TABLE

**Put the following conversations back into the right order. The first sentence is marked to help you.**

**Conversation 1:**

...... Susan: So your legal department said "no"? I thought we had made a deal. Now you are changing your proposal. I was planning to sign the agreement today.

...... Peter: I'm sorry Susan. I have to comply with company policy.

**1.** Susan: Peter, you cannot possibly go back on what you said. You promised that you would remove the confidentiality clause.

...... Peter: I disagree. In fact what I said was that I had to check with our legal department.

...... Susan: Well, if that's your company policy, I'm afraid that I have to withdraw our offer.

**Conversation 2:**

...... C.E.O.: Well, it looks like you got away with it this time then.

...... Brian: Well, I did offer him a compromise. I said if he would buy exclusively from us, we would give him a discount.

**1.** C.E.O.: Sit down Brian. Now, this is very serious. The customer is accusing you of bribery. What have you got to say to that?

...... Brian: That's strange because I heard from them this morning, and they are putting in a firm order for 20,000 parts.

...... C.E.O.: That was a gamble Brian, and it didn't pay. They say they can no longer work with us on a good will basis, and the purchaser is contacting his lawyer.

**Conversation 3:**

**1.** Charlotte: Did you put in a tender for the supermarket fittings last week?

...... James: Price reduction, short delivery deadlines, etc. I'm doing all I can to convince them that we are the right supplier.

...... Charlotte: Yes, their requirements are very demanding. Did you offer them a price reduction for regular orders?

...... James: I'll let you know as soon as I have any news.

...... Charlotte: Can you deal with it and come back to me by tomorrow afternoon?

...... James: Yes, I did. We'll have to stick very closely to their specifications.

**Conversation 4:**

...... Bob: You mentioned something about choosing your own freight forwarder, and putting in a penalty clause in case of late delivery. Is that all?

...... Sara: We must tie up a few loose ends before we finalize.

...... Bob: Of course. I'll get my lawyer to draw up the contracts tomorrow.

...... Sara: Just one more thing, we need to be sure that you can deliver from stock. That means you having a minimum safety stock all the time. Can you guarantee that?

**1.** Bob: Well, I think we've got a deal here, don't you?

## 18 WE'VE GOT A FEW MORE DETAILS TO GO THROUGH

### Choose the right answer: A, B, or C.

**1.** Our prices have to be highly .................................... if we are going to get the business.
**A.** competitive **B.** competition **C.** concurrent

**2.** To speed things up, we would be willing to accept a .................................... rather than the whole order at the same time.
**A.** pieces order **B.** part order **C.** semi-order

**3.** We cannot accept your offer so here is our .................................... .
**A.** counter-offer **B.** contra-offer **C.** content-offer

**4.** If you don't .................................... prices you will lose customers.
**A.** reduction **B.** descend **C.** decrease

**5.** We always require a .................................... for custom orders.
**A.** depot **B.** disclosure **C.** deposit

**6.** I'm afraid that we have to .................................... our prices this year to cover our costs.
**A.** augmented **B.** increase **C.** lower

**7.** Don't forget to remain .................................... during all your negotiations.
**A.** open-minded **B.** wide spirited **C.** inflexible

**8.** There are three main .................................... involved in this agreement.
**A.** partees **B.** parties **C.** partys

**9.** If we cannot .................................... a deal, we shall have to ask an arbitrator.
**A.** coincide **B.** concrete **C.** conclude

**10.** We should go over this again. We must .................................... what we have decided on.
**A.** review **B.** resee **C.** relooking

**11.** We have to .................................... our differences and move forwards.
**A.** regulate **B.** settle down **C.** settle

**12.** Could you please .................................... your agreement in writing?
**A.** confirme **B.** confirm **C.** conform

# 5. Job seeking

| | |
|---|---|
| *abroad* | à l'étranger |
| *application form* | dossier de candidature |
| *apply (to)* | postuler |
| *bonus* | bonus |
| *briefcase* | porte-documents |
| *candidate* | candidat |
| *closing date* | date limite |
| *company car* | voiture de société |
| *cover letter* | lettre de motivation |
| *CV / resumé* | CV |
| *day off* | journée de congé |
| *desk* | bureau |
| *drivers licence* | permis de conduire |
| *early retirement* | retraite anticipée |
| *earn* | gagner |
| *entail (to)* | entraîner, occasionner |
| *entitlement* | droit |
| *experience* | expérience |
| *fire / sack / dismiss (to)* | renvoyer |
| *fixed-term contract* | CDD |
| *fringe benefit* | avantage (en nature) |
| *go-ahead* | dynamique |
| *hard-working* | travailleur |
| *head-hunter* | chasseur de tête |
| *internal / (in-house) promotion* | promotion interne |
| *interview / interviewee / interviewer* | entretien / candidat / personne qui fait passer l'entretien |
| *job centre* | pôle emploi |
| *job-hunt / hunting* | recherche d'emploi |
| *lay off / make redundant (to)* | licencier |
| *leave (sick leave…)* | congé (maladie…) |
| *lunch / luncheon voucher* | chèque déjeuner |
| *openings* | poste disponible |
| *overtime* | heures supplémentaires |
| *part-/full-/flexi-time* | temps mi-/plein-/variable |
| *pension scheme / plan* | plan de retraite |
| *perk* | avantage (en nature) |
| *permanent contract* | CDI |
| *position* | poste |
| *promotion* | promotion |
| *qualifications* | qualifications |
| *recruit (to)* | recruter |
| *retire (to)* | prendre sa retraite |
| *retirement* | retraite |
| *shortlist* | préselection |
| *single* | célibataire |
| *spare time* | temps libre |
| *starting salary* | salaire de début |
| *strengths* | points forts |
| *take on / employ (to)* | embaucher |
| *task* | tâche, devoir |
| *train (to)* | former |
| *training* | formation |
| *training course* | stage de formation |
| *trial / probationary period* | période d'essai |
| *turn down (to)* | refuser |
| *unemployment* | chômage |
| *unsocial hours* | en dehors de l'horaire normal |
| *wage* | salaire horaire |
| *weaknesses* | faiblesses |
| *working conditions* | conditions de travail |
| *working hours* | temps de travail |

## ACTIVITÉS

### 19 WHAT WILL YOU PUT ON or WITH YOUR CV / RESUME?

**Add a vowel to make a word which might be useful on your CV.**

**1.** A letter to show how motivated you are: C _ V _ R L _ TT _ R

**2.** Previous working background: _ X P _ R _ _ N C _

**3.** Something which proves you can drive: D R _ V _ R'S L _ C _ N S _

**4.** An enterprising and dynamic adjective: G _ - _ H _ _ D

**5.** Diligent and assiduous: H _ R D – W _ R K _ N G

**6.** Diplomas, degrees…: Q _ _ L _ F _ C _ T _ _ N S

**7.** Married, divorced, or...: S _ N G L _

**8.** Free time: S P _ R _ T _ M _

**9.** Your assets: S T R _ N G T H S

**10.** Shortcomings: W _ _ K N _ S S _ S

## 20 WORKING CONDITIONS

**Choose the word that matches the definition.**

*day off – entails – entitlement – flexi time – full-time – overtime – part-time – sick / maternity leave – starting salary – task – unsocial hours – working hours*

**1.** A job to be done or undertaken. ................................................

**2.** The period of time to be spent at work. ................................................

**3.** The pay you receive when you start your job. ................................................

**4.** A job where you work less than 35 hours a week. ................................................

**5.** Leave of absence because you are unwell or expecting. ................................................

**6.** That to which you have a right. ................................................

**7.** A job which is at least 35 hours a week! ................................................

**8.** Includes or involves. ................................................

**9.** Working hours either very early in the morning or very late at night. ................................................

**10.** Hours worked over and above contracted hours. ................................................

**11.** A day when you do not have to work. ................................................

**12.** Varied time for starting or finishing work. ................................................

## 21 JOB HUNTING

**Put the following steps into the right order on the flowchart.**

**a.** Interviewee put on a shortlist and has final interview.

**b.** Interviewee turned down.

**c.** Go to see a head-hunter or a job center, and look at advertisements, etc.

**d.** Candidates may have to fill in an application form.

**e.** The company takes on the applicant.

**f.** Go back to squares 1, 2 and 3.

**g.** Look for openings in companies.

**h.** The employee gets a fixed-term or a permanent contract.

**i.** Write up a CV and a cover letter.

**j.** The applicant is offered the position.

**k.** Apply for a job.

**l.** The interviewee goes for an interview and is interviewed by the interviewer!

**m.** Look for companies which are recruiting.

**n.** Don't miss the closing date for applications.

**o.** The applicant has a probationary period.

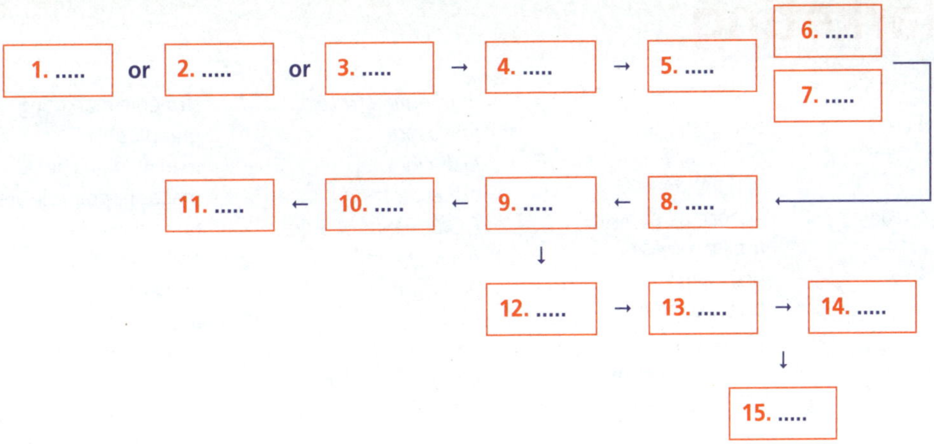


## 22 SOME ADVANTAGES

**Match a word from column 1 to a word from column 2. Then choose one to make a suitable answer to the question.**

| | |
|---|---|
| company | voucher |
| work | promotion |
| fringe | abroad |
| annual | scheme |
| luncheon | car |
| training | bonus |
| pension | course |
| internal | benefit |

**1.** What will you use to pay for your meal? ........................................

**2.** What will supplement your income when you retire? ........................................

**3.** What is a yearly sum of money for productivity / performance? ........................................

**4.** What can you drive around in at the company's expense? ........................................

**5.** What will help you improve your I.T. or other skills? ........................................

**6.** What could you do to get some foreign experience? ........................................

**7.** What are extra advantages on top of your salary? ........................................

**8.** What is it called when your career advances within the company? ........................................

## 23 NOT AT WORK (FOR NOW)

**Put the words below into groups by theme.**

*early retirement – employ – fire – job hunter – job-seeker – make redundant – retirement – sack*

| | |
|---|---|
| unemployment | |
| lay off | |
| dismiss | |
| retire | |

# 6. Marketing

| | |
|---|---|
| *ad / advert / advertisement* | une publicité |
| *adman* | publicitaire |
| *advertising* | la publicité |
| *advertising agency* | agence de publicité |
| *bargain* | affaire, occasion |
| *booth* | box, stand |
| *box* | boîte, coffret |
| *brand* | marque |
| *brand image* | image de marque |
| *campaign* | campagne |
| *competition* | concurrence |
| *E.D.L.P. Every Day Low Price* | prix bas tous les jours |
| *end-product* | produit fini |
| *end-user* | utilisateur final |
| *enhance* | mettre en valeur |
| *generic product* | produit générique |
| *hoarding* | panneau publicitaire |
| *launch (to)* | lancer |
| *leaflet* | dépliant, prospectus |
| *mail order* | vente par correspondance |
| *mailing list* | liste de distribution |
| *mark down (to)* | baisser le prix de |
| *market research* | étude de marché |
| *market survey* | sondage concernant le marché |
| *marketing research* | étude marketing |

| | |
|---|---|
| *marketing strategy* | stratégie marketing |
| *mass market* | grand public |
| *niche market* | marché de niche |
| *outlet, sales outlet* | magasin, point de vente |
| *P.O.S . Point of Sale* | point de vente |
| *package (to)* | emballer |
| *packaging* | emballage |
| *poster* | affiche |
| *press article* | article de presse |
| *price mark-down* | solde des prix |
| *prime time* | première partie de soirée |
| *product identity* | identité du produit |
| *product life cycle* | cycle de vie |
| *product range* | gamme de produits |
| *promotion* | promotion |
| *publicity* | publicité (gratuite) |
| *publicity stunt* | coup publicitaire |
| *reply coupon* | coupon-réponse |
| *store discount* | remise en magasin |
| *target / target (to)* | cible / cibler |
| *target audience* | consommateur cible |
| *teaser campaign* | teaser |
| *test market* | marché-test |
| *trade / brand name* | appellation commerciale |
| *trade magazine* | presse spécialisée |
| *TV commercial* | spot T.V. |
| *voucher* | bon (bon d'achat...) |

## ACTIVITÉS

The "7Ps": Product – Price – Promotion – Place – Packaging – Positioning – People.

### 24 THE MARKET

**Choose one of the words to complete the sentence.**

*brand image – competition – end product – end-user – generic product – marketing strategy – market survey – mass market – niche market – product identity – product range – target audience – test market – trade / brand name*

**1.** This is a very expensive and special product. We are aiming at the ........................................ .

**2.** You need to define the demographic and psychographic profile of your ........................................ .

**3.** Their ........................................ is very wide – they have so many different products.

**4.** Companies have to be careful to maintain a good ........................................ .

**5.** You need a good ........................................ .

**6.** It's a good idea to try a product out first on a ........................................ .

**7.** A ........................................ is one which does not use a brand name.

**8.** The ........................................ is the market for goods which are made in big quantities.

**9.** The look or character of a product, or ........................................ that leads to customer loyalty.

**10.** There is a lot of ........................................ between brands to get to the position of market leader.

**11.** We need a good ........................................ to make the most of all our resources.

**12.** The person who actually uses the product is really the ........................................ .

**13.** We need to carry out a ........................................ so we know all about our markets and customers.

**14.** The finished article off the assembly line is the ........................................ .

## 25 ADVERTISING

### Use the clues to find the right word from the list below.

*adman – advertising agency – flyer – hoarding – jingle – leaflet – poster – prime time – slogan – TV commercials – teaser campaign*

**1.** A printed sheet of paper, sometimes folded, with advertising on it. ........................................

**2.** An ad campaign that only shows part of the information, to make people interested in the product. ........................................

**3.** Someone who works in advertising. ........................................

**4.** The time when most people watch the television – usually between 8 and 11 pm. ........................................

**5.** A company that designs advertising. ........................................

**6.** The large posters for advertising you can see on the side of the road. ........................................

**7.** A big printed picture used sometimes for advertising. ........................................

**8.** An advertisement on the television. ........................................

## 26 PUBLICITY

### Choose the right answer in this little conversation.

**1. Boss:** We are lunching / launching the new product next week. Can we go through the checklist to make sure we have everything we need?

**2. Bill:** Of course. We have gone through the entire list of mailing / mailing list and sent information documents to all our customers and potential customers.

**3. Boss:** Did you send them vouchers / goods of purchasing with the mailshot?

**4. Bill:** Yes, and I also enclosed a responding coupon / reply coupon in case they need more information.

**5. Mary:** I have contacted all the trade magazines / trade volumes about a write up.

**6. Boss:** What about organizing and decorating the bath / booth at the trade fair?

**7. Mary:** I'm dealing with that. I've also sent press articles / pressed articles to all the local newspapers.

**8. Bill:** Of course the key is the stunted publicity / publicity stunt which I've planned. It's ready!

## 27 WHAT YOU CAN SEE IN THE STORE (or not in one case!)

### Put the letters back in the right order to find the word.

| | | |
|---|---|---|
| **1.** Somewhere for retailing goods. | ASSEL TLUEOT | ........................................ |
| **2.** To raise the beauty / quality of something. | NECNEAH | ........................................ |
| **3.** Something wrapped in a box, paper or plastic. | KPCEAAG | ........................................ |
| **4.** Selling goods using the postal service. | AMLI REODR | ........................................ |
| **5.** To reduce the price. | KARM ONDW | ........................................ |
| **6.** A (very) good deal. | RANAGIB | ........................................ |
| **7.** An activity to publicize a product. | RPOIMOTON | ........................................ |
| **8.** A reduced price in a shop. | OSTER SNCUTIOD | ........................................ |
| **9.** Materials used to protect / embellish goods | AAPIGGKNC | ........................................ |

# 7. Industry

| | |
|---|---|
| *0 defect* | zéro défaut |
| *assembly line* | ligne d'assemblage |
| *batch number* | numéro de lot |
| *breakthrough* | percée |
| *casual labor* | petits boulots |
| *clean room* | salle blanche |
| *closure* | fermeture |
| *components* | composants |
| *computer* | ordinateur |
| *factory* | usine |
| *foreman* | chef d'équipe, contremaître |
| *fork lift* | chariot élévateur |
| *gloves* | gants |
| *goggles* | lunettes de protection |
| *hardware* | matériel informatique |
| *hazardous* | dangereux |
| *industrial estate* | zone industrielle |
| *labor force* | main-d'œuvre |
| *layout* | disposition, mise en page |
| *lead time* | délai de production |
| *machinery* | machinerie, machines |
| *maintenance* | maintenance |
| *manufacture (to)* | fabriquer |
| *mass production run* | grandes séries |
| *N.P.I. (New Product* Introduction) | Introduction de nouveaux produits |
| *operative / operator* | opérateur |
| *output* | rendement, production |
| *outsource (to)* | sous-traiter |
| *pallet* | palette |
| *patent* | brevet |
| *pilot (run / plant…)* | pilote (production / usine…) |
| *plant* | usine, fabrique |
| *power supply* | alimentation électrique |
| *production capacity* | capacité de production |
| *production flow* | flux de production |
| *production rate* | cadence de production |
| *protective clothing* | vêtements de protection |
| *prototype* | prototype |
| *rack* | étagère métallique |
| *raw material* | matière première |
| *safety measures* | mesures de sécurité |
| *savings* | économies |
| *self-inspection* | auto-contrôle |
| *short and medium production runs* | petites et moyennes séries |
| *shortage* | manque, pénurie |
| *shut-down / closure* | fermeture |
| *skilled / unskilled worker* | ouvrier qualifié / non qualifié |
| *social unrest* | agitation |
| *software* | logiciel |
| *spare parts* | pièces détachées |
| *spot check* | contrôle inopiné |
| *stock-taking* | inventaire |
| *storage / warehousing* | entreposage |
| *streamline (to)* | rationaliser |
| *sub-contract (to)* | sous-traiter |
| *tooling* | outillage |
| *turn key plant* | usine clé en main |
| *unemployment black spot* | zone de chômage |
| *up-to-date equipment* | équipement moderne |
| *warehouse* | magasin |
| *warehouseman* | magasinier |
| *waste / waste (to)* | déchets, gaspillage / gaspiller |
| *wear and tear* | usure |
| *works* | usine (industrie lourde) |
| *workshop* | atelier |

## ACTIVITÉS

### 28 MIND MAPPING

**Put the words into the appropriate column: people, equipment, safety, the premises.**

*assembly line – casual labor – clean room – computer – foreman – fork lift – gloves – goggles – hardware – labor force – machinery – operative / operator – pallet – power supply – protective clothing – rack – skilled / unskilled worker – software – tooling – up-to-date equipment – warehouse – warehouseman – workshop*

| People | Equipment | Safety | The premises (factory / plant) |
|---|---|---|---|
| .......................... | .......................... | .......................... | .......................................................... |
| .......................... | .......................... | .......................... | .......................................................... |
| .......................... | .......................... | .......................... | .......................................................... |
| .......................... | .......................... | .......................... | .......................................................... |
| .......................... | .......................... | .......................... | .......................................................... |
| .......................... | .......................... | .......................... | .......................................................... |
| .......................... | .......................... | .......................... | .......................................................... |
| .......................... | .......................... | .......................... | .......................................................... |
| .......................... | .......................... | .......................... | .......................................................... |
| .......................... | .......................... | .......................... | .......................................................... |
| .......................... | .......................... | .......................... | .......................................................... |
| .......................... | .......................... | .......................... | .......................................................... |
| .......................... | .......................... | .......................... | .......................................................... |
| .......................... | .......................... | .......................... | .......................................................... |
| .......................... | .......................... | .......................... | .......................................................... |

## 29 WHAT'S THE RIGHT ANSWER?

**Choose the right answer between the two on offer.**

**1.** Do you think that we ought to rationalize our production system?

**A.** Yes, I think it needs streamlining.

**B.** Yes, I think it needs riverlining.

**2.** Are those products over there dangerous?

**A.** The label says they are "hazardful".

**B.** The label says they are "hazardous".

**3.** You say that the operatives are responsible for their workstations. How is that?

**A.** Each employee does self-control.

**B.** Each employee does self-inspection.

**4.** Is everything stored in this warehouse?

**A.** No, only the raw material.

**B.** No, only the first material.

**5.** Why is that person measuring up that metal sheet so carefully?

**A.** We are very strict about waste.

**B.** We are very strict about waist.

**6.** There doesn't seem to be enough sheet metal here, does there?

**A.** There is a market shortcut of metal.

**B.** There is a market shortage of metal.

**7.** Why does that machine look so very old and deteriorated?

**A.** It's a question of wear and tear.

**B.** It's a question of ware and tare.

**8.** Gosh, how do they manage to product so many items in an hour?

**A.** They do have a very high output.

**B.** They do have a very high outpouring.

**9.** How do you know how many spare parts you've got?

**A.** We do monthly stock-taking.

**B.** We do monthly store taking.

**10.** How do you make sure that nobody copies your inventions?

**A.** We take out a pattern of course!

**B.** We take out a patent of course!

## 30 TOP AND TAIL

### Match a word from list A to a word from list B.

**A:** *batch – lead – pilot – production (x3) – safety – spot – sub – 0*

**B:** *capacity – check – contract – defect – flow – measures – number – rate – run – time*

| | |
|---|---|
| **1.** ........................................ | **2.** ........................................ |
| **3.** ........................................ | **4.** ........................................ |
| **5.** ........................................ | **6.** ........................................ |
| **7.** ........................................ | **8.** ........................................ |
| **9.** ........................................ | **10.** ........................................ |

## 31 LET ME TELL YOU A STORY ABOUT A PLANT

### Put a right word into the gap in the story.

*breakthrough – closure – components – industrial estate – layout – maintenance – mass production runs – outsource – savings – short and medium production runs – social unrest – storage – turnkey plant – unemployment black spot – works*

We bought a **1.** ........................................ in the **2.** ........................................ near the old steel **3.** ........................................ just after R& D had the most amazing **4.** ........................................ and discovered a totally new nanomaterial. We paid great attention to the **5.** ........................................ and had a streamlined and efficient production system, with all new machines and low **6.** ........................................ We produced prototypes and **7.** ........................................ We did not start **8.** ........................................, because we thought the quantities would be too big.

Then we started to **9.** ........................................ to low cost countries, and by the end of 2008, over 80% of our **10.** ........................................ were sourced abroad. Our factory became more for **11.** ........................................, than production, which led to **12.** ........................................ but also led to job instability, and therefore **13.** ........................................ . Of course, what had to happen happened, and by the end of 2012, this resulted in plant **14.** ........................................ and a local **15.** ........................................ .

# 8. Written and oral communication



| | |
|---|---|
| *acknowledge receipt (to)* | accuser réception |
| *agreement* | accord, convention |
| *apologise (to)* | s'excuser |
| *apology (ies)* | excuses |
| *at / dot / com* | arobase / point / com |
| *backlog* | arriéré |
| *bandwidth* | débit |
| *best regards* | cordialement |
| *bounced e-mail* | un courriel qui revient |
| *broadband* | A.D.S.L. |
| *call back (to)* | rappeler |
| *capital letters* | majuscules (lettres) |
| *cell (US) (/ mobile(UK)) phone* | téléphone portable |
| *complaint* | plainte |
| *conference call* | téléconférence |
| *confirm receipt (to)* | accuser réception |
| *contact details* | coordonnées |
| *contract* | contrat |
| *double-check (to)* | vérifier à deux fois |
| *download* | télécharger |
| *enclose (to)* | joindre |
| *envelope* | enveloppe |
| *file / file (to)* | dossier / classer |
| *filing cabinet* | classeur (meuble) |
| *for the attention of* | à l'attention de |
| *further information* | plus d'informations |
| *get in touch (to)* | contacter |
| *grateful* | reconnaissant, gré |
| *headed paper* | papier à en-tête |
| *in the near future* | dans un avenir proche |
| *inconvenience* | inconvénient |
| *information* | information |
| *ink* | encre |
| *input / to input* | entrée (des données) / saisir (des données) |
| *inquiry / enquiry* | demande d'informations |
| *invoice* | facture |
| *keyboard* | clavier |
| *kind regards* | cordialement |
| *laptop* | ordinateur portable |
| *letterhead* | en-tête |
| *look forward to…(V-ing)* | dans l'attente de |
| *mouse* | souris |
| *office supplies* | fournitures |
| *on behalf of* | de la part de |
| *paperwork* | paperasserie |
| *please do not hesitate* | n'hésitez pas |
| *price list* | liste de prix |
| *quote* | devis |
| *recipient* | destinataire |
| *regarding* | en ce qui concerne |
| *reminder* | rappel |
| *ring back (to)* | rappeler |
| *search engine* | moteur de recherche |
| *small letters* | minuscules (lettres) |
| *spell-checker* | vérificateur d'orthographe |
| *tablet computer* | tablette |
| *to whom it may concern* | à qui de droit |
| *type (to)* | taper (au clavier) |
| *typeface* | caractère |
| *upload (to)* | mettre en ligne |
| *we regret to inform you* | nous sommes au regret de vous informer |
| *with reference to* | concernant |
| *written confirmation* | confirmation par écrit |
| *yours faithfully* | je vous prie d'agréer… (si vous commencez par Dear Sir or Madam) |
| *yours sincerely / sincerely yours* | je vous prie d'agréer… (si vous connaissez le nom) |

## ACTIVITÉS

Remember that when you write a letter or email, or put a power point presentation up on the screen, nothing is more visible than spelling or grammar mistakes. Do take care to re-read your documents thoroughly.

### 32 PLEASE DON'T MAKE ANY MISTAKES

**Choose the right answer.**

1. Remember to go through your orthography with the spell-verifier / spell-checker.
2. I got an NDR (Non Delivery Report) because my e-mail to you bounced / rebounded.
3. The whole email address is written in small / mini letters and not major / capital letters.
4. Bob, did you remember to double check / doubly check the presentation?
5. Please accept my apologies / apologize for any mistakes.

**6.** 6. Could you send a reminder / remainder about the unpaid invoice / factor?

**7.** We need to see the price list / price listing before we sign the contrat / contract.

**8.** I asked the manufacture for a quote / cote for 5,000 items.

## 33 ON THE TELEPHONE

**Find a word in the list below to replace the words in numbers 1-5.**

*conference call – contact details – get in touch – ring back – speaking*

**1.** Call back ..............................

**2.** To "contact" someone. ..............................

**3.** A telephone conversation between several people. ..............................

**4.** Phone number, address, e-mail address, etc. ..............................

**5.** This is me on the telephone. ..............................

## 34 A LITTLE BIT OF THE INTERNET

**Match the beginning to the end of the word and the definition.**

| | | | |
|---|---|---|---|
| band | load | A | a program for retrieving documents from the Internet |
| broad | load | B | taking data off the Internet onto a computer or disk |
| down | band | C | put data on a larger I.T. system or the Internet |
| search | width | D | A.D.S.L. |
| up | engine | E | the capacity of data transfer or range of frequencies |

## 35 EQUIPMENT FOR COMMUNICATING

**Put the jumbled up letters back into the right order.**

**1.** A computer you can carry around: ALOTPP ..............................

**2.** A small, flat touch-screen computer: AETTLB OUEPRTCM ..............................

**3.** A panel of keys for entering data: REDBAKOY ..............................

**4.** A small cupboard for putting files away: IGFNIL NAIECBT ..............................

**5.** A little animal to control the cursor: SMUEO ..............................

**6.** A container for a letter or document: NPEEEOVL ..............................

**7.** Writing paper with a letterhead: EDDHEA AEPRP ..............................

**8.** Essential for a fountain pen or a printer: NKI ..............................

**9.** Day to day consumables for an office: FCOEIF PLSIPSEU ..............................

**10.** A phone you can carry around (US): ELCL EHNPO ..............................

## 36 WHAT MIGHT YOU BE WRITING ABOUT?

**Match a need from the left hand column, to a word / expression in the right hand column.**

**1.** You need some information.

**2.** You are not happy about something.

**3.** You are writing for someone else.

**4.** You are very sorry about something.

**5.** You want to make sure someone has received something.

**A.** ON BEHALF OF

**B.** ENQUIRY

**C.** ACKNOWLEDGE RECEIPT

**D.** COMPLAINT

**E.** APOLOGIZE

## 37 WRITING A LETTER OR AN EMAIL

**Complete the letters and the email.**

Please note that for purposes of this exercise, the e-mail is written in less formal English than the two letters. However, everything must be taken in context – a letter can be informal, inasmuch as an e-mail can be formal.

Please note also that an e-mail address is given as follows:
charlotte.piper@xxx.com = charlotte DOT piper AT xxx DOT com

- *backlog – doing – enclosed – faithfully – inconvenience – input – output – paperwork – whom*

To ................................ it may concern

I am writing to apologize for the ................................ you were caused recently owing to an ................................ error by our sales staff, which caused an ................................ error on your invoice. I am afraid that they have a ................................ of ................................ at the moment owing to a changeover to new business management software.

Please find ................................ a credit note and a new invoice.

We look forward to ................................ business with you in the near future.

Yours ................................,

- *faithfully – Madam – reference – Sir – written confirmation*

Dear ................................ or ................................,

With ................................ to your request to put back the delivery deadline, we are willing to accept reception of the goods 10 days late, on condition that you guarantee there will be no further delays.

Could you please send us ................................ of these conditions?

Yours ................................,

- *attention – further – grateful – regret – sincerely*

For the ................................ of the purchasing department

Dear Mr Jones

We ................................ to inform you that the goods you ordered have been superseded by an up-graded version. However, we are pleased to inform you that we shall be able to offer you this new, high performance item at the same price as the one you ordered.

I would be ................................ if you would let me know your decision as soon as possible.

Should you require any ................................ information, please do not hesitate to contact us.

Yours ................................,

- *regarding – regards – near – typeface*

Dear Bob,

I'm writing ................................ our meeting about your publicity leaflet. I'm afraid that the ................................ just isn't right and we have to re-work the idea a little. The design department is working on a new mock up at the moment and they should have it finished by the end of the week.

I'll be in touch in the ................................ future.

Best ................................

Peter

# 9. Products

| | |
|---|---|
| *appliance* | appareil |
| *best-before date* | à consommer de préférence avant |
| *built-in* | incorporé |
| *cheap* | bon marché |
| *conform with / to (to be)* | être conforme à |
| *consumer durables* | biens de consommation durables |
| *cordless* | sans fil |
| *cost-effective* | rentable |
| *costly / expensive* | cher |
| *counterfeit goods* | contrefaçons |
| *custom-made* | sur-mesure |
| *cut-price* | à prix réduit |
| *cutting-edge* | de pointe |
| *defect* | imperfection |
| *defective* | défectueux |
| *device* | appareil / dispositif |
| *disposable* | jetable |
| *easy-to-use* | facile à utiliser |
| *end user* | utilisateur (final) |
| *environment-friendly* | respectueux de l'environnement |
| *eye-catching* | qui attire l'attention |
| *flawed* | qui présente des défauts |
| *foodstuff* | denrée alimentaire |
| *good / bad value for money* | bon / mauvais rapport qualité-prix |
| *hand-made* | fait-main |
| *harmless* | inoffensif |
| *high-quality* | de haute qualité |
| *improvement* | amélioration |
| *impulse buying* | achat d'impulsion |
| *innovative* | innovant |
| *item* | article |
| *labour-saving* | qui facilite le travail |
| *made-to-measure* | fait sur mesure |
| *man-made* | artificiel |
| *no-brand articles* | articles sans marque |
| *P.L.B. Private Label Brand* | marque de distributeur |
| *produce* | fruits et légumes |
| *reliable* | fiable |
| *removable* | amovible |
| *requirement* | exigence, besoin |
| *sample* | échantillon |
| *semi-finished* | semi-fini |
| *shelf life* | durée de conservation |
| *staple goods* | aliments de base |
| *supersede (to)* | remplacer |
| *upgrade (to)* | moderniser / actualiser |
| *useless* | inutile |
| *user-friendly* | facile à utiliser |
| *watertight* | étanche à l'eau |
| *well-known* | connu / célèbre |

## ACTIVITÉS

### 38 HOW WOULD YOU DESCRIBE YOUR PRODUCT?

**Put a word from the list with a word below to make a compound adjective.**

*catching – edge – effective – finished – friendly – friendly – in – known – made – made – made – measure – price – quality – saving – use*

**1.** built-..............................
**2.** cost-..............................
**3.** custom-..............................
**4.** cut-..............................
**5.** cutting-..............................
**6.** easy-to-..............................
**7.** environment-..............................
**8.** eye-..............................
**9.** hand-..............................
**10.** high-..............................
**11.** labor-..............................
**12.** made-to-..............................
**13.** man-..............................
**14.** semi-..............................
**15.** user-..............................
**16.** well-..............................

## 39 WHAT MIGHT YOU FIND IN A STORE?

### Add a vowel to complete the word.

1. Essential goods purchased on a regular basis: S T _ P L _ G _ _ D S
2. Something you can eat, which is edible: F _ _ D S T _ FF
3. A device or apparatus: _ P P L _ _ N C _
4. Goods which do not show a brand name: N _ B R _ N D _ R T _ C L _ S
5. Fruit and vegetables: P R _ D _ C _
6. Goods for consumers which last a long time: C _ N S _ M _ R D _ R _ B L _ S
7. Imitation products put on sale: C _ _ N T _ R F _ _ T G _ _ D S
8. Something you can have (for free) to test an item: S _ M P L _

## 40 OPPOSITE ADJECTIVES

### Find the opposite adjective.

One very good way of learning long lists of adjectives is to find the opposite (big vs. small). You can do this for most adjectives. Why don't you see if you can lengthen this list?

1. unreliable ................................
2. corded ................................
3. useful ................................
4. costly / expensive ................................
5. good value for money ................................
6. customary / uncreative ................................
7. penetrable ................................
8. harmful ................................
9. fixed ................................
10. flawless ................................

## 41 COMPLETE THE SHORT CONVERSATIONS

### Put a suitable word or expression from the list into the conversations.

*best-before date – conform with / to – defect – impulse buying – requirements – shelf life – superseded – upgrade*

1. **Husband:** "What are all those shopping bags doing in the hall?"
**Wife:** "You know I am a shopaholic darling, and just cannot stop ..............................!"
2. **Gillian:** "This yoghurt is not very good Bobby."
**Bobby:** "Oh dear, it's way past the .............................., put it in the bin."
3. **Customer:** "Why can't I have the rollerball pens that I usually buy? "
**Storekeeper:** "I'm afraid they have been .............................. by a later version."
4. **Salesperson:** "Could you please tell me why you are returning the product to the store?"
**Customer:** "Take a good look here. Can't you see the ..............................? There's a hole!"
5. **Jo:** "I want an improvement on cell phone because it's slow. But it's expensive."
**Bill:** "I agree. Did you know that in some countries you get a free .............................. every year?"
6. **Customer:** "It is very important that the product matches the end-users' needs."
**Manufacturer:** "We will follow your .............................. to the letter, sir."
7. **Buyer:** "Are you sure that this product is really safe?"
**Seller:** "Yes sir, it is .............................. all the norms and standards in force."
8. **Store manager:** "We need to keep these products in the store for as long as possible."
**Assistant:** "The product has a very long .............................. so there should be no problem."

# 10. Travelling

| | |
|---|---|
| *abroad* | à l'étranger |
| *air hostess* | hôtesse de l'air |
| *baggage / luggage* | bagages |
| *book (to)* | réserver |
| *booking confirmation* | confirmation de réservation |
| *bus lane* | voie de bus |
| *business trip* | voyage d'affaires |
| *cancelled* | annulé |
| *car park* | parking |
| *check out (to)* | quitter l'hôtel |
| *check-in* | s'enregistrer |
| *commuter train* | train de banlieue |
| *customs* | douane |
| *delayed* | en retard |
| *departure* | départ |
| *E.T.A. / E.T.D. (Estimated time of arrival / departure)* | heure estimée d'arrivée / départ |
| *elevator (US) / lift (UK)* | ascenseur |
| *excess baggage* | frais pour surpoids de bagages |
| *expenses* | dépense, frais |
| *first / economy class* | première / classe économique |
| *flight* | vol |
| *flyover* | pont autoroutier |
| *foreign currency* | devise étrangère |
| *gas (US) / petrol (UK)* | essence |
| *gate* | porte |
| *give someone a lift (to)* | prendre quelqu'un dans sa voiture |
| *hand luggage* | bagage à main |
| *high speed train* | TGV |
| *hire (to)* | louer |
| *hold luggage* | bagage en soute |
| *immigration (US) / passport control* | contrôle des passeports |
| *insurance* | assurance |
| *jet lag* | fatigue due au décalage horaire |
| *journey* | voyage |
| *leave (to)* | partir, quitter |
| *leg room* | place pour les jambes |
| *long-haul flight* | vol long courrier |
| *mileage* | kilométrage |
| *miss (to)* | louper / manquer |
| *one-way* | aller simple |
| *one-way system* | à sens unique |
| *over-booked* | surbooké |
| *over-charge (to)* | faire payer trop cher |
| *passenger* | passager |
| *pick up (to)* | aller chercher |
| *refundable* | remboursable |
| *rent (to)* | louer |
| *round trip* | aller / retour |
| *roundabout* | rond-point |
| *runway* | piste de décollage |
| *season ticket* | abonnement |
| *short haul* | court-courrier |
| *stand in line (to)* | faire la queue |
| *station* | gare |
| *stopover* | escale |
| *tickets* | billets |
| *time difference* | décalage horaire |
| *toll* | péage |
| *traffic jam* | embouteillage |
| *traffic lights* | feux tricolores |
| *travel (to)* | voyager |
| *travel agency* | agence de voyage |
| *trip* | voyage court |
| *voyage* | voyage |

## ACTIVITÉS

### 42 JOURNEYS AND TICKETS

**Match the word to the definition.**

| | | | |
|---|---|---|---|
| **1** | book (to) | **A** | a short journey or excursion |
| **2** | tickets | **B** | a company that looks after your travel needs |
| **3** | travel agency | **C** | travel from one place to another |
| **4** | travel (to) | **D** | reserve (to) |

| | | | |
|---|---|---|---|
| **5** | booking confirmation | **E** | to make a journey to one place or another |
| **6** | trip | **f** | able to be reimbursed |
| **7** | voyage | **g** | a piece of paper / card giving you the right to travel |
| **8** | business trip | **h** | validation that your journey has been reserved |
| **9** | journey | **i** | a short journey for work |
| **10** | refundable | **j** | a long journey by sea or in space |

## 43 TRAVEL TERMS

### Find a word to match the definition

**1.** fail to get your train or plane .....
**2.** "luggage" in US English .....
**3.** make someone pay too much .....
**4.** "return ticket" in US English .....
**5.** "single ticket" in US English .....
**6.** "lift" in US English .....
**7.** employee travel costs .....
**8.** where your passport is checked .....
**9.** not in your own country .....
**10.** the money of another country .....
**11.** where your luggage is checked .....
**12.** to leave and pay the hotel .....
**13.** to depart from somewhere .....
**14.** a rider on public transport .....

## 44 ON THE ROAD

### Complete the story with one of the following words. (Conjugate the verbs.)

*bus lane – car park – flyover – give (someone) a lift – gas / petrol – hire / rent a car – insurance – mileage – one-way system – pick up – roundabout – toll – traffic jam – traffic lights*

I had a bad journey yesterday. First, my car broke down so I had to **1.** .......................................... . I didn't have the right **2.** .......................................... so had to get my assistant to send them, and pay extra for unlimited **3.** .......................................... . I was meant to **4.** .......................................... the boss at the airport, I got stuck in a **5.** .......................................... so I was late. Moreover, I had no change to pay the motorway **6.** .......................................... so I had to queue. The boss was not very pleased.

We were running late so I drove down the **7.** .......................................... (buses and taxis only), and got fined by the police. When we stopped at the (red) **8.** .......................................... we saw Jack and **9.** ....... .................................. him .......................................... to the meeting.

We got lost and took the wrong exit off the **10.** .......................................... and then got caught up in the **11.** .......................................... (where you can only go in one direction). Then the fuel gauge in the car started flashing and we had to stop to fill up with **12.** .......................................... .

At last I could see where we were. I had a moment of vertigo as we drove over the **13.** ......................... ................ but there was lots of room in the **14.** .......................................... and I found a space easily. We were over an hour late for the meeting but as they say, "better late than never"!

## 45 TRAVELLING BY RAIL

### Choose the right answer.

**1.** That's because I have a season ticket / navigation pass so I don't need to get a ticket everytime
**2.** When there are a lot of people you have to stand in file / stand in line to buy your ticket.
**3.** We regret to inform you that the 9.45 train to Paris has been cancelled / annulled.
**4.** Owing to bad weather conditions, the next train at 10.14 has been differed / delayed.

5. He lives in the suburbs and takes the commuter train / suburb train morning and evening.

6. The best way to get from Paris to Brussels is to take the speedy train / high-speed train.

7. We pay first class / primary class tickets for managers, you go second class / secondary class!

8. OK, I'll meet you at the stationary / station on platform 5 at 8 am.

## 46 UP IN THE AIR

**Choose between A or B.**

**1.** "I'm flying to Scotland tomorrow."
**A.** "What fly are you on?" **B.** "What flight are you on?"

**2.** "I'm sorry, there are no seats left on the plane."
**A.** "You mean it's been overbooked?" **B.** "You mean it's been above-booked?"

**3.** "You look rather squashed in that seat there."
**A.** "Well, there's very little foot room." **B.** "Well, there's very little leg room."

**4.** "What time should I be at the airport?"
**A.** "You have to register in at 4pm." **B.** "You have to check in at 4pm."

**5.** "It takes about 12 hours 45 minutes to fly from London to Singapore."
**A.** "I know. It's a long-haul flight." **B.** "I know. It's a short-haul flight."

**6.** "But it only takes 45 minutes from London to Amsterdam."
**A.** "I know. It's a long-haul flight." **B.** "I know. It's a short-haul flight."

**7.** "When is this plane going to take off?"
**A.** "I'm beginning to wonder. We've been sitting on the runway for hours."
**B.** "I'm beginning to wonder. We've been sitting on the runaway for hours."

**8.** "I'd like a ticket for Orlando please."
**A.** "First class or ecology class?" **B.** "First class or economy class?"

**9.** "I really would like something to drink."
**A.** "You'd better ask the air host." **B.** "You'd better ask the air hostess."

**10.** "Where should I go for flight BA 135?"
**A.** "It goes from gate 45." **B.** "It goes from portal 45."

**11.** "That suitcase looks very large, sir."
**A.** "It'll be holed luggage please." **B.** "It'll be hold luggage please".

**12.** "However, that little bag can go with you in the plane."
**A.** "Yes, that's main luggage." **B.** "Yes, that's hand luggage."

**13.** "It's going to be a very long flight to San Francisco."
**A.** "We've got a stopover in Chicago too." **B.** "We've got an escalade in Chicago too."

**14.** "I can't decide which of all these flights on the website is the best."
**A.** "Did you look at the flight departure times?" **B.** "Did you look at the flight taking leave times?"

**15.** "Gosh, this suitcase is really heavy – it weighs a ton!"
**A.** "You'll have to pay excess luggage I'm afraid." **B.** "You'll have to pay excess baggage I'm afraid."

# Answers

## EX. 1

**1.** C – **2.** I – **3.** F – **4.** H – **5.** A – **6.** G (See also SMC – Small and Medium-sized Companies) – **7.** D – **8.** J – **9.** B – **10.** E

## EX. 2

**1.** Salary B / Wage A – **2.** Dispatch A / Delivery B – **3.** Stakeholder B / Shareholder A – **4.** Desk B / Office A – **5.** Earn A / win B – **6.** Advertising A / Publicity B – **7.** Jet lag B / Time difference A – **8.** Company A / Society B – **9.** Market Research A / Marketing Research B (A is in fact part of B) – **10.** Agenda B / Diary A

## EX. 3

**1.** Department (Service is only used where a service is performed, e.g. After-sales service)
**2.** Training (Stage is "une estrade, une scène")
**3.** Former (Old ("Ancien") is a question of age)
**4.** Fabricate (Manufacture is to make articles on a big scale)
**5.** Deadline (Delay means something is late)
**6.** Benefits (Profit is financial gain)
**7.** Current (Actual means in fact, something which exists)
**8.** Reunion (A meeting is for discussing a certain point)
**9.** Sum up (To resume is to start doing something again)
**10.** Exit (Issue is a topic or problem to be discussed.).

## EX. 4

**1.** B – **2.** B – **3.** B – **4.** A – **5.** B – **6.** B – **7.** A – **8.** A – **9.** B – **10.** A

## EX. 5

**1.** showroom – **2.** self-employed – **3.** branch – **4.** parent company – **5.** service – **6.** outlets – **7.** headquarters – **8.** subsidiary – **9.** sister company – **10.** department

## EX. 6

**1.** f – **2.** d – **3.** h – **4.** b – **5.** i – **6.** e – **7.** j – **8.** a – **9.** g – **10.** c

## EX. 7

The company was _founded_ by B.B. Bother in 1946. It was a small _partnership_ but soon grew to become a limited company. The _premises_ were firstly _located_ near Birmingham, but owing to considerable _growth_, we were able to buy real estate in the center of London. The _merger_ with PPL Ltd in 1953, followed by some exceptional _investment_ in R&D, enabled us to _strengthen_ our market position, increase our _turnover_ tenfold, and we became highly successful.
However, we saw our _market share_ decreasing and feared that we were going to go _bankrupt_. We were _taken over_ by Blue Brass Inc. who made a lot of changes which meant we could keep our heads above water. Many _cutbacks_ were made: first of all from a _payroll_ aspect – teams were _downsized_ and everyone in the company now has to _clock_ in or out. We also had to reduce our _overhead_ and the procurement and _purchasing_ departments improved supply chain management and found new low cost suppliers. This led to social unrest, and the night shift came out on _strike_ for three weeks.
Despite all these upheavals, our company _policy_ has never changed, "happy workers are good workers" and "customers rule ok".

## EX. 8

**1.** to – **2.** for – **3.** with – **4.** of – **5.** by

## EX. 9

| | | | | | | | | | | | | | | | | | |
|---|---|---|---|---|---|---|---|---|---|---|---|---|---|---|---|---|---|
| 1 | | | | | F | O | R | E | C | A | S | T | | | | | |
| 2 | | | | | | | | N | O | T | I | F | Y | | | | |
| 3 | | | | | | | M | I | N | U | T | E | S | | | | |
| 4 | | | | | | | | | F | I | G | U | R | E | S | | |
| 5 | | | | | | A | T | T | E | N | D | E | E | S | | | |
| 6 | | | | | | B | O | A | R | D | | | | | | | |
| 7 | | | | | | | M | E | E | T | I | N | G | | | | |
| 8 | | | | | T | A | K | E | N | O | T | E | S | | | | |
| 9 | S | T | E | E | R | I | N | G | C | O | M | M | I | T | T | E | E |
| 10 | | | | | | | B | R | E | A | K | | | | | | |
| 11 | | | | | C | H | A | I | R | P | E | R | S | O | N | | |
| 12 | | | | | | | | M | O | N | T | H | L | Y | | | |
| 13 | | | | | | | | M | O | T | I | O | N | | | | |
| 14 | | | | | | | D | E | M | O | N | S | T | R | A | T | E |

## EX. 10

bar chart – blueprint – dashboard – flow chart – line graph – organization chart – pie chart – polar graph – road map – spreadsheet

## EX. 11

**1.** C – **2.** B – **3.** C – **4.** B – **5.** A – **6.** C – **7.** C – **8.** B

## EX. 12

**P:** Bill, good morning. I'm calling because I'm afraid I have to _call off_ our meeting tomorrow. I'd like to _fix_ another meeting _A.S.A.P._ so we can get to the bottom of this supplier problem.
**B:** I agree Peter. Let me just look at my _diary_. What do you suggest?
**P:** Well, Monday morning would _suit_ me. How about you?
**B:** Sorry, Monday's a _public holiday_ in the UK, so I'll be _out of the office_ then. Can you do Tuesday?
**P:** No, I'll be _tied up_ all day Tuesday with the bankers. I'm pretty _booked up_ next week really. Wednesday's no

good at all. Let's see… What about a *breakfast* meeting at 8 on Thursday?
**B:** I'm supposed to be seeing the C.E.O. But I could see him *later*, at *noon* (then he can treat me to *lunch*!). He probably wants to talk about his favorite *topic*, streamlining the supply chain. I'll check and get back to you before the end of today.
**P:** You'll have to excuse me Bill, the auditor's just arrived. (Mrs. Jones, could you please *show him in*?) I'll get back to you later Bill.
**B:** Fine. I'll speak to you later.

## EX. 13

**1.** A. decade / B. fortnight
**2.** A. early / B. late
**3.** A. dinner (note there are 2 "n's) / B. tea (or teatime)
**4.** A. PM (post-meridian) / B. AM (ante-meridian)
**5.** A. date / B. appointment (for business, with a doctor, dentist, etc.)
**6.** A. busy / B. free
**7.** A. delay / B. deadline
**8.** A. schedule / B. Itinerary
**9.** A. meeting / B. seeing
**10.** A. out… / B. away… (In both cases, if it is an automatic e-mail response, it is better to say when you will be back).

## EX. 14

| | | |
|---|---|---|
| DELIVERY | DELAY | (Will be late) |
| | DEADLINE | (The final date for delivery) |
| | TIME / PERIOD | (The time it takes for goods to arrive) |

DISPATCH is the sending of something (for example when it leaves the factory / store), and not delivery, which is when it arrives.

## EX. 15

**1.** arrange – fix – set up
**2.** be off – cancel – call off
**3.** bring forward – put forward
**4.** defer – delay – put back – put off

## EX. 16

**1.** purchase order – **2.** order acknowledgement – **3.** sales price – **4.** quantity discount – **5.** certificate of origin – **6.** customs duties (import duties) – **7.** shipped – **8.** transport costs – **9.** handling charges – **10.** quality defects – **11.** sign – **12.** return

## EX. 17

**1. Susan:** So your legal department said "no"? Peter, you cannot possibly go back on what you said. You promised that you would remove the confidentiality clause.
**Peter:** I disagree. In fact what I said was that I had to check with our legal department.
**Susan:** I thought we had made a deal. Now you are changing your proposal. I was planning to sign the agreement today.
**Peter:** I'm sorry Susan. I have to comply with company policy.
**Susan:** Well, in that case, I'm afraid that I have to withdraw our offer.
**2. C.E.O.:** Sit down Brian. Now, this is very serious. The customer is accusing you of bribery. What have you got to say to that?
**Brian:** Well, I did offer him a compromise. I said if he would buy exclusively from us, we would give him a discount.
**C.E.O.:** That was a gamble Brian, and it didn't pay. They say they can no longer work with us on a good will basis, and the purchaser is contacting his lawyer.
**Brian:** That's strange because I heard from them this morning, and they are putting in a firm order for 20,000 parts.
**C.E.O.:** Well, it looks like you got away with it this time then.
**3. Charlotte:** Did you put in a tender for the supermarket fittings last week?
**James:** Yes, I did. We'll have to stick very closely to their specifications.
**Charlotte:** Yes, their requirements are very demanding. Did you offer them a price reduction for regular orders?
**James:** Price reduction, short delivery deadlines, etc. I'm doing all I can to convince them that we are the right supplier.
**Charlotte:** Can you deal with it and come back to me by tomorrow afternoon?
**James:** I'll let you know as soon as I have any news.
**4. Bob:** Well, I think we've got a deal here, don't you?
**Sara:** We must tie up a few loose ends before we finalize.
**Bob:** You mentioned something about choosing your own freight forwarder, and putting in a penalty clause in case of late delivery. Is that all?
**Sara:** Just one more thing, we need to be sure that you can deliver from stock. That means you having a minimum safety stock all the time. Can you guarantee that?
**Bob:** Of course. I'll get my lawyer to draw up the contracts tomorrow.

## EX. 18

**1.** A – **2.** B – **3.** A – **4.** C – **5.** C – **6.** B – **7.** A – **8.** B – **9.** C – **10.** A – **11.** C – **12.** B

## EX. 19

**1.** cover letter – **2.** experience – **3.** driver's license – **4.** go-ahead – **5.** hard-working – **6.** qualifications – **7.** single – **8.** spare time – **9.** strengths – **10.** weaknesses

## EX. 20

**1.** task – **2.** working hours – **3.** starting salary – **4.** part-time – **5.** sick / maternity leave – **6.** entitlement – **7.** full-time – **8.** entails – **9.** unsocial hours – **10.** overtime – **11.** day off – **12.** flexi-time

## EX. 21

**1.** Go to see a head-hunter or a job center, and look at advertisements, etc. – **2.** Look for openings in companies. **3.** Look for companies which are recruiting. – **4.** Write up a C.V. and a cover letter. – **5.** Apply for a job. – **6.** Candidates may have to fill in an application form. – **7.** Don't miss the closing date for applications. – **8.** The interviewee goes for an interview and is interviewed by the interviewer! – **9.** Interviewee put on a shortlist and has final interview. – **10.** Interviewee turned down. – **11.** Go back to square one. – **12.** The applicant is offered the position. **13.** The company takes on the applicant. – **14.** The applicant has a probationary period. – **15.** The employee gets a fixed-term or a permanent contract.

## EX. 22

**1.** luncheon voucher – **2.** pension scheme – **3.** annual bonus – **4.** company car – **5.** training course – **6.** work abroad – **7.** fringe benefits – **8.** internal promotion

## EX. 23

| | |
|---|---|
| ***Unemployment*** | job seeker, job hunter, employ |
| ***Lay off*** | make redundant |
| ***Dismiss*** | fire, sack |
| ***Retire*** | retirement, early retirement |

## EX. 24

**1.** niche market – **2.** target audience – **3.** product range – **4.** brand image – **5.** trade / brand name – **6.** test market – **7.** generic product – **8.** mass market – **9.** product identity – **10.** competition – **11.** marketing strategy – **12.** end user – **13.** market survey – **14.** end product

## EX. 25

**1.** Leaflet – **2.** Teaser campaign – **3.** Adman – **4.** Prime time – **5.** Advertising adgency – **6.** Hoarding – **7.** Poster – **8.** TV commercials.

## EX. 26

**1.** launching – **2.** mailing list – **3.** vouchers – **4.** reply coupon – **5.** trade magazines – **6.** booth – **7.** press articles – **8.** publicity stunt

## EX. 27

**1.** sales outlet – **2.** enhance – **3.** package – **4.** mail order – **5.** mark down – **6.** bargain – **7.** promotion – **8.** store discount – **9.** packaging

## EX. 28

**People:** casual labor, foreman, labor force, operative / operator, skilled / unskilled worker, warehouseman
**Equipment:** computer, fork lift, hardware, machinery, pallet, power supply, rack, software, tooling, up-to-date equipment
**Safety:** gloves, goggles, protective clothing
**The premises:** assembly line, clean room, warehouse, workshop

## EX. 29

**1.** A – **2.** B – **3.** B – **4.** A – **5.** A – **6.** B – **7.** A – **8.** A – **9.** A – **10.** B

## EX. 30

**1.** batch number – **2.** lead time – **3.** pilot run – **4.** production capacity – **5.** production flow – **6.** production rate – **7.** safety measures – **8.** spot check – **9.** sub-contract (/subcontract) – **10.** 0 defect

## EX. 31

**1.** turnkey plant – **2.** industrial estate – **3.** works – **4.** breakthrough – **5.** layout – **6.** maintenance – **7.** short and medium production runs – **8.** mass production runs – **9.** outsource – **10.** components – **11.** storage – **12.** savings – **13.** social unrest – **14.** closure – **15.** unemployment black spot

## EX. 32

**1.** spell-checker – **2.** bounced – **3.** small – capital – **4.** double-check – **5.** apologies (apologize (to) is a verb) – **6.** reminder, invoice – **7.** price list, contact – **8.** quote

## EX. 33

**1.** ring back – **2.** get in touch (with someone) – **3.** conference call – **4.** contact details – **5.** speaking

## EX. 34

**1.** bandwidth, E – **2.** broadband, D – **3.** download, B – **4.** search engine, A – **5.** upload, C

## EX. 35

**1.** laptop – **2.** tablet computer – **3.** keyboard – **4.** filing cabinet – **5.** mouse – **6.** envelope – **7.** headed paper – **8.** ink – **9.** office supplies – **10.** cell / mobile phone

## EX. 36

**1.** B (/inquiry) – **2.** D – **3.** A – **4.** E – **5.** C (/confirm receipt)

## EX. 37

To whom it may concern
I am writing to apologize for the inconvenience you were caused recently owing to an input error by our sales staff, which caused an output error on your invoice. I am afraid that they have a backlog of paperwork at the moment owing to a changeover to new business management software.
Please find enclosed a credit note and a new invoice.
We look forward to doing business with you in the near future.
Yours faithfully,

***

Dear Sir or Madam,
With reference to your request to put back the delivery deadline, we are willing to accept reception of the goods 10 days late, on condition that you guarantee there will be no further delays.

Could you please send us written confirmation of these conditions?
Yours faithfully,

***

For the attention of the purchasing department
Dear Mr Jones,
We regret to inform you that the goods you ordered have been superseded by an upgraded version. We are pleased to inform you that we shall be able to offer you this new, high performance item at the same price as the one you ordered.
I would be grateful if you would let me know your decision as soon as possible.
Should you require any further information, please do not hesitate to contact us.
Yours sincerely,

***

Dear Bob,
I'm writing regarding our meeting about your publicity leaflet. I'm afraid that the typeface just isn't right and we have to re-work the idea a little. The design department is working on a new mock up at the moment and they should have it finished by the end of the week.
I'll be in touch in the near future.
Best regards
Peter

## EX. 38

**1.** built-in – **2.** cost-effective – **3.** custom-made – **4.** cut-price – **5.** cutting-edge – **6.** easy-to-use – **7.** environment-friendly – **8.** eye-catching – **9.** hand-made – **10.** high-quality – **11.** labor-saving – **12.** made-to-measure – **13.** man-made – **14.** semi-finished – **15.** user-friendly – **16.** well-known

## EX. 39

**1.** staple goods – **2.** foodstuff – **3.** appliance – **4.** no-brand articles – **5.** produce – **6.** consumer durables – **7.** counterfeit goods – **8.** sample

## EX. 40

**1.** reliable – **2.** cordless – **3.** useless – **4.** cheap – **5.** bad value for money – **6.** innovative – **7.** watertight – **8.** harmless – **9.** removable – **10.** flawed

## EX. 41

**1.** impulse buying – **2.** best-before date – **3.** superseded – **4.** defect – **5.** upgrade – **6.** requirements – **7.** conform with / to – **8.** shelf life

## EX. 42

**1.** D – **2.** G – **3.** B – **4.** E – **5.** H – **6.** A – **7.** J – **8.** I – **9.** C – **10.** F

## EX. 43

**1.** miss – **2.** baggage – **3.** overcharge – **4.** round trip – **5.** one-way – **6.** elevator – **7.** expenses – **8.** immigration – **9.** abroad – **10.** currency – **11.** customs – **12.** check out (to) – **13.** leave – **14.** passenger

## EX. 44

**1.** hire / rent a car – **2.** insurance – **3.** mileage – **4.** pick up – **5.** traffic jam – **6.** toll – **7.** bus lane – **8.** traffic lights – **9.** give (someone) a lift – **10.** roundabout – **11.** one-way system – **12.** gas / petrol – **13.** flyover – **14.** car park

## EX. 45

**1.** season ticket – **2.** stand in line – **3.** cancelled – **4.** delayed – **5.** commuter train – **6.** high-speed train – **7.** first / second class – **8.** station

## EX. 46

**1.** A – **2.** A – **3.** B – **4.** B – **5.** A – **6.** B – **7.** A – **8.** B – **9.** B – **10.** A – **11.** B – **12.** B – **13.** A – **14.** A – **15.** B

Direction éditoriale : Christine Asin
Édition : Mélanie Schmitt / Emmanuelle Pellé
Maquette intérieure : Dany Mourain
Couverture : Vincent Rioult
Mise en page : Alinéa
Fabrication : Pascal Mégret


ISBN : 978-2-09-162902-5

N° editeur : 10195195 - Dépôt légal : septembre 2013
Imprimé en France par I.M.E. - 25110 Baume-les-Dames